Lost Youth in the Global City

What does it mean to be young, to be economically disadvantaged, and to be subject to constant surveillance both from the formal agencies of the state and from the informal challenge of competing youth groups? What is life like for young people living on the fringe of global cities in late modernity, no longer at the centre of city life, but pushed instead to new and insecure margins of the urban inner-city? How are changing patterns of migration and work, along with shifting gender roles and expectations, impacting marginalized youth in the radically transformed urban city of the twenty-first century?

In *Lost Youth in the Global City*, Jo-Anne Dillabough and Jacqueline Kennelly focus on young people who live at the margins of urban centres, the 'edges' where low-income, immigrant and other disenfranchised youth are increasingly finding and defining themselves. Taking the imperative of multi-sited ethnography and urban youth cultures as a starting point, this rich and layered book offers a detailed exploration of the ways in which these groups of young people, marked by economic disadvantage and ethnic and religious diversity, have sought to navigate a new urban terrain and, in so doing, have come to see themselves in new ways. By giving these young people shape and form – both looking across their experiences in different cities and attending to their particularities – *Lost Youth in the Global City* sets a productive and generative agenda for the field of critical youth studies.

Jo-Anne Dillabough is Reader at the University of Cambridge and Associate Professor in the Department of Educational Studies, University of British Columbia.

Jacqueline Kennelly is Assistant Professor in the Department of Sociology and Anthropology at Carleton University.

Critical Youth Studies

Series Editor: Greg Dimitriadis

Lost Youth in the Global City
Class, Culture and the Urban Imaginary

Jo-Anne Dillabough and
Jacqueline Kennelly

Routledge
Taylor & Francis Group

NEW YORK AND LONDON

First published 2010
by Routledge
270 Madison Ave, New York, NY 10016

Simultaneously published in the UK
by Routledge
2 Park Square, Milton Park, Abingdon, Oxon OX14 4RN

Routledge is an imprint of the Taylor & Francis Group, an informa business

Typeset in Minion by Wearset Ltd, Boldon, Tyne and Wear
Printed and bound in the United States of America on acid-free paper by
Walsworth Publishing Company, Marceline, MO

Library of Congress Cataloging-in-Publication Data
Dillabough, Jo-Anne, 1963–
Lost youth in the global city / by Jo-Anne Dillabough and Jaqueline Kennelly. – 1st ed.
p. cm.
Includes bibliographical references and index.
1. Urban youth–Social conditions–21st century. 2. Youth–Cross-cultural studies.
3. Globalization–Social aspects. I. Kennelly, Jaqueline. II. Title.
HQ796.D4815 2010
305.235086'942091732–dc22   2009050282

ISBN 10: 0-415-99557-4 (hbk)
ISBN 10: 0-415-99558-2 (pbk)
ISBN 10: 0-203-85833-6 (ebk)

ISBN 13: 978-0-415-99557-3 (hbk)
ISBN 13: 978-0-415-99558-0 (pbk)
ISBN 13: 978-0-203-85833-2 (ebk)

Contents

Series Editor Preface

Lost Youth in the Global City is a virtuosic scholarly achievement. In this rich and multi-layered text, Jo-Anne Dillabough and Jacqueline Kennelly focus on so-called 'lost youth', young people who live at the margins of urban centres – the 'edges' where low-income, immigrant, and other disenfranchised youth are increasingly finding and defining themselves. These young people live complex and bifurcated social lives. They are largely invisible in public discussions around youth – discussions often structured around the categories and imperatives of young people who live in more clearly defined centres (for example, the so-called 'urban youth' who have been the focus of much spectacular, subculture studies). Yet, these seemingly 'lost youth' become highly visible at key moments – moments of moral panic that crystallize public anxiety about youth, particularly in a post-9/11 world. One recalls here the violent protests of Arab and African youth that spread all around the outskirts of Paris in 2005 – the so-called 'Banlieue' that suddenly became the focus of worldwide media attention that Fall. Throughout this text, the authors look to name and understand this ambiguous and ambivalent condition. Their success is unqualified.

Taking the imperative of multi-sited ethnography as a starting point, this volume focuses on marginalized youth living in the surround of Vancouver and Toronto, Canada. As the authors demonstrate, these young people are often 'lost' in the self-mythologizing discourse of multicultural harmony prevalent in dominant Canadian discourse. Looking past these easy discourses of containment, Dillabough and Kennelly open up a discussion about the lived experiences of these young people. These youth are often poor or working-class. They often are immigrants or children of immigrants from across the globe: including countries in Southern and Eastern Europe, South and Central Asia, Central and South America, as well as First Nations. Moreover, these youth often identify with popular subcultural identities and forms. These include those of 'Nammers', 'Eminemers', 'Wannabe Asians', 'Ginos' and 'Nearly Black'. Several generations of work around youth culture have 'frozen' such young people at particular moments of time, often scripting their stories around one such key node in their lives. Dillabough and Kennelly avoid this temptation, focusing on the phenomenological experiences of these 'lost youth', in all their complexity. This includes new experiences of vulnerability, anxiety, risk and self-management associated with the loss of strong, central states and their attendant safety nets.

In so doing, Dillabough and Kennelly locate a generation 'in motion', moving between broader, overarching histories of immigration and class as well as more particular subcultural ones, as they navigate an increasingly diverse and fragmented cityscape. Dillabough and Kennelly use a supple set of theoretical and methodological tools, giving us a sharper perspective on these youth without calcifying them in time and place, as has so much work on youth to date. They chart out a new path here, looking at the narratives and phenomenological experiences of youth – finding and losing them again and again in this complex theoretical and empirical mix.

In the end, Dillabough and Kennelly accomplish much. They offer us a picture of young people as increasingly isolated, neo-liberal subjects self-managing and regulating their own identities, opportunities and outcomes. These youth live outside of the boundaries of a strong state, though they search for and live in large and small collective identities if only briefly and in passing. By giving shape and form to these lost youth – both looking across their experiences and attending to their particularities – Dillabough and Kennelly have set a productive and generative agenda for the field of critical youth studies.

Greg Dimitriadis

Acknowledgements

Like all ethnographies, it has taken some years for us to compile this cultural narrative about young people living on the hard edges of twenty-first century political economies in the global city. Hence the chapters were written in various draft forms in different places and times and put together formally as a book at a number of different institutions, including the University of British Columbia (Vancouver, Canada), OISE at the University of Toronto (Toronto, Canada), Deakin University (Melbourne, Australia) and the University of Cambridge (Cambridge, UK). We extend our gratitude to colleagues at each of these institutions for providing support and feedback on the work either in the form of early-stage presentations or on written text later in the process. A particular thanks is extended to the UBC thesis group and to the OISE thesis group, and the research assistants in both sites who carried out research with us or on behalf of the project. Carol Lynne D'Arcangelis and Anna Van der Meulen were the two research assistants at OISE and their background work and key contributions to the overall success of the ethnography cannot be overstated. Susan Sturman was particularly helpful in directing us towards key resources and individuals that helped us better understand and chart the policy context in Ontario; Yawei Cui offered important insights on the comparative dimension of our work. In Vancouver, Ee-Seul Yoon, Erin Graham, Jennifer Muir, Stephanie Skourtes and Eugenia Wang each provided essential contributions to the overall direction of the project, and we are most grateful to them for research assistance. Much of the work which implicates the intellectual likes of Hannah Arendt, Shoshana Felman and Wendy Brown was inspired by time spent at OISE and we owe Roger Simon much in expanding our reach, particularly by pointing us in the direction of new work.

We are also grateful to have received financial support for this work at a number of key stages in the writing of the book. We are particularly grateful to the Social Sciences and Humanities Research Council of Canada for funding this research across a seven-year period. This funding has provided the financial backbone of the comparative work and it goes without saying that research of this kind could never be done without such support. We have also been fortunate enough to have additional support throughout. The Deans' Fund from the University of British Columbia, the Spencer Foundation, a new Researcher's Grant from the Peter Wall Institute at UBC and a Killam Fellowship all provided either additional time and/or financial support for completing the monograph. A full year of writing support was also provided by the Faculty of Education at the University of Cambridge. We owe a special thanks to Mike Younger for ensuring that this time was granted and protected.

Similarly, there are a number of colleagues, individuals and/or groups who in one way or another were able to help us along the way, either by hosting conferences where the work was presented, as 'teachers', as critical friends or more general supporters of the work for us either together or independently. Julie McLeod, Andrea Allard, Andre Mazawi, Shauna Butterwick, Kathleen Gallagher, Diane Reay, Colleen McLaughlin, Mona Gleason, Madeleine Arnot, Kari Dehli, Handel Kalshope Wright, Kalervo Gulson, Sandra Acker, Kathy Bickmore, Meg McGuire, Gerry Pratt, Gabriel Ivinson, Greg Dimitriadas, Len Barton, Wendy Luttrell, Lois Weis, Don Fisher, Sue Fisher, Kjell Rubenson, Mary-Jane Kehily, Anoop Nayak, Christine Skelton, Rachel Thomson, Jill Blackmore, Johanna Wyn, Graham Smith, Linda Tuhiwai-Smith, Jane Gaskell, Fazal Rizvi, Bob Lingard, Martin Mills, Lori MacIntosh, Lisa Loutzenheiser, Sigal Speigal, Ze'ev Emmerich and Jane Kenway are just some of the many who have provided varying degrees of assistance along the way. The academic practice of naming important people in the writing of one's work is now a rudimentary task and yet we learn little in these long lists of the true lengths that some will go to to provide support when a writer suffers from illnesses, heartbreak, over-work, sheer exhaustion, university moves, losses or even writer's block. You have all been important to us in one way or another, and no book or publication is ever realized without a community 'without whom we would not be who we are'.

At more personal levels we are grateful to our family and friends for more general support.

From Jo: To Pascal and Dominique for enduring endless, blank staring into the computer, for forgiving mistakes and understanding limits. To Louis for standing by throughout. To my mother, Margaret, a supporter of young people, a teacher, an ardent unionist, an early feminist, an enlarged thinker and the central image of my life in terms of what I have learned about what it really means to 'think without banisters'. To P.S. Robinson and Mary-Clare Zak for the most exquisite of life-time friendships and to Judith Anastasia for unconditional emotional support. Special thanks also go to Aaron Davis and Candy Girling. To Robert, Celine, Michel, Marie and Tea Petazzi for providing extra childcare and more general relief from the routines of working life. Finally, a special thank you goes out to the *Village People* of Cambridge who cared for my children when I asked for help, and showed real kindness and friendship to us as newcomers. After many years of living as an urban dweller in the global city, the idea of the village has taken on a whole new meaning and I cannot say enough about how grateful I am to all those who opened their doors to us. Particular thanks go out to Chris Mann, Roger Mann, Beverley Carruthers, Bettina Furnee-Horton, Catherine Barnese, Neil Dysan, Ian Horton, Emma Giddens, Sigal Speigal, Ze'ev Emmerich, Bee Wilson, and David Runciman.

From Jackie: First and foremost, with utmost love and gratitude to my spouse, Cuc Duong, for coaching me in the art of finding balance, and for providing unwavering support even in the midst of the most difficult circumstances. To our daughter, KaiLin Duong, who spent her first year of life growing alongside this other baby, 'the book'. To Caroline Liffmann, my fountain of wisdom and friendship. To Lu Ripley and Elaine Arrowsmith, fellow mothers and lifelong friends. To my community of friends in both of our 'global cities' – Toronto and Vancouver (and some scattered elsewhere) – for listening ears, e-mail chats, visits and support. You make life so much richer. Finally, with eternal gratitude to my parents, who have given me what I needed to get to where I am: Barbara Kennelly, Lawrence Cornett and Ken Arenson.

Finally, a big thanks to the cheerful Richard Smith (for editing), and to Catherine Bernard and Greg Dimitriadis for being patient and supportive throughout.

Some sections of this book have been substantially revised from portions of published papers and presentations from elsewhere, and permission to publish them here in revised form has been granted as follows:

Dillabough, J. (2009). History and the making of young people and the late modern youth researcher: Time, narrative, and change. *Discourse: Studies in the Cultural Politics of Education, 30*(2), 213–229.

Dillabough, J., Kennelly, J. & Wang, E. (2005). 'Ginas', 'Thugs', and 'Gangstas': Young people's struggles to 'become somebody' in working-class urban Canada. *Journal of Curriculum Theorizing, 21*(3), 83–108.

Kennelly, J. & Dillabough, J. (2008). Young people mobilizing the language of citizenship: Struggles for classification and new meaning in an uncertain world. *British Journal of Sociology of Education, 29*(5), 493–508.

This book is dedicated to Phil Gardner. Every sentence is infused with his thinking, his mentorship, his brilliance and his kindness.

Part I: Introduction

A key power of narrative, claims Ricoeur, is to 'provide ourselves with a figure of something' [...]. So doing, we can make present what is absent. Translated into the idiom of historical time, we are dealing here with the capacity to liberate ourselves from the blind amnesia of the 'now' by projecting futures and retrieving pasts. Projection is an emancipatory function of narrative understanding, retrieval a testimonial function. Both resist the contemporary tendency to reduce history to a depthless 'present' of 'irreference'.

(Kearney, 2004: 99)

In this book, we seek to narrate an account of a new social group that has begun to gather both at the edge of the inner core and at the suburban fringes of late-modern Canadian cities. These are young people who have come to be seen by the media and even by some youth studies scholars as the 'lost young people' of the post-industrial global city, and who are thought to pose substantial threats to national order (see Nayak, 2003a, for theoretical and sociological critiques).[1] The youthful agents of these growing threats, which are presumed to be facing the 'West' at this moment, are seen principally to be deeply disaffected low-income young people, characteristically, but not always, from ethnic or religious minorities, and increasingly presumed to constitute a 'homegrown' problem of post-war multicultural nations, perceived – to use the much-quoted words of the former British Prime Minister Margaret Thatcher – as an insidious 'enemy within' or, more recently, as a highly mobile worldwide threat.

In making such young people the focus of this book, we must begin by asking: what does it mean to write about a group of people who are often sensationalized in the wider public arena as 'lost'? Are they to be described in this way because of the impact on their lives of state retrenchment, with all its bleak prospects for the future? And are they thereby constituted as the objects of another impending moral panic? Or perhaps the 'loss' is to be understood more in terms of an academic failure – of the inability of theory adequately to represent the complex interrelation of youth and youth cultures with social class and new scales of global change. Or, finally, to draw upon the now seminal work of Paul Ricoeur, have we simply failed as researchers to give young people's accounts some figurative depth because of our own amnesia of the 'now'?

1

In this book we attempt to address these questions. We do so by focusing particularly upon the cultural experiences of diverse groups of young people in two radically transformed modern urban centres: the Canadian cities of Toronto and Vancouver. Through a close engagement with the daily life experiences of 50 young people in these two urban concentrations, we hope to arrive at new conceptual understandings of the ways in which the 'losses' of which we have spoken are tied to both traditional and quite new forms of moral regulation in the 'global city' (Sassen, 2007; Skeggs, 2005; Skeggs & Binnie, 2004). We also explore the manner in which youth cultures are shaped by urban exclusion, specific local histories, diasporic shifts and migration flows, experienced by young people otherwise sensationalized away into a depthless mythology of the present. In revealing these elements of change, we seek to better understand how new class distinctions and cultural practices in youth groups emerge as they navigate discourses of zero tolerance, increasing surveillance, and new policing and media practices in re-ordered global neighbourhoods, schools and cities increasingly marked by a sense of loss (see Gallagher, 2007). Whilst increasingly unable to access the forms of mobility associated with global capitalism, these young urban dwellers have emerged as the symbolic locus for the general breakdown of life in the late-modern city.

Reporting on the urban riots in France in the summer of 2007, CNN offers us the following vivid and characteristically lurid expression of the prevailing mood of loss and disorder, together with the clear implication that particular groups of youth are still not to be seen by the wider public as a legitimate part of Western nations:

> The violence has spread to poor neighbourhoods across France, *shocking French society.* 'The response of the government is firmness,' said de Villepin. He said that Monday night 8000 police backed up by 1500 reserve police will be deployed to quell the violence. De Villepin said that so far more than 1200 arrests had been made. He blamed some of the violence on 'criminal networks' but said much of it was carried out by 'gangs of very young youths' who feel they have suffered discrimination and deprivation [...] [A]cting under a 1955 law, city leaders would be able to 'apply a curfew to ensure a return to peace and calm'. Asked who was causing the violence, the prime minister responded, 'They are delinquents.'
> (CNN online news, CNB@www.cnn.com/2005/US/11/07/
> monday/index.html)

It is with these twenty-first-century moral fields in mind that we must necessarily begin our account by examining the question of the 'lost generations' of young people who live on the fringes of the urban core in the new global cities of today. We do so by pointing to the historical paradoxes associated with the common fixation, exemplified by much of the corporate media, upon the new 'folk devils' of today. Accounts based on these assumptions do nothing so much as to highlight the capacity of the social 'world of the text' to generate distorted images of young people through the lens of moral assumptions. For us, what this means is that we will need to look beyond the representation of economically disadvantaged young people as being ever in need of rescue from the clutches of vice and criminality, towards a temporal and spatial narrative of youth experience which does not leave these young people frozen in the text or in 'historical time' (see Ricoeur, 1981).

Such a recognition of temporality and historicity, alongside that of more dominant theoretical concepts in the study of youth cultures such as 'culture', 'spatial imaginaries', 'discourses' or 'structures', calls for sustained attention to some of the wider theoretical debates concerned with youth subculture and post-subcultures and their very limited presence in contemporary youth studies research (see Shildrick, 2006; Shildrick & MacDonald, 2006). For example, some argue that, along with the supposed death of class as a category of social analysis (the post-subculturalists), the utility of subcultural theory has now run its course (see Muggleton, 2000; Redhead, 1993, 1997, 2004). Others, by contrast, have retained an interest in analyses of the symbolic elements of youth cultures as they might remain connected to global variations in social class relations (see Nayak, 2003c; Pilkington, 2004; Shildrick, 2006). And still others argue for 'next wave cultures', 'can do' cultures or post-subcultures (see Harris, 2009).

Our approach here is to pursue a middle course, arguing that the residual weight of the past retains a hold over young people's cultural expressions and social practices at the same time as change infiltrates and reconfigures those symbolic practices that form the basis of youth identity work. To talk of dispensing with the material, temporal and cultural forms of subject narration is to dispense with the power of meaningful experience through which any potentially displaced or de-centred subject must necessarily speak. In other words, we seek to show the relationship between the existence of what Paul Ricoeur refers to as an 'opaque subjectivity' which expresses itself through countless mediations – signs, symbols, texts – and meaningful human practices which are narrated across time and place.

At the same time, and regardless of place or temporality, young people are always the bearers of something which must necessarily exceed their own frontiers. To understand these frontiers and their excesses requires us to pay adequate attention to the temporal and spatial complexity which lies at the heart of narrative identity,[2] and to accept that there are uneven degrees and scales of global change which impact on young people at the level of local experience. The complexity and unevenness of youth culture across waves of change and context ultimately require us to turn towards the narrative accounts of young people themselves. We can thereby offer a temporalized comparative account of late-modern life that is able to incorporate the contemporary conditions that young people face as they navigate urban social arrangements which are 'more than local and less than global' (Pinney, 2001) and in no simple way linked just to the present. In our attempt to assess these frontiers, we hope to capture novel forms of youth culture which not only operate at the edge of our exemplar cities – Toronto and Vancouver – but which point to quite new 'forms of selfhood and patterns of social life' (see McDonald, 1999) associated with being young in global cities at the start of the twenty-first century.

In looking to the idea of narration and young storied lives, our concern is directed to moving away from 'trauma narratives' (see Felman, 1992, 2000) and 'voice accounts' of young people, and towards the idea of the young person who is always in the process of becoming someone through the relational practices of recognition. This is a storied process which operates through deeply symbolic, often invisible and sometimes quite unremarkable practices of recognition as young actors compose their experiences in particular places and temporal moments. This means that, for us, the story of being young forms the object of representation rather than the identity of the young person. And, in embracing this idea of the story of youth selfhood as operating somewhere between truth and fiction, myth and legend, and between the objective and subjective, we seek to show how youth narratives encode and recode 'human time'. As Caverero (2000: 37) writes: 'the identity that materializes in a "life story" has no future that is properly its own if it has no past in the present of its memory'.[3] That is to say, that human time is a temporalized account of one's life as represented in a story.

The paragraphs above encapsulate some of the major dilemmas and challenges which have led towards our thinking on youth narratives and social class, seen here as forming part of the 'social world of the text' and serving as a partial reflection of late-modern narratives of state life. If the narratives (e.g. visual, linguistic, aesthetic, written) we had encountered in our *spatial ethnography* had a clear substantive dimension, opening previously unexplored connections between the lives of young people in the post-industrial city and the lives of young people from an unknown past, they also spoke directly to larger theoretical concerns about the need for a temporally and geographically bounded account of youth culture. For us, young people's accounts of life at the edge of the global city spoke to the need to find new ways of working towards a localized expression of that 'temporalised sociology' of youth cultures about which

Patrick Baert (1992: 1) has so thoughtfully written. These expressions are not free-standing accounts of youth *identity* – as in sameness or in the same place – but instead represent the shifting moral registers of time and place as they are embodied and performed by young people themselves.[4]

All of these considerations lead us to our key questions: Why does the spectral image of late-modernity's 'lost youth' sit so close to the core of public consciousness in 'the new global city'? How are we to understand this image, penetrate its meanings and relate it to radical urban transformations? Such questions point us towards the kind of contemporary narrative account that appears here – the stories related by the *Gangsta Girls and Boys*, the *Thugs*, the *Nammers*, the *Hardcore Asians*, and the *Ginas* and the *Ginos* of today's urban Canada – and that we place at the heart of the book.

Our hope in invoking contemporary accounts from young people is that we might begin to view youth narrations of contemporary cultural practice in the global city as a 'mode of emplotment which synthesizes heterogeneous elements' (see Kearney, 2004: 34) which unfold in the face of time and space, as well as simultaneously visualizing the official and unofficial forms of classification and governance of young people from a distant past and its modes of operation (see Foucault, 1977). Significantly, then, these youth narrations are not best seen as origins or as wholly unbounded discourses. Rather, they may be better understood as 'effective' narrations which help us recognize that

> if everything is an effect of historical accident rather than will or design, then we are, paradoxically, both more severely historical and also more plastic than we might have otherwise seemed [...]. We are more sedimented by history but also more capable of intervening in our histories.
>
> (Brown, 2001: 102)

Our point here is that in contemporary political dialogue about young people, the association of the present to the past is typically cast through 'idealizations and demonizations in particular epochs and/or [classed] individuals' (Brown, 2001: 102; brackets our addition). How, this leads us to ask, do these representations hide, elide, defer or symptomize the place of young people in the present? How do they mask the most challenging questions about young people who live at the edge of twenty-first-century political economies, largely ignored by the nations who claim still to care for them whilst simultaneously mourning their own losses of apparent stability and tradition? In addressing such questions we hope to reveal the identity work in which young people themselves engage as they interweave lived experience in the twenty-first-century city with the landscapes, rituals and legends of the urban past.

Youthful Subjectivities of Cultural Loss, Risk and 'Individualized' Failure

At the same time as we endeavour to track novel patterns of youth cultural activity, we also seek to uncover what Willis (1977), three decades earlier, referred to as the forms of 'caged resentment' or what we call, following Raymond Williams and Frederic Jameson, the deep structures of ambivalent 'feeling' experienced by economically disadvantaged young people.[5] In so doing we do not, however, wish to return to the factory shop floor, a pre- and post-war site of labour now also lost to the project of global change on a vast scale. And nor do we wish to remain tied to the other post-subcultural polarity of 'lost youth', entertaining seemingly oblivious and apolitical twenty-first-century lives on the techno dance floor or on the Ecstasy-driven global and digital transdance beaches of a once 'distant East'. Grossberg's (1997) 'Dancing Despite Myself' or the Ecstasy-driven phrase 'I'd Rather Feel Bad than Feel Nothing at All' come to mind here as apposite metaphorical devices for entertaining 'lost youth'.

Clearly, the space of observation or of change is long past a fixed labour site, an apparently selfish Ecstasy-driven club culture, and an overly simplified account of territorial class practices of protection, kinship control and resistance. Instead, what we witnessed comparatively as we encountered the young people in our study was, on the one hand, the spatialized unfolding of a story about a wholly new group of young people, a group which still undoubtedly carried the historical burdens of social resentment towards a state which remained substantially tied to class (a class that was not yet dead but rather still mired in boredom or 'anomie').[6] On the other hand, and often simultaneously, we also recognized youthful experiences of quite substantial post-war diasporic movement leading to new spatialized and localized forms of youth classification (see Nayak, 2003b). Here was a spatially and culturally reconfigured 'urban imprisonment', a kind of 'dancing in the dark' which was most typically expressed as ambivalence about one's place in the city in the past, present and future. These 'structured planes and scales of affect' or 'mattering maps'[7] emerged most particularly in response to radical changes taking place in immediate neighbourhood locales and in relation to wider global scales of popular culture. Using our comparative dual-sited ethnographic lens, we attempted to tease out the complex relations between space, history and identity that we witnessed unfolding on the ground.

In our comparative spatial ethnography, the personified feelings of loss of visibility and failure which young people often embodied were deeply felt and expressed as a 'classification struggle' (see Bourdieu, 1984) in which they engaged with themselves and others. In this respect, the dominant regulating force was a heightened emphasis upon late-twentieth-century forms of liberalism and mobile narratives of panic and risk management which had infiltrated and changed the nature of youth cultural activities and of nation, as well as concepts of citizenship and culture. Some part of their complementary influence also incorporated an enhanced emphasis on the idea of self-perfection and self-making, new micro-nationalist forms of self- and group 'identity' governance, alongside a re-ordering and recoding of earlier subcultural hierarchies, sometimes, though not exclusively, in the direction of post-subcultural or 'next-wave' hybridity.

A further significant feature we noted was the return of forms of moral regulation which were not straightforwardly traditional but re-traditionalized (see also Adkins, 2002) such that traditional forms of moral regulation were packaged and represented in new forms. These forms emerged often as a form of presentism, primarily in relation to the 'war on terror' which seemed critical in tipping the balance towards a new gendered form of racialization and new patterns of race relations in relation to youth communities in particular urban spaces (Ahmed, 2003, 2004a). The prevalence of these new moral regimes and classifications of exchange and value (see Skeggs, 2004, 2005) in the governing of the lives of young people can be seen as tied in part to the folding of new 'crisis' content into the practice of traditional discourses of morality which young people and their families were already negotiating (i.e. re-traditionalization). In such cases, we were able to witness the simultaneous operation of both self-governance (as a new way of thinking of oneself in relation to the state, including the symbolic language of individualized selfhood such as 'I can be who I want to be', or 'next year I'm going to be more like myself', 'I'm equal to boys and better so I can be tough'), and more traditional forms of subcultural authority ('we stick together to watch our back', 'you gotta do right by your gang').

These re-traditionalized forms of classed morality could not be understood without some attention to the ways in which moral regulation remained substantially associated with both inherited and new class relations (such as urban retrenchment or the redrawing of new neighbourhood boundaries in the urban city, Safe Streets legislation, etc.), as well as with the power of particular and local geographical arrangements. There are, of course, different styles of self-governance and modalities of authority among youth cultural groups across distinct geographical spaces, and in relation to the twenty-first century's new moral registers. It is the distinctions of these styles and modalities that we particularly wish to explore and, where possible, to historicize.

Alongside re-traditionalized forms of self-regulation, a further spatial constant was a powerful need for young people to identify with a wider and sometimes symbolic figure of authority in a rapidly changing city. In our study, not unlike Cohen's (1972) argument in earlier times, and against Willis' (1977) contention that resistance is the most powerful form of class reproduction, young people living in tightly bound first- and second-generation immigrant communities demonstrated no straightforward resistance to the most visible forms of educational or social authority. Many recognized that, for example, teachers were 'doing their best', 'were trying to help'. Many would also comment that: 'I want to graduate and the teachers are trying but I don't think I will', or 'it's probably too late', or 'I'm gonna feel excluded in university like because I'm gonna see all these people that have high marks and like they know a lot of stuff and I'm gonna be, like, *lost*.'

In most cases these young people were aware that larger systemic problems served as uncomfortable barriers to class mobility and dictated a prospect of the future that seemed likely to keep them firmly contained in their working-class neighbourhoods. *Resistance through rituals* (Hall & Jefferson, 1976) was not what was going on here. Rather, what young people were left with was a profoundly spatialized ambivalence which rendered them uncomfortable about geographical mobility, the school, the city and their futures. Whilst clearly recognizing the failure of the state (and middle-class forms of authority) to support them and their families, rituals of self-doubt and class and race denial were in many cases more common among these young people, particularly in relation to shoring up and evaluating friendship groups, conceptualizing legitimacy and belonging, and contemplating their futures.

In new urban arrangements, young people often classified themselves and their not-so-distant others as 'unworthy', as 'space invaders', or as trespassers, but neighbourhood boundary crossing 'or breaking out' represented uncomfortable urban imaginaries of social risk. Indeed, the psychic costs of doing something different in the new city, where boundary markers of social class were much clearer and symbolically marked than in an earlier period, were so great that ambivalence about moving on became profoundly immobilizing (Baumann, 2007). Young people expressed feelings of being 'lost' to a world that no longer recognized them ('gotta look out for yourself now', 'nobody gives a shit about the kids in the *ghetto*', 'you got to watch your back', 'the cops don't even come here anymore', or 'there are never any cops here, never and the dealers are right outside my door!') at the same time as performing deeply spatialized and new authorized versions of class, race and cultural protection in relation to, for example, school authorities and surveillance cameras. The symbolic expressions were heavily mediated by rising moral registers about, for example, 'gang' activities, black/white violence, indigenous land claims, new gender relations and increasing anomie associated in part with a post-9/11 world.

New Folk Devils, Urban Security and the Global–Local Nexus

As we stated at the outset, a pervasive social anxiety has been circulating in public consciousness about the emergence of terror threats and in relation to 'real' political events in major urban centres (e.g. 7/7 London bombings, 2005 French suburb riots). These growing social anxieties have, to varying degrees, been explored by criminologists, urban studies scholars and sociologists interested in surveillance (see Ahmed, 2003; Thompson, 1998). However, within the sociology of education, youth studies and youth cultural studies, very few questions have been asked about the cultural manifestation of new moral economies of social life, and their associated regulatory or mediating impact on young people – those who are often identified as the 'new folk devils' in urban concentrations. As cultural sociologists we were therefore faced with the dilemmas of ascertaining how to broach questions about new moral economies of the city and young people simultaneously. The kinds of questions and associated dilemmas which emerged were: How might we seek to conceptualize the character, as well as the dimensions, of the consuming combination of suspicion and dread which are posed by post-9/11 urban youth? How should we endeavour to understand this largely uninvestigated constituency in sociological, cultural and educational terms in order to afford some systematic purchase both upon its genesis and upon any possibility for its sustained engagement? How do low-income young people navigate new cultural fields of moral regulation and flows of migration and change? And how are such navigations related to particular spatial locations in the global city and emerging forms of youth subjectivity, youth cultures and youth classification?

In contemplating these questions we recognized that youth cultural studies afforded some potentially very helpful conceptual tools which, with some revision and nuance, might still be put to some good analytical use. Though now more than three decades old, Stan Cohen's (1972) challenging dualism, 'folk devils' and 'moral panics', still offered us an important starting point for such an exploration. Indeed, the expansive conceptual power of the notion of moral panic (although organized differently in the twenty-first century), with all its intimations of moral uncertainty and impending crisis, afforded a starting point for addressing the novel problems posed for excluded, low-income youth by, amongst other contemporary trends, globalization, global economic crises and large-scale migratory flows.

In its original configuration, the threat of those constructed as youthful 'folk devils' provided the symbolic focus for the concentration of a general social perception of uncertainty, loss and anxiety. But, in conducting our research, like others we recognized that now, three decades on in the twenty-first century, the basis for moral panic no longer resides in the localized and often over-determined class threats issued by Mods and Rockers battling on the beach at Clacton, the under-determined class practices of the virtual clubber or 'wannabe' black Goa Transdancer, or any straightforward and easily identifiable 'folk devil' in new times (see Ahmed, 1999, 2004b; Spooner, 2006). Rather, it invoked the behaviours, practices and strategies – now global as well as local and transnational – seen to be available to excluded urban youth.

At the same time, the basis for today's claims about being young are not the same as they were in the time of Britain's factory shop floor or Toronto's Clearhousing and post-war 'slum' sanitization projects. In the 'new' times of the twenty-first century young people are navigating the movements of culture and people, as well as the ideas of what constitutes the so-called 'world-class' city. Here we witness new media-generated fears of highly sensationalized accounts of white working-class tattooed Chav boys and their pitbull dogs, sensationalized media accounts of South American and Asian street gangs lifted by air and by sea from their homelands 'knifing' and 'shooting' their way to North American success, and Muslim Jihadist boys terrorizing the 'West'.[8]

Cohen's original notion of moral panic has always retained the material and symbolic charge of its particular association with the de-stabilizing challenges presented by youth in terms of the late-twentieth-century 'revolt into style' which dominated early understandings of the concept. But the true power of the idea of 'moral panic' lies in its enduring promise for engaging the radically changed conditions of a new, transnational economic and cultural world (see Thompson, 1998; Ungar, 2001; Hier, 2003), as well as in recognizing its continued power as a regulatory force and symbolic economy of urban social class relations (see Jameson, 2000; Miller & Rose, 2008). However, as class continues to be diminished as a sociological concept worthy of investigation, so too does the investigation of increasing youth stratification and its links to the affective and moral geographies of youth culture. Consequently, conceptions of moral regulation, governance and the re-ordering of both cities and youth cultures still await systematic revision in relation to those contemporary youth groups substantially affected both by exclusion and by the scale of current increases in security measures directed against them, powerfully perceived but indeterminately conceived. We therefore argue that these are precisely the groups for which a revivified conceptualization of the notions of 'folk devil' and new moral registers have some real analytical utility, albeit reconstructed here in new ways.

Cumulative recent research work demonstrates that urban Canada represents an example of urbanizing and globalizing sites where 'moral panic' about urban youth is visibly on the rise, largely in response to: recent political challenges to the idea of the liberal democratic state; the rise in urban and suburban economic disadvantage, sometimes accompanied by racial tension (e.g. see Poynting, 2006); and recent documented changes in local security measures and migration patterns in urban concentrations of poverty (e.g. Vancouver and Toronto crime crackdown, Safe Streets legislation). Alongside these social changes, the apparent promise of life in the new global city has been constantly undermined by very strong indications that rising levels of youth marginalization are closely associated with the pronounced anti-welfare stance many urban centres have adopted in relation to economically disadvantaged youth over the last decade. In ideological terms, such policies can be seen to draw powerfully upon globally dominant currents and scales of neo-liberal social thinking (see, e.g. Dei & Kurumanchy, 1999; Dillabough et al., 2005; HRDC, 2007; Weis, 2008).

But if growing media attention and urban educational and social policies have been directed towards linking youth economic disadvantage with new dangers in urban centres, both in Canada and internationally, it has also become increasingly evident that those identified as the most disadvantaged are precisely those who are being pushed off the global economic agenda and who are obliged to live on the often unrecognizable fringe of the urban core. While there are clear signs that incipient contemporary anxieties are growing alongside wider social changes – and emerging as a powerful cross-national phenomenon – very little research has investigated how the consequences of such changes have been conceptualized, understood, negotiated and narrated by low-income young people in comparative Canadian urban contexts.

Equally problematic is that, within the sociology of education, attention to the new forms of moral regulation now circulating has remained largely outside the study of urban youth cultures, youth exclusion and young people's urban imaginaries of the city,[9] being found more typically in the fields of criminology, cultural geography, cultural sociology and mainstream sociology. Moreover, the idea of moral panic is now seen by many contemporary youth culture scholars as a deeply constraining term. But throughout the entire discipline (Skeggs et al., 2004), powerful questions about social change, such as the shifting character of moral regulation and urban conflict in the lives of economically disadvantaged young people, still remain yet are substantively ignored by the majority of youth studies and youth culture scholars. As Kelly (2000) and others have observed (see Shildrick, 2006), 'pathways and transitions' seems to be the dominant mode of youth research as our obsession with the future and with progress predominates. Whilst much of the work in this mode offers important indicators of change, it tends to pass over the larger context of morality, urban youth cultures, national imaginaries and their associated links to urban class conflict. One of our key goals is therefore to bridge this gap between sociology of education, youth culture research and the wider social sciences. Of course, in so doing, we do not wish to remain wedded to the idea of 'panic' as the primary mechanism for thinking through the challenges of exploring the formations underlying current urban youth exclusions. Rather, we hope to build on this early work and take it forward in new ways.

Rationale: Global Scales of Change, New Minority Nationalisms and the Late-Modern Canadian City

In addressing wider scales of globalization, we do not support the idea of the 'end of nationalism' which has so long been predicted through globalization processes in the sociology of education literature. Rather, we follow Saskia Sassen (2007; see also Apparadurai, 1996, 2000) in her assessment that globalization also inhabits the national and the local. The new task of sociological research is thus to 'detect the presence of globalizing dynamics in thick social environments that mix national and non-national elements' (Sassen, 2007: 5). In this way, we might suggest that the contextual, class and spatial realities of young people's lives in cities are negotiated in relation to wider scales of global change which have resulted in the localized re-ordering of cities within nation-states. Consequently, urban contexts can no longer be seen as straightforwardly reflecting early-twentieth-century and post-war ideas of the nation as either coherent or as a largely abstract and empty term. This is a particularly important point to make in relation to the documented widening disparities in class relations, the scale, sheer volume and movement of ideas, people and finances, and the subsequent refiguring of political economies and immigration policies through the very mobility of panic as a global urban imaginary.[10]

As our research with young people shows, these new registers of panic and anxiety often take the form of new minority nationalisms (or micro-nationalisms) at the scale of the city and neighbourhood, and change the ways in which young people in these locations classify themselves and others. In charting these classifications, we focus particularly upon 'the affective and cathectic' (see Ahmed, 2003, 2004a; Lawler, 2005, 2008) aspects of being young and economically disadvantaged in contemporary urban contexts. From this perspective, moral disdain can no longer simply represent an encoded classification for middle-class feelings of disgust towards the white working class – that is, 'inter-class' distinctions of taste (see Bourdieu, 1984). Rather, such terms need to be understood as pervasive features of the urban fringe, as everyday intra-class distinctions tied to the wider moral registers of the 'foreign other' (see Kennelly & Dillabough, 2008), and organized historically in ways which sometimes operate as fragmented forms of micro-nationalism(s). Lawler writes:

George Orwell famously declared 'the real secret of class distinctions in the West' is to be summed up in 'four frightful words': 'The lower classes smell' [1937]. What was at issue for Orwell was less literal (real or imagined) than what smell signifies – the alterity, for the middle classes, of working class existence. [...] [Being disgusted] is at the very core of their subjectivity: their very selves are produced in opposition to the low and the low cannot do anything but repulse them [...]. This is not simply a matter of cognition but is bound up with middle class identity. Orwell continues (in a phrase that prefigures Bourdieu's concept of the habitus): The fact has got to be faced that to abolish class-distinctions means abolishing part of your self [1937].

(Lawler, 2005: 429; see also Lawler, 2008a, 2008b, 2009)

While Orwell's observations about class distinctions in the 'West' might have been incisive in 1937, we need to look more closely at his intimation (and, by association, that of Lawler, 2005) that in order truly to grasp the nucleus of class imaginaries in new times, it is necessary to expose the residual surplus meanings, social structures and the new geographies of power associated with the feeling of being disgusted by others, and which allow for new classifications of young people to emerge or to be sustained and recast in new ways.

In responding to increasingly heightened degrees of hysteria and anxiety associated with these changes in urban Canadian cities, we take a number of key starting points. The first is the plethora of recent global media outputs linking youthful urban cultures with incipient terrorist activity, violent crime, school failures or individualized disengagement from the state or city altogether. The second is the range of contested policy debates contrasting 'integrationism', citizenship, migration and devolved urban cities with Anglophone 'multiculturalism'. And the third is that body of current European, Canadian and wider international research which posits growing generational fears and increasing public anxieties about young people perceived as fundamentally disengaged from conventional political structures (e.g. Institute for Public Policy Research, 2006).

Finally, the widespread belief that Canada represents one of the last bastions of social welfare and public support for young people has also been exaggerated – mythologized – beyond acceptability. It is necessary to provide some understanding in global terms of the ways in which urban retrenchment in Canadian cities substantiates and parallels wider international research findings on the relationship between youth and social exclusion. For example, recent policy work indicates that the incidence of poverty – particularly child and youth economic disadvantage – has risen dramatically in Canada and other post-industrial nations in recent years, and continues to do so (see Human Resources and Development Canada (HRDC), 1997, 2001; First Call: BC Child and Youth Advocacy Coalition, 2008). Similar concerns have been raised in the US, Europe and other western nations about the relationship between rising urban poverty, growing urbanization and regeneration practices, and new rural–urban migration patterns and class and ethnic conflict (see also Ungar, 2001). As Weis (2008: 2) writes: 'with a clear turn in the global economy, one accompanied by deep intensification of social inequalities, the need for serious class based analysis of schooling [...] and social structure could not be more pressing.'

It is also manifestly clear that the social groups most profoundly affected by increasing levels of economic disadvantage and associated social conflicts are children and young people, principally in urban settings. The Canadian Council on Social Development (CCSD, 2000) and Human Rights Watch (2009) have reported that the numbers of young people living in poverty or deprived social conditions in urban centres have nearly doubled over the last two decades (between 1989 and 2008). Those sectors of youth which appear to be most affected by this increase are visible minorities, Aboriginal, first- and second-generation migrant youth, asylum-seeking youth and young lone mothers (CCSD, 2000; Frankish et al., 2005). These same groups are often seen as providing the representational apparatus for both the public projection and the embodiment of class disgust and moral anxiety, highlighted by media and government institutions alike. To put this in another way, those principally affected by some of the trends we have documented here constitute the 'lost' groups which remain almost wholly outside those social changes associated with middle-class advantage, and largely beyond the reach of any positive features associated with global mobility or burgeoning national wealth in the 'West'. Yet they remain targets for the repository of middle-class anxiety about young people and their presence in the 'world-class' city.

Broad Objectives and Organization of the Book

In light of the above discussion, *Lost Youth in the Global City* may be seen to have two overarching objectives. The first is to build, layer by layer, an intimate and detailed ethnographic picture of the everyday lives and experiences of today's urban youth and to assess these cumulative accounts in relation to wider theories of youth selfhood, culture and global cities. The second is to understand the ways in which such everyday experiences have been translated into cultural expression and, where relevant, into new systems of youth classification. We seek to uncover how these experiences are interpreted, on the one hand, through desires for belonging, for security, and for a twenty-first-century idea of citizenship;

and, on the other, through novel forms of youth class-conflict, changing gender relations, new national imaginaries, race relations and peer rivalry.

Our study centres upon the two Canadian cases we identified from the outset – Toronto (Tower Hill) and Vancouver (Beacon Park). Each represents particular national contexts and specific histories and geographies, generating policies which shape the experiences of the young people confined within their metropolitan and national borders. Each also represents particular scales of the global, each sharing characteristic elements of the new and emergent form of urban space called the 'global city' (Sassen, 2007). Located in central and Western Canada, respectively, both Toronto and Vancouver have experienced rising waves of immigration largely from countries of the 'Global South' and Southern and Eastern Europe, are increasingly enmeshed in international trade and are the settings for hotly contested retrenchment policies. In earlier periods, each of our neighbourhood sites also witnessed the commonly shared history of the twentieth-century industrial 'working classes' (including post-war clearance zones) and both housed industries and factories where many immigrant and white working-class groups and their children were employed.

Though having much in common, our two sites also exhibit some important differences. For example, in Toronto a much more locally contained post-war history of European immigration – particularly from Southern Europe (e.g. Italy, Portugal, Greece and Macedonia) and, to a lesser degree in recent years, Eastern Europe (particularly from Poland) – was evident in the local neighbourhood and the surrounding locales. By contrast, the Vancouver neighbourhood is shaped by the flow of much South Asian and Central Asian immigration and associated diasporic movements (the Pacific Rim borders), and has more recently been a locus for Central and South American youth arriving in Vancouver, often unaccompanied by their immediate or extended families. This site was also home to a much larger percentage of low-income First Nations families, many of whom were living on the economic fringes of the modern Canadian city. In terms of both comparative similarities and differences, Vancouver and Toronto proved to represent eminently suitable urban arenas for our study, serving as exemplars for similar sites in countries with a broadly similar history of liberal democratic traditions and rapidly globalizing and increasingly post-industrial economies.

The broad research objectives we set for ourselves resolved themselves into a series of discrete but interlinked questions for investigation: What is it like to live in a world where intimations of incipient terrorism, whether considered or casual, have become the new channel for everyday racism and ethnic hysteria? What does it mean to be subject at one moment to unseen and unknown surveillance from the formal agencies of the state, and at another, to the constant gaze of competing youth groups in school and on the street? What is life like for economically disadvantaged young people of late-modern Canada, no longer at the centre of city life, but pushed instead to a new marginal existence at the edge of the urban core? How are shifting and still conflicted gender relations and expectations changing the contours of life in the school and on the street for young people? How are changing patterns of migration, race relations and work making themselves felt among marginalized youth in the radically transformed urban city of the twenty-first century?

In coming to grips with these cardinal questions, we have had to move outside what McDonald (1999) refers to as the current impasses in the field of youth studies. We have sought to do this by drawing strongly upon the disciplines of cultural studies and human and cultural geography in order to achieve more nuanced accounts of youth cultures which simultaneously embrace the concepts of change, fluidity and sedimentation. This amounts to a conceptual apparatus with the potential to challenge earlier youth studies accounts resting upon uniform and classed analyses of youth subcultures. At the same time, we also highlight the need to 'rethink social class' (see Skeggs, 2004) and wider sociological questions concerning 'value exchange' by exploring their moral, spatial and phenomenological dimensions. In so doing, we assess in particular the role of class and new urban geographies of power in shaping what we have witnessed as the deeply 'spatial structures of locale' (see Stahl, 1999) and their impact on the reconfiguration of youth communities as a late-modern social phenomenon.

In practical terms, this means that we have sought to allow the ethnographic and empirical dimensions of our work shape the specific claims we make about youth cultural configuration and forms of social conflict and fragmentation experienced by young people at the turn of the twenty-first century.[11] Yet, as Ricoeur tells us, the power of residual surplus meanings to shape the narrative accounts of urban exclusion and youth cultures retain considerable force as young people navigate new times. In this respect, new times are not always as new as might be supposed (see McLeod & Yates, 2006). With these comparative and contextual structures in place, it is possible to chart key elements of global change as one new 'subterranean channel' (see Hebdige, 1979) and to attempt to assess their impact on contemporary youth cultures, emphasizing their links, as Nayak (2003a) suggests, to the temporal geographies of place and globalization.

In terms of intellectual lineage, this book is perhaps best understood as developing and augmenting aspects of the rich intellectual legacy of the highly influential phenomenological tradition established three decades ago by the Birmingham Centre for Contemporary Cultural Studies, alongside the hermeneutic approach developed by Paul Ricoeur. Following the innovative cultural approaches mapped by writers such as Sarah Ahmed, Phil Cohen, Stan Cohen, Stuart Hall, Anoop Nayak, Lawrence Grossberg, Mary Jane Kehily, Beverly Skeggs, Paul Gilroy and many others, the book can be seen as a contribution to understanding the ways in which urban geographies of change are currently shaping new forms of youth identification. However, 30 years on, the Birmingham tradition needs to be reconfigured both in relation to recent theoretical developments in youth studies, and against the background of very different historical circumstances, shaped by sweeping new currents of globalization, radically different economic policies and crises, and manifestations of urban malaise.

In this way, our approach seeks to draw not only upon established youth subcultural theories, but is also centrally informed by those contemporary theories about youth cultural identification which, through a sociological and phenomenological approach, highlight the significance of the direct cultural and spatial experiences of young people themselves. Such an approach further recognizes that conditions of social exclusion and youth cultural formations are not only subject to a high degree of external regulation and political socialization but are also simultaneously mediated intersubjectively through sedimented histories, social communities and local–global spaces. A key epistemological approach here draws upon the phenomenological hermeneutics of Paul Ricoeur (1981). Such a theoretical interdisciplinarity we believe to be appropriate for the complex tasks we have identified for understanding the unprecedented challenges facing urban youth in the early twenty-first century.

At the methodological heart of the book is what we have termed a 'spatial ethnographic' (Chari, 2005) approach, drawing heavily on elements of visual sociology, and highly influenced by phenomenological, cultural and geographical concerns (described in greater detail in Chapter 2). This approach has equipped us with the methodological tools to chart mobile patterns of globalization as they are manifested locally and are seen to 'fit' into the local scales of urban life we have researched. Here, we particularly emphasize the importance of both the enduring and changing elements of youth cultural practices associated with race, gender, class and space.

In the first part of the book, we begin by setting the scene and laying the groundwork for exploring and challenging prevailing impasses in the field of youth cultural studies, as well as outlining our theoretical and methodological orientation for the work.

Chapter 1 elaborates our theoretical frame, focusing primarily upon cultural and geographical accounts of youth cultural activity, which allow for an assessment of the relationship between schooling (as a regulative social institution), social exclusion (as a social and cultural practice), and the formation and development of youth cultures in urban spatial contexts. The chapter rests primarily upon a framework which embraces elements of classical youth subcultural theory (Clarke, 1976; Hebdige, 1979; Cohen, 1997; Willis, 1977), geographical theories of the relationship between youth identity, urban space and social exclusion (Jameson, 2000; Massey, 1994, 1999, 2005; Nayak, 2003a, 2003b, 2003c) and cultural sociology (see Ahmed, 2004b; Bourdieu, 1997; McNay, 2000; Skeggs, 2004, 2005: Skeggs & Binnie, 2004) – particularly the idea of education as a spatial site and moral field of meaning-making which young people must necessarily draw from. From this vantage point, such meaning-making among youth is seen to be manifested in the complex narrations and experiences of young people themselves. At the same time, we chart a theoretical approach that necessarily moves beyond a subcultural theory of youth. To do this, we focus on the wider contemporary significance of symbolic culture, history, geographies of risk and exclusion, and young people's sedimented cultural narratives as regulating elements in the formation of youth cultures.

The theoretical frame occupies an integral place in our methodological approach, detailed in Chapter 2. In keeping with the phenomenological concerns of the classic youth cultural theorists, and consistent with Bourdieu's ethnographic approach to field work, our methods incorporate not only the standard semi-structured interview, but also involve the self-reflection and symbolic repertoires of participants through visual channels such as photography, archival material, self-portraits, critical media analysis and other written cultural texts. We also draw heavily upon the spatial dimension of our work in further developing what we identify as a spatial ethnography through the use of maps, accounts of urban space and wider urban zoning policies.

In Chapter 3, we offer a much more detailed account of each of the comparative research sites, as well as distinguishing between the concepts of context and space. In so doing, we work towards challenging dominant perceptions of Canada as a fundamentally harmonious site for the cultivation of social welfare and the future of young people. Instead, we locate Canada in a wider context of neo-liberal change, growing class conflict, heightened urbanization, changing migration patterns and the developing forms of urban malaise associated with urban retrenchment on a much wider scale. While our accounts of the young people we encountered as the 'lost youth of the global city' do not imply a future without hope and in no way presume an individualized 'loss', we maintain that a cultural, social and affective language of 'loss' remains the most appropriate and accurate one for understanding wider urban imaginaries and repositories of often elusive change.

For us, what this means more precisely is that loss must be seen on a much wider scale, indeed on a global scale, and in relation to the very idea of the global city. It must not be understood as a loss which is bound by the interiority of the young people we encountered. Nor does it stand in any straightforward way for the death or loss of collective subcultures or for the simple endurance of traditional accounts. Indeed, patterns of migration, rising moral anxiety and shifting gender relations serve as part of what Nayak (2003b) has referred to as a 'creative reworking' of local youth identities which are commonly misunderstood by the wider public. Among youth cultures, our research discerned many elements of that which McNay (2000, 2008) has referred to as class and gender sedimentation, helping us to understand loss as Carolyn Steedman (1986, 2000) has expressed it – as the loss of legitimacy and visibility in a post-industrial city. Taken together, Chapters 1 to 3 form the first part of the book.

In the second part, we focus much more substantially upon young people's urban narrations of the global city and their cultural manifestations as they are expressed in both distinct and more fluid youth formations in localized settings. Our aim is to draw primarily upon the highly variegated but still interrelated scales of urban space such as the school corridor, the neighbourhood, the border terrain of these neighbourhoods, the city, the nation, and emergent national imaginaries and symbolic micro-nationalisms. We begin the second part of the book with a focused revisiting of our core theoretical ideas, outlining the main conceptual tools that we have applied to the ethnographic case studies explored in the chapters that make up this second part.

In Chapter 4, we make our first evaluation of the ethnographic data. We focus in particular upon the interface between moral anxieties and modalities of youth representation which are associated with space-based class performances of peer rivalry in the school corridor. In so doing, the chapter charts the ways in which youth subcultural and post-subcultural identification is shaped by the new forms of gendered and racialized peer rivalries operating on the margins of the 'new global city'. We also attempt to answer questions which account for changes in youth subcultural formations; our focus here is specifically on schooling as a heavily invested site of sexualized meaning for young people. The primary emphasis here is on the Toronto case study (Tower Hill) as a pre-9/11 context which highlights the sometimes necessary theoretical and empirical defence for a subcultural effect among young people.

Some aspects of the complex geographies of exclusion lie outside the range of schooling or the more obvious forms of peer rivalry associated with the school. In Chapter 5, we move away from the 'corridors of power' in urban schools to the local contexts of urban neighbourhoods and urban spaces. Following Reay (2008) and Reay and Lucey (2003) once more, we seek to explore young people's experiences of space 'as deeply ambivalent understandings of their social context'. In so doing, we concentrate much more substantially upon the structural and cultural dimensions of anxiety, as a 'structure of feeling' (Williams, 1977), experienced by young people living in demonized fringe areas of the Canadian urban core. Our aim in this chapter is to demonstrate how elements of urban space play some part in framing the forms of alienation or anomie, class denials and class contradictions which economically marginalized young people embody and narrate. In examining these experiences, we deploy our visual sociological data (e.g. photo-narratives of urban cities, self-portraits, visual portraits of young people's future, timelines) which offer novel indications of the ways in which young people currently imagine and draw upon the changing urban environments of modern Canada as they reinvent their lives. Following Jameson (2000), a focal point is to capture young people's urban imaginaries of their neighbourhood.

In Chapter 6 we sharpen the focus to look at the ways in which the class-based expressions of youth subculture encountered in the research fieldwork have also been shaped by histories of racism, colonialism and multiculturalism within the global city. Rather than 'becoming somebody' as a straightforward distinction between different 'races', youth subcultures can be seen to exploit the highly symbolic elements of racialized identities in order to specify the boundaries and putative membership of various sub-groupings. Our intention here is to pose questions about the links between urban space, the national imaginary, post-9/11 security discourse (see Poynting & Morgan, 2007) and the ways in which racialized young men and women express a 'structure of feeling' (Williams, 1977) as they navigate urban terrain and schools at the economic fringe. Following Bettie (2000, 2003), we ask: What does it mean to perform 'black' or 'white' in the urban city? And how might we explore the manner in which racialization becomes tied to a new class imaginary in urban centres? In so doing, we outline ways to re-think the concept of 'social class with a clarity' which might enable us better to 'read' the geographies of race and youth subcultures in urban centres. Like Bettie (2003), we focus on the idea of race as a performance and as a symbolic expression of temporal existence that is grounded in the racialization of geographical space.

Continuing the book's analytical trajectory outwards from school to neighbourhood, Chapter 7 moves to a consideration of national and supra-national settings. It focuses upon questions related to belonging, identity and feelings of the security of young people in relation to the nation-state. Making connections to larger issues pertaining to citizenship, exclusion and state discourses about the aspiring 'good citizen', the chapter examines the ways in which young people have appropriated the prevalent language of the neo-liberal state as an element of their own classification struggles. Our primary argument at this point is that we cannot approach questions about youth within the state through a straightforward analysis of young people's conceptions of the 'good citizen'. We instead concentrate upon the ways in which the expressive, symbolic elements of youth culture function in part to translate the idea of political legitimacy and the 'legitimate person' into elements of young people's own class struggles under the dynamics of radical urban change and as a response to new class and race relations and formations. This chapter serves to complete the movement across distinct levels and scales of change within the overarching analysis of Canadian youth cultures and exclusions, from school-centred (Chapter 4), to the spatial contexts of local neighbourhood (Chapter 5) and thence to the national, supra-national and global arenas (Chapters 6 and 7).

1

Theoretical 'Breaks' and Youth Cultural Studies

Post-Industrial Moments, Conceptual Dilemmas and Urban Scales of Spatial Change

In serious, critical intellectual work, there are no absolute beginnings and few unbroken continuities [...]. What we find instead is an untidy but characteristic unevenness of development. What is important are the significant breaks – where old lines of thought are disrupted, older constellations displaced, and elements, old and new, are regrouped around a different set of premises and themes.... Such shifts in perspectives reflect not only the results of an internal intellectual labour but the manner in which real historical developments and transformations are appropriated in thought, and provide Thought, not with a guarantee of correctness but with its fundamental orientations, its conditions of existence. It is because of this complex articulation between thinking and historical reality, reflected in the social categories of thought, and the continuous dialectic between knowledge and power, that the breaks are worth recording.

(Hall, 1980: 57)

In this chapter, we provide an overview of the interdisciplinary theoretical approach we have developed in relation to our comparative youth studies research. Before setting this out in detail, however, it is worth paying some attention to Hall's (1981) idea about the problematics associated with categories of social thought and his notion of broken continuities in critical theoretical work, particularly in relation to research impinging on our own concerns about youth culture(s). A key argument we wish to put forward is that, while it may be true that theoretical 'breaks are worth recording' as well as engaging with creatively, youth researchers must also be conscious that this recognition must not undermine our efforts to account for the power of 'residual surplus meaning(s)' (see Ricoeur, 1981) in shaping the present. In other words, theoretical orientations cannot offer us 'a guarantee of correctness'. They should instead be seen as useful tools which allow us to 'read' or to interpret our data in particular kinds of ways. In critically engaging the complex questions at the heart of our study, it is also important to maintain an ethical striving towards genuine openness in our interpretations.

With the conceptual challenges associated with the categorical nature of social thought and youth cultural studies in mind, we seek to address three aims in this chapter. The first is to provide a brief overview of some of the major theoretical positions relating to the broad question of youth cultures, together with an account of the principal theoretical and conceptual shifts which have taken place in the field of youth cultural studies in recent years. We do not offer a full-scale overview of the field, primarily because there are now many useful accounts of the landscape of both youth subcultural and post-subcultural studies (see Bennett & Kahn-Harris, 2004; Muggleton, 2000, 2003; Nayak, 2003a; Redhead, 1997, 2004; Shildrick, 2006; Shildrick & McDonald, 2006; Stahl, 1999; Thornton, 1996, 1997). As Griffin (2009: 1) has argued, the 'legacy of these approaches remains an arena of much heated debate and contestation'. Here, our aim instead is to utilize a brief discussion of now well-established debates to highlight some of the impasses within the field, along with their connections, still largely unexplored, to the wider field of youth studies and the study of youth exclusion. We focus particularly upon debates between those who remain wedded to the concept of subculture cast primarily as class resistance and those who have sought to take the partial turn towards the idea of post-subcultural studies in which youth cultures may be seen as hybridized cultural formations, global neo-tribes, and/or fluid, ever-changing and unstable forms of identification (following scholars such as Muggleton & Weinzierl, 2003; Redhead, 1993, 1997). Our discussion endeavours to locate this debate within the larger contexts of moral regulation and low-income youth, the new global city and wider currents of urban change in the affluent 'West'. This emphasis allows us to work towards identifying the ways in which some elements of the theoretical debate may have lost sight both of their original purpose and their continuing potential for establishing an interdisciplinary frame through which to bring forward new explanations for any reconfiguration of urban youth across time and place (see Chatterton & Hollands, 2003; Nayak, 2009).

A second and related aim is to point to the power of paradigmatic or conceptual dominance and the effects of conceptual polarization in the field of youth cultural theory over recent years. Here, we seek to develop the argument that while theoretical shifts in youth cultural studies have been powerful and creative (as well as ethically responsive to wider debates in social theory), a particular kind of theoretical formalism may have undermined our ability to engage with powerful interdisciplinary work or to follow Hall's injunction to reconfigure 'old and new' and to regroup 'around a different set of premises and themes', particularly in relation to rethinking new social class formations. In discussing questions of conceptual dominance, we do not seek to undermine existing work in the field. In fact, the process of invoking such dominance is to show that a particular conceptual idea may itself have wide and enduring value (and even theoretical dominance can be over-determined) and constitutes a powerful interpretive frame. However, there is danger in paradigmatic dominance, just as there is in all forms of dominance and conceptual polarization, and we believe that we are at a critical point in rethinking our responses in relation to the case of economically disadvantaged youth, particularly in relation to new spatial scales in cities and their contested boundaries (Roy & Al-Sayad, 2004). In so doing, we do not wish to set concepts of class or culture or cohesive subcultural identity against post-subcultural identity, or 'discourses of the self' against discourses of individualization in any antagonistic sense. Rather, we seek to show how polarizing these very ideas can be problematic, and how the notion of 'true' breaks may elide or silence other creative responses to the positioning of young people in any system of classification. In sum, we hope to take Hall's reflections seriously in addressing both the strengths and limitations of a theoretical and conceptual 'break' with social class in relation to the youth research we are undertaking here.

Our final aim is to provide some detail on the relationship between the identification of these impasses and the development of our theoretical framework. We therefore link the wider domain of youth culture with emergent debates in social theory about the 'subject', urban space and moral regulation, particularly as they pertain to excluded young people in the late-modern Canadian city. Each of these issues necessitates careful consideration of the very particular challenges facing youth cultural studies in the contemporary moment, and will highlight the reasons why we have moved in the direction of a wider interdisciplinary approach. Here we hope to highlight some potentially novel regions of theory which have yet to be tapped fully in addressing the larger questions of heightened moral regulation, conceptions of 'loss' and injury, and urban youth exclusion. We see it as particularly important to demonstrate the ways in which young people have been 'lost' not only to the project of conceptual dominance (and therefore sometimes lost to theory and research itself). For us, then, this calls for an examination of the ways in which current debates and approaches in youth cultural studies may weaken a closer understanding of the contemporary issues we have encountered in the course of our research. The need for an exposition of cultural meaning of youth exclusion which is not only tied to theory but also to a particular local space and scale of change provides one entry point into a 'thicker' account of youth culture on the ground. It also allows us to determine as far as possible the impact of local geographies on youth formations, at the same time as accounting for new political theorizations of wider global change and the transformative nature of youth cultures (see Chatterton & Holland, 2003; Connell, 2007).

In accounting for scales of local change, analyses of the modalities of youth representation across place and space enable us to witness the differentiated impact of, for example, transnational flows and local meanings on the very constitution and landscape of youth culture as well as on the manner in which we come to think about the 'urban' or the 'city' in new times. Often, theoretical texts invoke and impose a certain kind of reality on the meanings associated with youth culture (and our work is also burdened by this difficult theoretical challenge). However, we strive to show in this chapter how the process of focusing upon a set frame or urban scale might open a window upon the alterity of youth cultures themselves. From this vantage point, our conceptual optic is not only preoccupied with youth cultures but also with their differentiated relationship to forms of youth exclusion in cities and schools which are re-scaling their 'strategic territories' of meaning. As Willis (2000: 12) writes:

> Globalisation is not a singular, unilinear process, fatalistically unfolding towards inevitable ends: it entails gaps, contradictions, counter-tendencies, and marked unevenness. And just as capital flows more freely around the globe, so do human ideas and imaginings, glimpses of other possible futures. These elements all interact in really existing sites, situations and localities, not in outer space or near-earth orbit. Unprefigurably, they are taken up into all kinds of local meanings-makings by active humans struggling and creating with conditions on the ground, so producing new kinds of meanings and identities, themselves 'up for export' on the world market.

In the remainder of this chapter, we shall expand upon each of these three aims, investigating the manner in which they assist us in imagining new ways of exploring the realities of economically disadvantaged young people living in the late-modern global city.

Subcultural Landscapes of Youth Selfhood and Cultural Turns: Locating the Dialectic of Culture, Class Conflict and Post-subcultural Hybridity

1964: Mod or Rocker – *You had to be one or the other.*
(http://bbc.co.uk/onthisday/hi/dates/stories/may/18/
newsid_2511000/2511245.stm accessed on 23 June 2008)

These long-haired, mentally unstable, petty little hoodlums – these sawdust Caesars – seem to find courage, like rats, by hunting only in packs.

(www.time.com/time/magazine/article)

We begin with the landscape of a recent history before us, briefly showcasing some of the early and indeed dominant debates and images linked to some of the most sensationalized youth subcultural groups – the Mods and Rockers – of post-war Britain. We do so with the aims both of capturing that once-present history as an aesthetic exercise in studying youth cultures as well as placing our current work in a historicized, international context beyond the confines of the Canadian city.

Many early studies concerned with the Mods and the Rockers highlight the post-war framing of morality and its links to young people, as well as the misapprehension that youth subcultural groupings were ever in any sense straightforwardly singular or essentialized in their positional standing.[1] They also speak to the wider apprehension of loss that is manifested over time through mobile forms of nationalism and memories of home and place which young people inherit as that which is already 'latent', and which emerges through the embodied history of youth performances and their links to symbolic culture. As Hall himself wrote about the nation: 'sometimes cultures are tempted to turn the clock back to retreat defensively into that lost culture when the nation was great' (1996: 54). Perhaps loss – as a deeply sociological reaction – then is most powerfully evident at those moments when young people are obliged to confront their own and their families' increasingly mythical origins as they navigate new scales of change and social division at the level of the local. In considering the idea of mythical origins and their links to young people's urban imaginaries, we agree with Steedman (1995: 3) when she argues:

> I proceed on the assumption that it is helpful to make an analytical separation between 'real children/young people', living in the time and place of particular societies, and the ideational and figurative force of their existence (which necessarily frames loss as either the loss of innocence or the loss of potential past and future).

Here, of course, we do not make a realist separation between the ideational and the performative elements of being young but rather endeavour to show that a cultural sociology of young people and longstanding ideas of being young can never be wrenched apart in realist terms but that, following Steedman, we cannot objectify young people as the repository of losses. Once we accept this condition, we are required to engage with different ways of representing the present.

Our starting point – while in no way representing a substantial historiography – is to offer some account of the kinds of distinctions that have been made between young people as powerful categories in social thought, and which have emerged in public life and indeed in theory itself. Additionally, by offering a past of subcultures in this way, we may also better understand how illusory and firm divisions between various youth groups and indeed conceptual thinking have come to be. From our vantage point, such divisions are tied above all to moralizing 'structures of feeling' which are embodied in what Steedman (1995) has called 'lexes of feeling' in both public life and social thought, and which impact directly upon the lives of young people: the social structuring of ways of thinking about youth groups, and the bringing of feeling and associated intellectual and cultural responses into use in particular contexts. A key point to emerge here is that such concrete and over-determined divisions which were thought to exist between youth groups both then and now are used in part to express a kind of historicity of youth which is in some way essentially linked to these groups operating in relation to nationhood (however uncomplicated such descriptions appear to be in the sociology of young people in the past and present). We hope to raise questions therefore about how such divisions came to emerge in the 'social psychologies of place' and public consciousness both at the level of youth cultural theory, and in real social circumstances where young people loomed large. For us, this move involves some consideration of the ways in which groupings of spectacularized youth, such as the Mods and Rockers (or the Skinheads, Chavs, Real Geordies, Teddy Boys or Punks), could become detached from their origins or indeed from the mythical origins of 'nation' itself. A key emphasis must therefore lie upon how such strict categorical understandings of youth culture(s) allowed for some questions to be asked and others to be silenced or unsayable, given the degrees of conceptual dominance and theoretical alterities in the field. As we hope to demonstrate, such questions about the formation of theoretical categories of young people ultimately rest upon the 'symbolic order' and 'horizons of meaning' associated with theory itself (see Connell, 2007).

Post-war Subcultures as Storied Accounts of Social Change: Narrating the Mods and Rockers as the Centrepiece of Twentieth-Century Youth Cultural Theory

In *Quadrophenia*, the well-known 1979 film inspired by the iconic rock band The Who, a story is told about the endemic conflict between two of the most prominent youth subcultures of the late 1960s. These groups apparently represented two radically different working-class youth styles. The first, the Mods, were seen to symbolize the aspiring post-war working class, sharp suits, motor scooters, R&B and soul music, and desires for sophistication. The second, the Rockers, were leather-jacketed bikers, rock'n'rollers, defenders of a more traditional perception of the working-classes (see Pearson, 1983). Who were these apparently 'deviant' and 'unstable' young people, famously reported in the media as 'sawdust caesars' (now a UK punk revivalist band) and 'juvenile yobs' and why should they remain of enduring interest to youth studies scholars today?

As Cohen (1972) argued in his classic text, *Folk Devils and Moral Panics*, the Mods and Rockers were always likely to retain their importance as metaphors of youth transition (or of the changing nature of youth cultures) because they told us something about the impact of wider social change (including the rise of new media, music, social mobility and affluence in the post-war period) on young people in post-war Britain and elsewhere, and about the ways in which young people responded to the growth of the mass media and new forms of consumption. The activities of the Mods and Rockers also raised important issues about the part played in their cultural making by class (often spectacularized to the wider world), the labour market and patterns of kinship. As far as youth subcultures go, they were seen as a quite unanticipated and unprecedented post-war cultural presence and, consequently, were often linked in the public record, with quite unprecedented visibility, to moral accounts of, for example, rising rates of juvenile delinquency and teenage pregnancies.

In reality, these young people did not represent 'deviance' or 'folk devil' status as the media or sociologists of deviance had prominently suggested. They were instead, as cultural theorists such as Cohen and Hebdidge argued, better understood as frustrated young people facing the consequences of economic dislocation, fears of unemployment and a growing conservative moral pressure to conceive family and social stability in highly traditional terms. The ensuing moral panic was a socially constructed phenomenon which revealed more about the embodiment through culture and nation of traditional conceptions of Britishness than it did about young people living in a deeply divided classed society. We need to ask, therefore, in what ways could these youth cultures be seen to reflect a form of what Willis has called 'symbolic creativity' which ultimately challenged any such conceptual duality or binary (subculture versus post-subculture, for example) – as a dynamic response to class stratification – or, by contrast, as a form of accelerated adulthood? How might that which Cohen, three decades ago, so insightfully referred to as the 'sociology of moral panic' – as a reactive form of national myth-making or, more accurately for the twenty-first century, as a form of transnational, mobile and persistently reconfigured rhetoric – help us better understand the place of today's young people in the 'movable equilibrium' of wider social relations (see Hebdige, 1979)? More importantly, how did the very segregation of young people into particular categories of leisure and pleasure, and danger and criminality, expose sedimented ideas about young people and serve to mask the importance of social class as a major and continuing influence in youth cultures (see Nayak, 2009)?

It is precisely because of the persistence of these questions about social class and youth that we revisit, for the sake of clarity as opposed to theoretical interest, the arena of youth and class struggle. In their earliest incarnations, class struggle and structure, like the more general theoretical dominance of neo-Marxism in social theory, were primary concepts for understanding youth subcultures of the post-war period. Despite the theoretical weight placed upon culture and the idea of the sign, the semiotic or the symbol as 'the arena of class struggle' (see Hebdige, 1979: 17) in much of this early work, the primary reason for a sustained emphasis on class in youth subcultural studies was the persistence, in the mid-twentieth century, of a neo-Marxist concern with the political economy of nation-states and the mid-twentieth-century dominance of structuralism in sociology. This was accompanied by a simultaneous though sometimes disassociated interest in the role of class in socializing young people into an apparently stable labour market through institutions such as the education system. However, against a background of changing migration patterns and new diasporas, alongside a clearer recognition and understanding of the variegated dimensions of social inequality, researchers interested in youth subcultures began to turn towards development of analytical frameworks sufficiently refined for addressing the interrelated issues of youth culture, identity and exclusion. A key aim – particularly from the 1980s onward – was to move beyond class struggle in order to capture the 'subterranean channels of broad cultural exchanges' (see Hebdige, 1979) taking place among working-class youth.

As part of this cultural turn in youth studies, a new constellation of questions was brought forward and addressed from various angles and vantage points. Were youth subcultures re-organizing in line with late-modern social changes under the dynamics of global reform and flows of migration (Muggleton, 2000)? Were youth identities representations of global mobility and fragmentation and, if so, could they still represent objections to an apparently dominant moral order as a form of symbolic refusal – 'a symbolic violation of the social order' (Hebdige, 1979: 19)? Had mass consumption torn youth collectives and subcultures into fragmented and individualized, fluid cyber transdance figures? Were scales of globalization shifting youth identity away from an essentialist class culture, towards a more 'crystallized' trans-local, but still partial, identity paralleling wider spatial changes? Could some or any of these changes be seen as tied to the idea of moral panic, if reconfigured or paradigmatically and conceptually re-constituted in new theoretical ways as regulation, re-ordering, surveillance and policing (as opposed to social control)? And what role might the idea of the nation or the mobile memories of nation play in all of this, particularly as the diaspora and its 'frontier effects' (Gilroy, 2000; Hall, 1997; Redhead, 1993) had widened beyond post-war imaginings?[2]

In response to some of these questions in wider theoretical debates, a particularly powerful turn in the late 1970s in continental social theory emphasized the 'death of the subject', and by extension in the wider field of cultural theory, the death of subcultures and the apparent death of social class. These various conceptual turns in the social sciences and humanities produced a new conceptual frame for thinking about the subject which posits, for example, that a coherent narrative of selfhood or the collective poses challenges to elements of particularity. For example, in a powerful and creative 'post' moment, post-subcultures, 'new wave' cultures, individualizing youth and the concomitant perception of youth selfhood as an ever-changing discourse, primarily constituted through language all, one way or the other, bear the mark of some of these interesting turns (e.g. Buckingham, Bragg & Kehily, 2009; Kehily & Nayak, 2009; Redhead, 1993, 1997, 2004). The work in this field is vast and we could never do justice to another rehearsal of all the innovative work that emerged from this point. Suffice it to say that such work has been an extremely powerful theoretical resource for studying young people and without it contemporary youth cultural analysis scarcely seems possible.[3]

Within the field of youth cultural studies, one very noteworthy and arguably dominant theoretical approach – or indeed conceptual break – for studying representations of youth culture as a 'post-subculture', as 'image, style or global productions has been derived from this turn' (see McRobbie, 1982; for review, see McRobbie, 2009). There has been, as a consequence, a quite comprehensive (although not exclusive) movement away from examining youth subcultures as temporalized elements of material culture or as the straightforward reproductive bearers of ideological sub-texts, in the style of Althusserian, psychoanalytic and materialist/Marxist.[4] Recent approaches have more readily emphasized; for example, Foucauldian, Deleuzian, Butlerian or Derridian understandings of youth identity, concerns over and/or with the body, forms of cultural hybridity (scapes and tribes, Apparadurai, 1990) and the ways in which young people's language and leisure activity – as opposed to the positional rules of youth subcultures – has become the operative form of power. Here, the subject of youth cultures is typically understood as more fundamentally distanced from cohesive class and kinship groups and instead points to high levels of fragmentation, global flows and inconsistent membership which regulates, rather than determines, youth identity in a broad sense (see Redhead, 1997).

At the same time, the question of identity within youth subcultural contexts has moved towards the idea that the search for 'magical solutions' can no longer frame the positional rules in operation through youth subcultural activities.[5] In short, a key argument is that class identities no longer predict and/or determine the cultural activities of the young person. This very creative movement in theoretical perspective has allowed many of the post-subcultural theorists and other youth researchers to move beyond any notion of retrieving an objectifiable representation of youth subcultures as true authentic collectives bound by class rituals, leading to their own class reproduction (*pace* Willis).

Arguably, such approaches stand as examples of a 'break' with an earlier structuralist moment emphasizing more uniformly class-directed forms of youth activity. And indeed this break dramatizes some of the fundamental grievances that many post-war youth studies scholars (see Chatterton & Hollands, 2003; Griffin, 2009) in the late twentieth century had expressed about the ramifications of the narrow focus on class, and the lack of emphasis on racialization, gender, sexuality and all those associated emergent contradictions within youth subcultures which could not be accounted for by a model of class resistance. And here too this turn has played a partial role in, and influenced, our collective theorizing. But while these approaches have undoubtedly constituted a powerful reading of new youth cultures, we are suggesting that the idea of a true 'break', or the complete death of very important conceptual tools in the study of youth cultures, has resulted in some quite substantial dilemmas in contemporary youth culture and youth studies research (see also Buckingham et al., 2009). The primary problem emerges when we consider the relationship between youth cultures and ideas about choice which seem implicit within post-subcultural analysis – the choice to be 'who you want to be', the choice to go clubbing and do leisure large, or the choice to engage in heavy 'Chav' drinking – as if they are true choices or straightforwardly 'fluid' youth identities of the post-subcultural era. As Muggleton (cited in Stahl, 1999: 14) writes:

> Post-subculturalists no longer have any sense of subcultural authenticity where inception is rooted in particular socio-temporal contexts and tied to underlying structural relations. Indeed, post-subculturalists will experience all the signs of the subculture of their choosing time and time again. Choosing is the operative word here, for post-subculturalists revel in the availability of subcultural choice [...]. This is something that all post-subculturalists are aware of, that there are no rules, that there is no authenticity, no reason for ideological commitment, merely a stylistic game that must be played.

However, as Stahl goes on to suggest (and it is worth quoting him at length here):

this [particular] formulation of post-modernism, [...] (which includes the ability to occupy a multiplicity of subjectivities) obscures the effects that difference and differential access to power have on producing meaningful contexts (and contexts of meaning) for cultural activity. In Muggleton's estimation, the gravitation of individuals and groups to sites of emotional investment, whether they be real or imaginary, is evacuated of all meaning and affective value.

(Stahl, 1999: 15)

To put this somewhat differently, the consequence of focusing on the global style industry or leisure activity as the mainstay choice of youth post-subcultural theory has meant that rethinking social class relations and their impact on young people in re-ordered urban spaces has become more challenging. This is a particularly important point in relation to wider questions about how both young people and space come together to serve as mediators of meaning, new social class relations, affective investments in space and associated styles and group naming practices. For example, if post-subcultural youth cultural affiliations (such as 'Nammers', ' Eminemers', 'Wannabe Asians', 'Ginos' or 'nearly Black') now predominate among some young people, are there not underlying material investments in those affiliations, as well as in how the positional rules of participation might change in relation to global and diasporic culture (such as allowing one white member to take the namesake of a group) or at trans-local levels? Would not the meaning of 'being' post-subcultural be deeply invested in particular exchange values and resources which are shaped by wider 'differentials of power' and geographical shifts? Is this theoretical practice not a somewhat over-determined 'symbolic erasure of older registers' of youth subcultures (see Nayak, 2009).

More importantly, the links between the moral rules young people affiliate with and conform to out of some loyalty to the idea of an imagined ideological 'collective' – although provisional, fluid and always in an ad hoc form – have become to greater or lesser degrees yet further removed from our empirical and conceptual reach. Consequently, many of the theoretical ideals associated with a critique of subculture could be seen as failing to expose the temporalized nature of young people's deeply invested activities and moral commitments which remain linked to urban imaginaries. As Grossberg (2005: 12) has suggested, youth cultures operating in particular territories still consistently demonstrate a 'structured distribution of practices, moral codes and effects' which are spatially organized.

Finally, it is now well established within the field of geography that scales of change in the particular places where young people live are of substantial importance to the explanatory power of any theorization of youth cultures. Yet we would argue that in post-subcultural terms the differential meanings invested in new places are all too often evacuated from the research. This is primarily because the idea of the global is somehow conflated with fragmentation in every urban space which carries with it a kind of totality without a historicity of place and particularity intact. And in this conflation of place and fragmentation we may mask uneven changes in cities in relation to scales of global transformation, or in relation to migration biographies and a young person's imagination and memory of nation and place. Consequently, the cumulative effect of focusing *solely* upon the global language of post-subcultures or their associated fragmented, fluid activities and individualized multiple groupings may be to undermine how we come to think about young people as still tied in part to locales (even if such locales are linked to global change). It might also obfuscate our understanding of how newly structured distributions of resource, forms of urban regeneration and degeneration, and rescaled urban spaces might impact on youth cultures and their experiences of exclusion across contexts. To put this in more philosophical terms, it may have the unintended effect of reducing the importance of an unfolding, storied yet still materially bounded *youth narrative* in time and space, moving us away from recognizing the figurative depth of a temporally and materially contingent 'who' rather than a 'what', a thing, a 'discourse', or a string of unbounded youth performances, however important these may all seem to be at different theoretical moments in time (see Caverero, 2000).

As Felman (1992) suggests, we need to engage the idea that young people embody – as a cultural performance – an important site for the 'enactment of memory'. In other words, within such approaches we may fail at times to witness some of the temporally bound experiences of young people through whom memory and history must necessarily speak as a narrative form of social differentiation – as something that always exceeds, but which does not get beyond, a discourse as it appears in the present (see Kearney, 2004). In cultural terms, this kind of narrative bears the mark of what Raymond Williams (1977) refers to as 'residual meaning' and what Paul Ricouer (2004) refers to as 'surplus meaning'.

Conceptual Polarizations and Theoretical Dilemmas in Youth Cultural Studies: A Critical Analysis of Problematics

To summarize our key points thus far, we have argued that research on youth cultures has in more recent years represented quite polarized positions.[6] Within youth subcultural and post-subcultural theory, for example, these polarizations between two possible accounts of youth culture are frequently evident. On the one hand, there is the post-subcultural account, focusing on tribes, landscapes and global flows of hybridity. Here, not only is there often an intrinsic, if generally implicit, theory of youth – as hedonistic, as indulging in self-worship, as individualized and choice-making, and sometimes as essentially unethical and uncommitted (see Brake, 1985; Chatterton & Hollands, 2003). There are also significant underlying theoretical assumptions about the major roles that individualization and consumption are seen to play in the making of youth cultures.

On the other hand, there are those remaining defenders of historical materialism who argue that class (even if barely visible) remains significant, not least because it exposes the ways in which wider society is bent to the expression of various forms of disgust ('poor white trash', 'the working classes smell'; see, for example, George Orwell, 1937, as cited in Lawler, 2005) circulating about young people in the present (see also Lawler, 2009). And of course there are also some overlapping approaches, although these seem far less evident than the surface polarities which are expressed through associated research (see Shildrick & MacDonald, 2006). Noteworthy, however, is that these two broadly distinctive bodies of work share an odd unity in the negative fact that neither is much interested in the notions of spatially organized class sedimentation or deeply felt, *embodied* forms of social conflict grounded in the long history of moral regulation. Whilst it is beyond argument that the organizational characteristics of youth groupings have changed and will continue to do so, it is essential that our thinking within theoretical polarities should continue to be fully problematized.

Emergent Theoretical Dilemmas in Contemporary Youth Cultural Studies

In thinking through these issues, we now move forward to identify a number of specific emergent theoretical, practical and conceptual dilemmas which framed our ethnographic fieldwork, and raised key theoretical problematics in need of some response. Below, as a partial response, we outline some key limitations associated with these problematics.

First, whilst post-subcultural accounts of young people may unearth illuminating insights into the changing global relations of power embodied by young people, they may not always account for the part that they play – in highly varied urban spaces – in the formation of new micro and macro social processes (e.g. novel policing practices and broader public perception). These very modes of post-subcultural representation, ironically, may influence just those reproductive processes which play some part in the making of both new spatial arrangements and class divisions among urban youth. It may be the case, for example, in scrutinizing a group of young people in their rave activities, stylistic performances or gendered peer rivalries that we find that by comparison with earlier years and depending on location, they would no longer appear to be or really never were solely determined in their self-representations by class,[7] nor as merely resisting dominant cultural forms (Muggleton, 2000). Rather, in particular contexts, they may be seen to have been more or less substantially impacted by the forms of individualization and fragmentation which are associated with late-modern social formations and could indeed support an argument for a quite new post-subcultural effect. Here we might witness – as material and cultural effects – not only elements of fluidity and transgressive forms of identification, but also a dis-identification from class (or even a denial of class) as a potentially grounding principle in shaping youth subcultural activity.

A theoretical recognition of this sort would constitute, and has indeed constituted, an important intervention. However, in charting the novel pattern of these forms of identification, we may still unintentionally mask the role of new class divisions and the part they play in this very dis-identification. In other words, we might want to ask what social relations made such dis-identification possible? We may similarly remain uncertain about the forms of social harm which might be directed towards young people when they have been unable to 'dis-identify' or to 'choose' who they want to be, particularly those who are living on the economic fringes of the global city.

We might also be limited in understanding how the intersections between space and place interface with social class to shape youth reconfigurations across time, and how they might be tied to quite new moral fields of the urban. For example, we might fail to see how the social conflicts experienced by young people demand – as narrative contextualization – a form of temporalization and comparative spatialization which takes them beyond the isolated moment of a fragmented post-subcultural activity such as drug use and dance, whether as twenty-first-century hedonism or as real presentism. We might think to move, instead, towards the 'space of appearances' (Arendt, 1968, 1971, 1998) or a phenomenology of narrative selfhood where a more meaningful story of youth cultures may appear, confronting not only the present, but also acknowledging the power of past time upon the present performances of young people themselves.

In addition, youth subculture research in the past has been preponderantly directed towards young people who were either attending secondary school or of secondary school age. In focusing on these groups, it was both possible and logical to advance the kinds of claims that were commonly made about youth subcultural activity as cohesive, resistant and specifically age-related.

By contrast, much of the post-subcultural research of recent times has been conducted with groups of young people who constitute, whether by class circumstances or by age, a more mobile and, typically, an older presence (youth, as a category, has widened its chronological remit in this respect). This may account in the research for a characteristically lower emphasis upon the more traditional subcultural practices of territoriality or positional thinking and rule-taking. In other words, it might simply be too elusive or even ahistorical to report that new youth cultures are effectively hybridized with no real social class ties, when the young people in question have attained the mobility that may come with age and experience rather than as a consequence of a radical shift or sharp rather than tenuous break in the fundamental structures of youth cultures and theories themselves. Or, as we demonstrate, it may be that any related shifts may be more tightly bound to the place, space and temporal contexts which young people find themselves occupying. Importantly, too, as the French theorist Canguillem (1989) has noted, we might also see that Hall's theoretical break and turn is really more of a conceptual break and innovation than a radical alterity in theories of subcultures or post-subcultures themselves. These concepts always bear the traces of the past even if we, once blinded by the techniques of theory, fail to witness these traces directly.

With the exception of a very small number of studies (e.g. Brake, 1985; Chatterton & Hollands, 2003; Nayak, 2003a, 2003b, 2003c; McLeod & Yates, 2006; Pilkington, 2004; Pilkington & Johnson, 2003; Kehily & Nayak, 2009)[8] and some powerful contemporary travel writing ethnographies, there is still very little comparative multi-sited research on youth cultures operating at the cusp of the twenty-first century. For these exceptions, a key element of the work is to illuminate the ways in which spatial variations and context play a decisive role in understanding the formation of youth cultures. Outside this small but very important corpus of work, the bulk of research has been grounded in single-case ethnographies which constitute the evidential platform upon which the death of class and youth subcultural groupings has frequently been announced. In view of this, comparative research is clearly important if we are to understand the sustained and reconfigured cultural power of social class in reshaping youth cultural responses to the experience of heightened levels of social retrenchment and the changing nature of the 'global' city.

An additional problem is that much youth cultural research has remained somewhat isolated from the broader field of youth studies and those other areas of the humanities and social sciences embracing wider conceptual apparatuses, such as larger questions of affect, moral regulation and youth subjectivity as it relates to geographies of place (Ahmed, 2004b;

Skeggs, 2005). As a result, we may fail to recognize that youth groups always operate at the edge of an already inherited set of social conditions which invokes particular performances and dramatizations of identity. In these performances, class is remade and re-aligned in new ways, yet we may not have all the necessary tools to assess these cultural forms of remaking. However, in changing times, the relationship between the re-making of class and the power of symbolic residues or the 'symbolic fit' between class performance, youth activity and moral positions seems increasingly important. As Skeggs (2004) argues, morality is clearly central to the cultural remaking of class relations. This suggests that we need to widen our theoretical reach such that we can better understand the interaction between structure, place and culture in ways which can account for both urban spatial change and new forms of moral regulation, together with the constraints which young people must navigate in yet another epoch of increasing anxiety about youth themselves.

A further problem is that the temporal and spatial effects of global transformations, particularly as these relate to the geographical dimensions of urban life (e.g. street, housing project or 'urban slums'), may not be as easily uncovered through a discursive analysis of 'youth identity', nor can they be easily revealed through traditional sociological methods, such as voice research, or straightforward class research. Our contention is, rather, that whilst a focus upon discursive approaches may provide a conceptual apparatus for breaking down the essential nature of youth subcultural identity generated through more traditional forms (a very important task), the spatial configuration of youth discourses also asserts enduring class configurations and remains central to the symbolic order of youth cultures.

In overestimating the power of the turn in relation to the interpretation of young people's performances of culture (as well as overestimating a theoretical rather than conceptual break), we may also be poorly placed to address the notion of distanciation – as introduced by Gadamer and developed by Ricoeur. Distanciation is the recognition that we always feel alien to the 'social text' of youth culture or any social text from another time or place, primarily because of our cultural and temporal distance from it. This must not be seen negatively; indeed, it is the very recognition of this alienation that allows us to keep the text from perishing from the moment and permits new interpretations. Put differently, any interpretation of the symbolic repertoires of youth expressions must function in part to connect the social structures and cultural spaces of the past and the present through traceable interpretive configurations and modes of narrative transmission (Ricoeur, 1991: 75–88).[9] Without this, we may forfeit some partial conceptual purchase upon the tensions which exist between culture, space and time when considering modalities of youth culture. And relating to this are the still elusive questions about the interface between geography, colonial ideas and changing urban structures in shaping public theories of economically disadvantaged young people.

Taken together, these limitations in no way seek to undermine the excellent youth post-subcultural accounts now circulating within the realm of cultural studies. Rather, they are designed to suggest the extent to which any cultural configuration remains bound to that imaginary nucleus which may hide its own rules from itself and therefore elude us (see Kearney, 2004: 117). If we are to address at least some of these dilemmas, we may come to witness those geographies of youth performance which are being redrawn as the local impact of global forces on the city is experienced at the level of feeling and thought. At the same time, we may witness how the spatialization of ethnographic thinking can provide vivid phenomenological descriptions of comparative spaces where young people creatively experience their world as a partial response to collective, fragmented and individualized narratives about community and self in both local and trans-local ways. Such emotional geographies of experience are never simply of the descriptive kind. They are always grounded in symbolic differentiations and particular classed fantasies about that space, and such fantasies are transformed in relation to scales of global change (Jameson, 1998b, 2000). Following Jameson (2000), we view young people's connection to each other in space as in part an imaginary about the city which necessarily represents the intermingling of the present and history, retaining salient rituals and practices from the past, and reconfiguring new symbolic orders from a trans-local space. In this way, geographies of space become organized moral fields of social practice where young people negotiate their status, recognition and their futures.

A final problem encountered in our theoretical engagement with notions of the death of the classed subject, and associated subcultural tools, is their relative conceptual incapacity to address questions of young people's capacity to act with others in the social world, and their ontological status in the state. Consequently, it may be that accounts both of youth cultures and their related vocabularies may ultimately denote nothing but an empty space which is simply occupied by 'narrowly defined linguistic discourses' (McNay, 2000) or that which Felman (2000) describes as 'liberal trauma narratives'. Such discourses or narratives exist without structural, spatial, phenomenological or temporal musings as to why they possess such substantial force.

Approaches in this vein cannot, as Arendt and Ricoeur would each insist, signify a mark of struggle or detour, contestation or change in the public meanings generated about youth cultural groups across diverse contexts. Nor are such approaches easily able to indicate a storied 'who' that has been constructed as 'stateless', 'impoverished' or illegitimate (as some selves carry higher moral value than others in particular places and are more or less kept under surveillance or 'lost' to forms of globalizing moral panic). Our concern with such approaches is how this lack of 'whoness' means that young people are denied the possibility of legitimacy, a story or visibility. Here, ultimately, any notion of the active construction of narrative selfhood through memory is lost in favour of the assumption that young people are simply passive victims of a narrowly defined urban discourse of the street, the urban Ecstasy rave, the slum or, for example, the global cyber village. As Villa (1997: 190) writes of Arendt: the 'disclosure of the agent in speech and action implies [...] an abiding subject, a reality, behind appearances'. In this view, youth cultural groups need to be seen as both suffering and acting, if as necessarily constrained subjects, in a larger symbolic order. With these concerns in mind, we now turn towards the kind of interdisciplinary responses signalled in the work we outline below.

Interdisciplinary Approaches: Moral Registers, Temporality and Spatial Imaginaries

Our task in this final section is to offer broader yet still partial theoretical interventions into the study of youth cultures, the global city and young people's associated forms of exclusion. Our primary argument rests upon the claim that youth subcultures are certainly not dead and neither is class. Class and youth urban imaginaries remain important elements of youth subcultural and indeed post-subcultural practice, including the ability or 'choice' to be 'fluid' in the forms suggested by post-subcultural theorists. Degrees of fragmentation or the concept of post-subculture can certainly be defended, but such a defence must be mounted explicitly in relation to the dual effects of spatiality and temporality and their impact on the moral reconfigurations of youth expressions. The former engages the spatial divisions of the global city, and the degrees to which 'lost youth' are implicated in such divisions under the effects of global forces. The latter looks to the residual weight of the past as it bears upon the enactment of contemporary youth cultural activity on the urban fringe.[10]

In bridging these ideas, we are not forced to accept a self locked in time, a fixed and immobilized narrative of selfhood or space but rather a person who must navigate and interpret time and space as it appears for them in new ways. There can be no youth identity which is merely global or local; rather, a form of youth selfhood emerges that is intersubjectively constituted and contains a capacity for forms of self-ascription that must always be seen as differentiated through highly variable and material scales of change. Arguably, then, it is only through comparative research that we can identify the persistent activities of cohesive subcultural groupings as well as rather less cohesive youth community groupings of the kind that we will consider in later chapters.

The reason we wish to argue for a form of interdisciplinary openness in our engagement is that we cannot assume that any one theory or empirical account can, in and of itself, explain the new or sedimented forms of youth identification which currently operate within the new global city. Nor can we simply assume that the binary and somewhat artificial breaks in youth cultural theory are adequate in explaining changes in youth culture. Instead, we need a wide, essentially hermeneutic repertoire for understanding new youth cultures which function both as a response to, and a connection between, macro and micro forces of change which are spatially organized and reconstituted under the dynamics of urban change.

At the same time, we also wish to offer a phenomenological reading of youth cultural formations which represents neither the view of an outsider nor that of an insider, but which instead reflects a mediated reflexive and distanciated view. Such would be a view which both accounts for youth culture in its contemporary expressive forms (that is, as it reveals itself on the ground) but also remains ultimately tied to a form of distanciation with the capacity to uncover the temporal character of these forms. An account of this kind is important in showing how young people negotiate, in the world of the everyday, the varying degrees of alienation they experience and 'what they do with the cultural commodities they encounter' (Williams, 1977: 17) as they navigate highly moralized forms of change. We believe that anomie still remains central to such navigations. In common with Goffman's (1959) concern with modes of representation in everyday culture, we too are interested in the ways in which anomie impacts upon the particular modes of representation young people construct for themselves, and for each other, as constituting the ground for particularly powerful forms of cultural identification.

In addition to the phenomenology of quite new youth cultural practices, we also endeavour to address a persistent concern with what we see, borrowing from McNay (2000), as sedimented cultural narratives. The importance of sedimentation points to the power of narrative identity to exceed its own cultural meanings as expressed in the present. Each contemporary expression of youth culture holds within it deep resonances with earlier symbolic forms from past time and it is here that we remain wedded to earlier accounts of subcultural reasoning. As Kearney (2004: 31; brackets our addition) writes: 'the [youth cultural] text breaks the circle of internal reflection and exposes us to intersubjective horizons of language and history.' It is these intersubjective horizons which take us beyond the 'speaking subject' in the present. Rather, as Kearney (2004: 4) writes in relation to Ricoeur:

interpretation is described [...] by Ricoeur as the process by which, in the interplay of question and answer, the interlocutors collectively determine the contextual values which inform their conversation. Interpretation explodes the confines of the timeless reflective subject and discloses us as language-using beings in a world with others.

This is why

a hermeneutic model of the text reveals complexities of meaning beyond the face-to-face of spoken dialogue. It goes beyond the direct reference of two interlocutors co-presenting to one another in an immediately identifiable situation 'here and now'. This involves a long intersubjective detour through the sedimented horizons of history and tradition [...]. Ricoeur demonstrates how the short intersubjective relation (or two speakers in conversation) is invariably intertwined with various long intersubjective relations and cultural traditions [...]. In short, hermeneutic explication coincides with the broadest historical and cultural connections.

(Kearney, 2004: 30)

This kind of approach permits us to embrace simultaneously historicity, regulation and contemporary forms of youth intersubjectivity, precluding any idealist or realist claim to an autonomous speaking young person, a strongly bound 'true' collective, or a totalizing standpoint. In embracing these positions we hope, as researchers, to be in a position not merely to defend theory as a form of cultural reading, but also to open ourselves to new worlds emerging from the study of young people in the present. We understand our encounters with urban youth cultural narratives as intersubjective relations, the characteristic forms of everyday meaning-making that young people undertake, and which carry within them the sedimented cultural residue of times past. We perceive the researcher's role in such work as engaging in a radical interrogation of the meaning systems young people draw upon to make sense of their contradictory worlds and in response to particular moral imperatives circulating in new urban spatial arrangements.[11] These contradictory worlds can only be understood through a spatial lens such that we can see the wider and comparative effects of the global at the scale of alterity at the level of local space.

We also argue that inherited mechanisms of earlier forms of symbolic domination (see Bourdieu, 2001) persist as a sedimented element of social conflict, continuing to shape the morally invested sites of meaning upon which young people draw in urban cities and schools. What this implies is that neither deeply entrenched inherited culturalist formations nor modernizing global forces can be seen as solely responsible for the formation of youth subcultural identity. The relational negotiations achieved by youth, along with their associated phenomenologies of meaning, are rendered possible precisely through their daily exposure to complex cultural, spatial, moral and historical milieux, organized at local, national and global levels.

Cultural Phenomenology and Symbolic Narratives: Narrating Time Through Youth Culture(s)

In order to engage in a cultural 'reading' of the narrative accounts and visual expressions of exclusion and youth cultures which we encountered in our fieldwork, we draw extensively upon the field of cultural phenomenology. We have sought to link cultural phenomenology and youth cultural theory debates with contemporary theories of social class in a spatial ethnography of young people living at the edge of the global city.

We have made these connections for a number of reasons. First, each of the thinkers we related to as we interpreted our data has a direct or indirect link to phenomenology either as students of the approach itself (e.g. Arendt, Brown, Bourdieu, Ricoeur, Miller, Rose, Nayak, Cohen) or as those who interpret culture, the body and social class through a radical hermeneutic lens (e.g. Ahmed, Bettie, Lawler, Hall, Skeggs, McNay). Each also shares an interest in understanding both the sedimented and the novel metaphors of social conflict which have been overlooked in more recent post-subcultural accounts emphasizing fragmentation as the primary basis for subject formation. A hermeneutics of the self argues for an 'opaque subjectivity which expresses itself through the detour of countless mediations – signs, symbols, texts, and human praxis itself' (Kearney, 2004: 32). Our task then has to be seen in terms of an identification of the relationship between young people and the mediation of their social meanings in a particular time and place. Our aim, in short, is to profit from a return to the 'imaginary nucleus' of youth cultures themselves (Kearney, 2004).

We see phenomenological readings of youth cultural activities as one means to bridge the insights of youth subcultural theory and post-subcultural accounts. Historically, youth subcultural theory emanating from the intellectual work of the CCCS was linked to the turn towards constructivism, class, culture and language in post-war social thought, seen and reported by history of ideas scholars such as Foucault as the 'unhappy bride' of Marxism (see Foucault, 1980). Whilst the turn away from deterministic notions of social class was very valuable and served as a creative example of Hall's 'break', the domain of phenomenology (particularly as linked to wider debates about the interrogation of meaning systems) was 'lost' primarily because the field as a whole was seen as a 'discipline' which was overly concerned with structures.[12] This perspective may be challenged through the bridging of the gap between ethnography, youth cultural studies and cultural phenomenology in an attempt to strengthen youth cultural research in each of these domains.

In seeking to do this, we draw heavily from those, such as Ricoeur, who have made key contributions in the areas of phenomenology, narrative and time, alongside youth cultural theorists, with the goal of a necessary displacement and theoretical recontextualization of ethnographies of youth culture, particularly but not exclusively within education. We seek not only to chart the contemporary 'maps of meaning' and 'mattering maps' young people draw up for themselves and others living in deprived urban centres, but to address ontological questions about youth narratives, morality and youth subjectivity in different spaces. Our primary argument here is that retrieval of meaning among youth cultures requires a detour into cultural phenomenology. A key aim is to assess the very persistence of narrative in the face of cultural fragmentation, and what that narrative may tell us about youth in late-modernity. Like Ricoeur, we believe that young people 'are in search of a narrative' and we seek to better understand the very nature of these narratives as elements of youth classification (Kearney, 2004: 158). We therefore follow Ricoeur in setting out a 'hermeneutics of imagination' which sees youth culture as an open set of interpretive performances of 'non-totalization' (Kearney, 2004: 46). The notion of a cultural repertoire of performances is designed to encourage us to avoid binaries of thinking over the very nature and essence of youth culture. However, in attending to this repertoire as a phenomenological event, we wish to assert, following Althusser, that elements of youth culture remain tied to both ideologies and utopian visions as young people necessarily navigate the gaps between memory, projection and possible futures (see Kearney, 2004: 88). As Kearney (2004: 88) writes:

> In so far as we remain aware of this gap, it can remind us that society's self-representation is an open ended process. The gap is also an indispensable and unsurpassable horizon of our finite hermeneutic understanding. To deny its existence would be absurd, even ethically dangerous.

Bringing together phenomenology and youth cultural studies also necessitates an attempt to understand the logics of action and associated imaginaries generated by young people as a form of social transformation both in the city and in youth subjectivities (see McDonald, 1999). As Dubet tells us:

> in a decentred world, social actors face the challenge of forming some sort of unity from their experiences in a context where the logic of actions is not necessarily coherent. Constructing such coherence is not necessarily the achievement of the social system, as

classical sociology postulated, but an increasingly urgent imperative facing the social actor.

(Cited in McDonald, 1999: 21)

From this vantage point, a major theoretical aim of expanding the terrain of phenomenology as it relates to the study of youth cultures is to better understand the interpretive dilemmas underlying young people's struggle to 'become somebody' in times of urban retrenchment and significant, if variegated, degrees of moral regulation. An understanding of how young people struggle to hold together the identities they must construct for themselves and with others as they navigate complex social terrain is also particularly well suited to the project of phenomenology.

At the same time, an investigation of the kind we have undertaken does not reside outside the frame of what Raymond Williams, Paul Gilroy or Stuart Hall might refer to as the 'cultural ordinary' – the idea that the meaning systems young people express symbolically are both ordinary and extraordinary. They may be seen as ordinary to the extent that they represent cultural elements of the symbolic order and are ritualized in everyday lived experience in the present; hence the attraction of a subcultural focus. They may be seen as extraordinary in that such meaning systems represent both something from the past and something new. This is because a reconfiguration of the past through a cultural expression in the present leads to the interruption of traditional systems of meaning which change the course of an existing social narrative and open up new worlds of understanding. Social change and youth identity therefore emerge as mediators of social meaning.[13]

In this way we endeavour to approach meaning-making practices or modes of representation and *emplotment* (see Ricoeur, 1981) among contemporary urban youth, at the same time as commenting on the larger cultural forms of *symbolic violence* (Bourdieu, 1999) which operate within the moral 'fields' where the lives of young people are played out. In so doing, we are responding particularly to Nayak's (2003a) concern over the contemporary flight from the study of subculture and from its articulation with stratification. He writes:

> more recently there has been an abandonment of subculture altogether as a viable concept for exploring the temporal, fluid and open-ended construction of youth identification. The end of subculture has been hastened by new technologies and processes of globalization that have been said to have led to new forms of youth subjectivity. With the rise of postmodern theory there has been a marked shift from cultures of production to cultures of consumption, from the local to the global, from resistance to conformity and from subculture to tribes.
>
> (2003a: 10)

In taking a middle ground bound by a phenomenology of youth cultures, we learn that young people neither represent lone authors of a singular story nor are they merely floating receptacles for their symbolic expressions of selfhood. Rather, they carry the burden of the durable effects of the social order with them as they attempt to live their lives in a changing world. In so doing, they mediate and recontextualize these effects in the present: 'meaningful action outstrips its unique situation' (see Ricoeur, 1981). Young people may therefore be seen as neither author nor subject of their own narratives. Youth expression emerges instead as a form of mediated interpretation which draws simultaneously upon the past, the present and an anticipated future in particular spatial arrangements.

To understand young people's actions, we need to move in the direction of viewing young people's accounts as forms of social and spatial text. In keeping with such a position, we do not concern ourselves with language so that it can only be critiqued or deconstructed. Instead, we view the full range of youth cultural activities as social vocabularies which are attempting – in their unfolding – to open up new worlds. As Ricoeur reminds us, hermeneutics is the 'capacity of world disclosure yielded by social texts' (Kearney, 2004: 41). The phenomenologist is not looking to the object of youth culture or to its deviant subject but to the capacity to better understand the worlds that are opened up through their deeply felt cultural experience.

Key Concepts and Conceptual Ideas

In engaging these elements of cultural phenomenology, we draw upon three key principles impinging upon our research findings. The first of these concerns our interest in uncovering the sometimes hidden meanings in the youth cultural text of 'apparent meanings' which are generated by young people living on the fringe of the inner-city. In this way, and following Holloway and Valentine (2000: 9), we can begin to link the hidden meanings generated through expressions of youth cultural identity with the 'importance of place, everyday spaces and spatial discourses'. We can also begin to understand how class imaginaries may emerge in racially and economically divided urban arrangements and may be translated – as hidden meaning – into youth cultural practices. In this respect, identity, invested sites of meaning and space may be seen to intersect and offer an important symbolic site for understanding some of the hidden elements of youth culture and associated practices. Essentially what this means is that texture and nuance can be added to a phenomenology of the spatial meaning-making practices which young people undertake. It also implies that we may gain deeper understandings of how young people negotiate the circulation of particular discourses within and across spaces, and the meanings and symbolic expressions they accord to such discourses.

Second, we argue that symbolic meanings generated about or within youth cultures will always exceed the direct or apparent meaning of any articulation, and that the interpretation of such surplus meaning is a task for hermeneutics and the researcher of youth culture (Ricoeur, 1976). We must struggle to interpret the symbolic meanings expressed through youth culture because they tell us something about young people's place in the social order as they are articulated as a form of youth subjectivity, as well as affording a temporalization of the state that does not derive from an official documentary account. We are therefore called upon to bring the symbolic language of youth to the level of meaning for others. We can assess this language – as part of youth cultural formation – both in relation to its expressed meaning but also in relation to an inherited set of meanings which date back to earlier forms of social inequality.

Third, a phenomenology of youth cultural activity in the global city is here seen to represent an aspect of complex narrative identities which are bound to hidden and often unrecognizable rituals, spatial forms of governance and new aspects of moral regulation.[14] Seen in this way, we can begin to locate young lives as temporally, morally and spatially bound. Young people can also be seen as initiating and sustaining something new as well as representing what may appear, at surface levels in the present, as lost time or involuntary memory (see Curtis, 1997, 2003; Proust, 2003). Therefore, every action that a young person engages in or every story they narrate may be understood as taking place in a temporal context of meaningfulness. Thus youth action and associated symbolic expressions take place in 'historical time'. Historical time, as expressed by young people, is seen through their narratives and modes of representation, which 'attain their full significance when they become a condition of temporal existence' (Simms, 2003: 102).

In working with these three principles, we witness how notions of youth selfhood emerge as social metaphors which point to young people's struggle to classify and to be recognized. And throughout we point to the key concept of classification as central to understanding one's social position in the city. It is through the very practices of classification that we can begin to gain some purchase upon a cultural understanding of how youth existence arrives at expression and emerges as a 'structure of feeling', and as what Marcel Mauss (2006) has identified as a 'body technique'. We can also witness how new social class arrangements and urban re-arrangements are inscribed onto bodies through performances and symbolic practices which can only be understood in relation to other categories of youth. In so doing, we can begin to identify the moral and cultural investments young people make at the level of the symbolic meanings, with the cultural dimensions of a particular space providing – as a site of exchange and classification – one context for inscribing a particular moral register onto the body. As Skeggs points out: 'class insinuates itself into structures of representation and operates in relation to the body of others and is consolidated at a powerful symbolic level' (2004: 54). Space therefore emerges as the imaginative platform for revealing different selfhoods through symbolic expressions, collaborations, conflicts and differentiations.

Conclusions

This chapter set out to chart some of the major positions relating to the broad question of youth cultures and aporias in the field, and to document the principal theoretical shifts which have taken place in the field of youth cultural studies in recent years. Having outlined the key theoretical innovations, we have highlighted the power of both paradigmatic and conceptual dominance and effects of polarization in the field of youth cultural theory over recent years. We then moved forward to showcase elements of our own theoretical apparatus linking the wider domain of youth studies with emergent social theory debates on social space, temporality and moral regulation, as understood through the powerful lens of phenomenology.

In the second part of the book, we shall return with a more detailed eye to the specific conceptual tools that we drew upon to analyse the ethnographic data. At that point, we shall also return to the ideas outlined here, in keeping with the epistemological approach outlined above, which is designed to offer a better understanding of the complex meanings expressed by economically marginalized young people living on the urban fringe of the global city. To return to Hall's ideas about breaks, we hope to show that 'there are no absolute beginnings and few unbroken continuities' in the expression of youth cultures and their performances of identity and classification at the level of local experience. If any such radical break is thought to exist, arguably it is not theoretical per se but is instead operating at the level of what Alain Touraine refers to as the 'sociology of experience': that is, at the level of our very understanding of the very complex dimensions of being young in any given time and place.

2

Spatial Landscapes of Ethnographic Inquiry
Phenomenology, Moral Entrepreneurship and the Investigation of Cultural Meaning

It is very unusual for an attempt to be made to bring the social and the symbolic into a common analytic frame, but it is precisely this that the ethnographic imagination of life as art requires.

(Willis, 2000: 23)

Tis the eye of childhood that fears a painted devil: anti-relativism has largely concocted the anxiety it lives from.

(Geertz, 2000: 46)

In this chapter, we build upon the theoretical interventions described in the previous chapter and seek to illustrate how our interdisciplinary frame has been translated into a coherent methodological approach. At the heart of our research is an attempt, animated by a desire to keep epistemology and method entwined, to uncover the deep meanings underlying young people's narrative accounts of the everyday, of the cultural ordinary, of anomie and even the sub-ordinary in comparative urban contexts. Of central importance for us was to develop a range of methodologies that could capture what Ricoeur referred to as a social imaginary:

> that body of collective stories, histories and ideologies which informs our modes of socio-political action. Social imagination, he argues, is constitutive of our lived reality [...]. The social imagination serves both an ideological role of identification and a utopian role of disruption. The former preserves and conserves; the latter projects alternatives.
>
> (Kearney, 2004: 86)

In striving to capture young people's social imaginaries in urban space, a particular feature of our efforts across the entire ethnography has been a sustained attempt to extend our methodological reach to engage larger questions of time, place and space. And perhaps more specifically to pose novel questions capable of linking the temporal expression of local youth cultures to prevailing currents and spatial scales of globalization. As Thompson and Holland (2003: 3) note:

> an attendance to the specificity of place thwarts the development of meta theories, and some of the most interesting studies of the young as moral agents are those that seek to document the processes of identity-making in small scale local cultures.

In bridging time, place and space, we seek to touch levels of youth experience which may at first glance seem distant from late-modern experience, perhaps even 'archaic' (Kearney, 2004). What we mean by this is that, while we have been primarily concerned with young people's contemporary conceptions of exclusion and the associated modalities of their subcultural and post-subcultural practices, we are also interested in how young people encode and practice 'historical time' (that is, how they engage symbolic practices from past time) in the present. Such approaches to the investigation of cultural meaning show us how forms of youth cultural regulation and classification, and associated forms of ambivalence and interpellation, come to represent real social practices which are governed in part by urban rituals and legends which, to borrow the words of Ricoeur, 'exceed their own frontiers' (see also Rose, 1999). If we see cultural meaning as a representation of the past and the present in discontinuous tension, then our methodology ought to highlight both the paradoxical modes of representation and forces of ambivalence which give the symbolic expression of youth culture its currency in the present. We do not therefore see any mode of youth representation as fixed but instead as an 'ambivalent mode of knowing' which opens and exposes those very processes of regulation, exclusion and cultural production which impinge so directly upon contemporary youth. This in turn allows us to witness prevailing narrative conventions and their symbolic force as they operate through the moral fields of youth cultures.

As previously noted, the core epistemological and philosophical approach driving our methods is founded upon a renewed critical tradition of phenomenological hermeneutics, and most particularly a radical hermeneutic interrogation of meaning as it is expressed by young people. Ricoeur (1981) and Arendt (1971) describe phenomenology as an inherently hermeneutic endeavour. In the case of our study, the description, analysis and representations of the social world offered by young people are generated from within the positions of those who are tied to these social worlds, and who appropriate and reinvent past time as they perform their cultural identities in the present. These appropriations and reinventions are tied to the meaning-making processes (phenomenology) young people apply to the world as they engage in the interpretation of the everyday of city life (hermeneutics), and most particularly in relation to the crystallization and local scales of global flows within transnational social formations. To put this differently, for a study such as ours, one cannot uncouple the project of radical hermeneutics from the need to imagine the interpretive repertoires operating within those spatial contexts upon which youth cultural groups draw (Gille & O'Riain, 2002).

As the lifetime work of Ricoeur so impressively demonstrates, the project of phenomenology must necessarily make its long detour through hermeneutics, through the attempt to understand the other; that is, 'beyond a phenomenological idealism of pure reflection to a phenomenological hermeneutics of cultural interpretation which acknowledges that meaning is never first and foremost for me'.[1] For the study of youth cultural activity and the narrativization of youth subjectivity, such an injunction suggests that an emphasis (however important now and in its own time) upon the 'discourse(s) of the self' as one way to identify state governance can never be enough. To study the lives of young people phenomenologically is to seek to identify their symbolic worlds as a detour through other spatial, structural, moral and temporal narratives and registers which are not bound by a coherent notion of the subject but which point instead to their boundedness within the complexities of a global metropolis. To say 'self', then, can never be merely to say 'I'.[2] The private subjective accounts of young people as communicated are always symbolically produced in a specific space and time – 'the symbol gives rise to thought' (Ricoeur, 1967: 348).

As researchers, we have engaged a range of methods consonant with our goals and designed to access the symbolic, spatial, temporal and cultural/subcultural processes of meaning-making performed by young people. The theorists we particularly follow here, while very different in particular ways, have by and large made use of phenomenological and hermeneutic approaches to access the 'sense-making' processes of their research participants, generally through diverse and largely cultural forms of ethnographic practice.

We have likewise drawn strongly upon ethnography as one means through which to generate greater insight into the daily lives of our research participants; our ethnography incorporates field observations and semi-structured interviews, similar to those of the classic ethnographies we considered earlier. However, in keeping with Ricoeur's, Benjamin's (1937), Sekula's (1984, 1986) and Evans and Hall's (2007) insight into the cultural role of symbols and systems of representation in revealing the surplus meanings inhering within phenomenological and hermeneutic approaches, we have integrated methods into our ethnography that are intended to access these alternative modes of symbolic meaning. For example, visual accounts provide a window of illumination upon the field of moral identification to which young people have access as they navigate the urban city. We therefore combined the visual and the spatial in order to witness the unevenness of both imaginative ideals and essential ideas associated with particular urban locales. Through the visual and the spatial, we were also afforded some purchase on the forms of 'radical realism' which lend currency to young people's accounts of themselves and others within youth cultural communities.

Finally, we have incorporated methods that access historical time, linking these methods to the present as a way of signalling the importance of the temporal to present-day youth cultural configurations. In the absence of these multiple ethnographic forms, we felt we would be unlikely to capture the localized and uneven ways in which wider global relations stretch across place and time, and lead to specific forms of social differentiation both between youth cultural groupings and within them. Such an absence would also result in the neglect of the sense-making and place-making activities of young people which can be performed only in relation to particular spaces and times. In short, moving beyond linguistic description through the visual, spatial and temporal methods we employ provides some access to the kinds of youthscapes to which Nayak (2003a) refers, affording important insights into the strategic actions of young people as they develop new scales of youth cultural activity in multiple sites.

Our integration of these multiple methods has allowed us to generate an approach that is broadly consistent with our epistemology, offering insight at the ethnographic, symbolic, temporal and spatial levels simultaneously. Guided by these four dimensions, we hope to outline a more ethically attuned account of methodological thinking which may hold out opportunities for the emergence of more complex narratives about young people in relation to contemporary class disadvantage. In bridging the spatial, the symbolic, the temporal and the ethnographic, we also generated a conceptual and methodological breadth which responds to wider debates in social theory about the still deeply classed nature of youth cultures operating across time, place and space, and the associated cultural narrations of identity which link these sites (see Dillabough, 2008). It was through this bridging exercise that we were able to position the young person not as fixed or essentialized but instead as only a partial draft of the person who must necessarily unfold in the face of time and place in the present (Ricoeur, 1981). In this case, we can see that young people's actions can be understood intersubjectively through regulatory webs of social relations and constrained historical narratives in a deeply material sense. Arendt writes:

> to identify an action is to tell the story of its initiation, of its unfolding, of its immersion in a web of relations constituted through the actions and narratives of others. Likewise, the wholeness of the self is constituted through the story of a life – a coherent narrative of which we are always the protagonist but not always the author or producer.
>
> (Arendt, 1968: 150; see also Cavarero, 2000)

Following such injunctions on the part of both Arendt and Ricoeur, we have sought to create a methodological approach which answers to our recognition that isolated representational narratives of young people conceived as outside of time and place may fail to generate the knowledge that we, as researchers, seek. Such narratives will be limited in what they offer for understanding new horizons of youth subjectivity, which not only reflect the conditions of late-modernity, but also reflect the sedimented past. Youth 'voices', on their own, cannot offer us an account of 'who' economically disadvantaged youth are (see Arendt, 1971: 151: 'when the one that speaks also acts, she shows her words are not empty'). We have therefore sought to avoid, as far as possible, an emphasis on atomized individual accounts, whether attained through traditional forms of one-off interviewing in the context of research accountability cultures, or as a form of 'insider politics' or putative expressions of researcher solidarity with young people. We have also sought to distance ourselves from the position where young people are characterized through research conceived solely in terms of a narrowly defined linguistic discourse of an ungrounded, immaterial kind. This has been an approach, as for example in discourse analysis and particular forms of deconstruction, which has held sway 'as a fixed critical space' (Lather, 2007) in the study of youth identity over the last decades, and more recently in the study of post-subcultures, and particularly perhaps, within educational research. Here, by contrast, we seek to escape some of the potential limitations of a straightforward 'discourse' analysis of youth cultures and social class, whilst still recognizing its place within our work and the vast body of scholarship it has incited.

We now go on to describe in more detail, drawing upon examples, the means by which our epistemological positions and associated methodologies were translated into the pragmatics of method. For the sake of clarity, we have divided our description by means of the four sub-categories we have already described: the ethnographic, the symbolic, the temporal and the spatial.

The Ethnographic

Ethnography is a research method which allows the researcher to interpret the meanings of thematic findings. Its core function as a mode of qualitative representation is therefore fundamentally a phenomenological one. The use of (a symbolic–temporal–spatial) ethnography as our central methodological approach is highly consistent with the questions that drove our comparative research, questions which pertain to young people's everyday cultures and negotiations within rapidly shifting urban contexts and intensified degrees of moral regulation. We see ethnographic approaches as providing a framework for exploring particularly important aspects of youth cultural identification as it is manifested in localized and spatially divided settings, and as it responds to wider and intensified forms of moral panic associated with youth practices. Likewise, it is only through comparative ethnographic means that the rich aspects of what Williams (1977), and Pilkington and Johnson (2003), and other youth cultural theorists term 'the cultural ordinary' can be accessed, along with the uneven effects of wider changes. As Willis (2000: 6) writes:

> The point remains that there is something rare and special about the symbolic stresses of the common and everyday that ethnography so routinely picks up and records. The fact that these experiences are both repeated and common does not make less of them, or make them any less human defining. They are an essential part of the creative finding of symbolic place and identity, of recognizable time and place in out-of-scale and baffling historical structures.

This nexus between everyday cultures, global flows and the 'baffling historical structures' that shape them is precisely the interconnection that our methods are designed to reveal.

In pursuit of this interconnection, the first author spent over two years in the Toronto site, spent time on a weekly basis 'hanging out' at the school, and shadowed a small sample of the students in their classrooms, in the hallways, and, where possible, in the wider neighbourhood. This was combined with 12 months (two six-month terms) of action research and team-teaching with both the English and Social Studies classroom teacher in the classrooms where the study took place (some of the students in these classes were classified as 'remedial' learners). This fieldwork was augmented by a sample of one-on-one and group interviews with young people over a two-year period, alongside interviews with teachers and administrators within the school.

At the Vancouver site, both authors and two graduate students spent six months working within a grade 10 vocationally bound English classroom, interacting with and observing students both inside and outside the class, as well as carrying out one-on-one interviews with students and teachers. In each case, the authors and researchers generated copious fieldnotes, which, coupled with interview transcripts and substantial media, journalistic and visual photo work, formed the bulk of the ethnographic data.

Open-ended individual interviews with the young people in both cities concentrated upon students' accounts of their schooling and social experiences across aspects of urban space and schooling in times of change; their view of themselves in relation to peers and peer rivalry, popular culture and issues of cultural identity; and the impact that urban life had on their school experience, as well as their sense of security, nation, citizenship and belonging in the radically changing city. The interviews further traced, where possible, young people's relationship to wider accounts of social class, race, and emergent forms of masculinity and femininity.

Finally, and perhaps most importantly, we incorporated visual representations that participants had created themselves through classroom projects or that we had found in media or archives as elicitation tools. These activities were designed to help us and the young people deepen their exploration of their experiences in relation to past, present and future (these processes and methodologies are described in much greater detail in the section that follows).

In carrying out interviews over the duration of the ethnography, we were persistently reminded of Reid's caution in relation to the interviewing process: 'sociologists' queries are likely to be alien to interviewees' ways of understanding their world – and to be successful, sociologists must pose and answer their own questions without simply imposing their own problematics.' As researchers, we therefore faced the challenge of finding ways of interpreting youth accounts which 'do not allow the discipline simply to find itself in the other it studies' (Reid, 2002: 344). In attending to this warning, the data represented throughout the book explicitly focus upon young people's reflections on their ties to urban arrangements and the ways in which their experiences of exclusion and/or belonging have been structured by the spatial and moral practices of the urban school, neighbourhood and localized territory. While it remains the case that we read this work through particular theoretical lenses, we hope that the range of methods provides a rich and perhaps more vivid impression of young people who are perhaps more heavily surveilled and governed than ever before.

All the young people who participated across both sites were aged between 13 and 16, and came from a range of ethnic backgrounds and cultural and religious identifications. This range varied depending on the histories of migration and urban biographies of change in each of the cities where the research was conducted. Each attended the same secondary school within their respective cities. Many had recent histories of family migration or had parents or grandparents who had arrived in Canada in the post-war period with refugee or asylum status. Some were second- and third-generation immigrants as well, with families and entire villages sometimes migrating as specialized labourers from the turn of the twentieth century into the same neighbourhood (particularly Tower Hill, the Toronto neighbourhood). A minority of white and Aboriginal students also participated. Another minority of students was represented by communities of Eastern-European migration (non-visible minority groups, e.g. from Poland, Macedonia, the Ukraine).

One unifying factor for almost all participants was their social location as either 'working class', 'economically disadvantaged' or 'working poor' living at the edge of the urban core of an affluent 'world-class' city. Parents of participants held occupations such as taxi drivers, babysitters, cleaners, factory workers, fish farmers, construction workers or agricultural labourers. Many parents held multiple part-time or seasonal jobs, and often youth participants were expected to care for younger children at home while parents worked. Some participants also lived with extended families, particularly if they had arrived as immigrants or refugees and were reliant on extended family networks, rather than direct parental supervision. In both sites, students habitually referred to their schools and neighbourhoods as a 'ghetto', 'warehouse' or 'slum' for 'poor kids'. A more detailed account of the specific spatial context navigated by participants in each site is given in Chapter 3.

The Symbolic

> For as Ricoeur submits, 'I am convinced that we must think, not behind the symbols, but starting from symbols, ... that they constitute the revealing substrate of speech which lives among [humans]. In short, the symbol gives rise to thought.' Hermeneutics is thus the route to philosophical reflection, to reflection premised on the assumption that by following the indication of symbolic meaning one will arrive at a deeper understanding of human existence.
>
> (Thompson, 1982: 6)

In drawing upon a phenomenological approach to interpreting the realities of class disadvantage, youth cultures and new terrains of moral regulation, we take as our guiding principle the epistemology captured by Thompson in his reflection on Ricoeur's work above. That is to say, in attempting to generate greater understanding (for both ourselves and our readers) of the realities faced by the young people in this study, we take as central the power of the symbol as a mediating structure in understanding youth cultures and view these symbols as powerful narrative devices which are a 'trigger to telling' (see Harrison, 2002). Such symbols are expressed polyvalently and contextually through the social text of semi-structured interviews, the images generated by both media and young people themselves,[3] and the wider symbolic order that has come to be associated with marginalized young people and youth cultures in a neo-liberal era.

Here we acknowledge that epistemology represents a form of visual meaning and provides access, through associated methods, to a symbolic identity and form of moral classification predicated as much on the idea of a human need (not only that of young people) for mastery, as well as by the anxiety created through novel moral registers of fear and panic which often drive these needs. These moral registers, unlike the Mod–Rocker disputes at Clacton, can now be seen as highly spatialized and mobile, and are arguably changing the relationship between self and other in local urban contexts. Our visual data particularly possessed the power to bring our attention to the challenges young people face when confronting the play of difference, feelings of security and belonging and the accompanying 'myths of origin' which are associated with a denial of difference. This form of data helped us better to understand some of the distinctions between the global epicentre, its imagined peripheries and the associated unevenness of their combined effects.[4]

Indeed, until relatively recently (and actually as a still dominant research practice), sociology of education and related methods have been preoccupied with charting narratives of exclusion through the means of language or the 'spoken word', leaving behind its commitment to draw upon the image and even writing to better understand the social life world of young people. At one level, we feel compelled to suggest that the text or the spoken word on its own constitutes an important resource for youth research. However, it can also constitute (and we believe that all researchers in education have faced these realities) that which Arendt might call banal and paralysing if it cannot move us beyond the traumas and reproductions of essential categories of youth selfhood in late-modernity.

We also utilize the symbolic (the visual, the archive and the narrative account) in our methodological approach as a humble way to engage in what Patti Lather (2007) identifies as a very partial 'generative undoing' of more traditional youth research methods in seeking to widen methodological discussions (Bloom, 1998; Britzman, 1995a, 1995b, 1998).[5] In other words, the scope of ethics in methodology should not here be seen as tied only to 'reflexivity', apparently 'equal' research relationships, 'open-ended insider approaches', subcultural shadowing, participant observation, dialogue and the like, but also to our understandings of historicality and to ethnographic research as addressed, conducted and expressed within the terms of a symbolic temporality. Research relationships are fundamentally temporal to the degree that we are able to learn from a very particular past which has remained elusive to us, but which never fails to point to our connection to that past (Simon, 2005). Indeed, as Walkowitz (2007) argues, the meanings and relations of power through conceptualizations of methodology always deepen with the specificity of each research account, and the 'truth value' (not 'truth' itself) of any research lies in its interpretation of the symbolic within particular contexts. As Fyfe and Law (1988: 1) write (in relation to the work of symbols through the creation of images):

> to understand a visualization is thus to enquire into its provenance and into the social work that it does. It is to note its principles of inclusion and exclusion, to detect the roles that it makes available, to understand the ways in which they are distributed, and to decode the hierarchies and differences that it naturalizes.

Our emphasis upon the symbolic allows us to start from the premise that our research participants are acting yet still regulated subjects who do not reside outside the social, cultural and bodily conditions within which they circulate. That is, by applying a hermeneutic analysis of the symbols developed by, and applied to, young people in urban concentrations of economic disadvantage, we follow Ricoeur in effecting 'an initial displacement of the primacy of the subject' (Thompson, 1981: 18). This is done, in part, by 'subordinating the subjective intentions of the author [in this case, both the young people and images they generate] to the objective meaning of the text' (Thompson, 1981: 18). Additionally, following Ricoeur (1981) in his leap from the hermeneutic analysis of texts, understood traditionally as bodies of written work, to the same method applied to what he terms 'meaningful action' within the context of our research, we understand the symbols generated by youth participants – often in response to methodologies we have presented to them – to be one of the necessary objects of analysis.

To access the residual symbolic meanings associated with young people's experiences of exclusion, being 'warehoused' in failing urban schools and neighbourhoods, and the use of epithets associated with contemporary moral panics about terrorism and migration, we made use of a variety of methods. These generally took the shape of classroom-based projects and media and urban studies approaches, completed within the context of the ethnographic fieldwork described above. For example, participants in both research sites were asked to draw 'timelines' of themselves, with a representation of themselves from 10 years previously, one in the present, and one projected 10 years into the future (an example is given in Figure 2.1).

Figure 2.1 Self Portrait of Past, Present or Future: Beacon Park, Vancouver, BC.

Participants at the Vancouver site were asked to create images of the 'good citizen' and the 'bad citizen,' and associated 'folk devils', which elicited images such as Figure 2.2.

This emphasis on the production of visual culture, as well as reflections on it, helped us to access the symbolic meanings young people attributed to such highly conceptual notions as 'citizenship', social class and security, together with reflections on their own aspirations and expectations for

Figure 2.2 Student Image of the 'Citizen': Beacon Park, Vancouver, BC.

the future. These visual projects often generated deeply symbolic images that represented more complex, ambivalent and contradictory elements of young people's experiences and regulatory categories of the social world than they would express through spoken interviews. Indeed, as Hall (1997) has argued, we were able to witness those modes of ambivalent knowing that young people expressed about the changing nature of the city, their place and future within it, and associated youth cultural activity. We also used the visual images as elicitation devices within interviews, with a resultant deepening and widening in the scope of reflection by participants.

Additionally, we made use of both alternative and mainstream media in order to draw responses from participants and encourage reflection on their own lives in the city and the lives of those represented. Participants were shown a video entitled *Kelly Loves Tony*, a documentary by US-based documentary film-maker Spencer Nakasako (1998) which followed a teenage couple whose families had migrated from Laos and were currently living in housing projects in Los Angeles, USA. The young people showcased in the documentary faced many of the urban social issues encountered by the research participants themselves. After watching the video, participants were asked to produce written reflections on it, and asked what advice they would offer to Tony and Kelly.

WRITE YOUR OWN STORY ABOUT THESE CHILDREN

Settling in Canada at such a young age from a foreign country makes these childrens life better. Although there have been hardships for them for being different, the good outweighs the bad. But at a young age they shouldn't be scod, they don't know whats going on. Though from a different country, these are our future, the next generation.

Figure 2.3 Student Response to Archive Photo of Young People Portrayed on the Street in Urban Toronto in the Early Twentieth Century (source: *Children of the Ward*, Fonds 1244, Item 8028, William James Collection. Permission granted by the City of Toronto Archives).

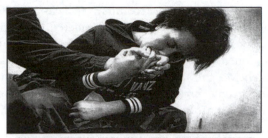

Figure 2.4 Student Response to Media Photo from the *Toronto Star* (source: ©
Peter Power/GetStock.com, Image Number 2083215602).

In a similar vein, participants were asked to write captions for archival
and media images of child and youth economic disadvantage (see Figures
2.3 and 2.4). Participants in Vancouver were also asked to write letters
to imaginary young people who were immigrants to Canada, soliciting
their advice for these new arrivals. Each of these strategies generated rich
data sources in their own right, as well as serving as further grounds for
deepened reflections within the interview context.

The Temporal

> Every image of the past that is not recognized by the present as one
> of its own threatens to disappear irretrievably.
>
> (Benjamin, 1968: 255)

One distinct manner in which the visual was engaged within this project
was through the use of historical archival images, specifically images of
other low-income young people in different temporal periods (a larger
image of 2.3 is given in Figure 2.5). In examining these photos, it became
apparent that any ethnography which posed questions only about the
present threatened to degrade the 'art of seeing' (if one sees ethnography,
as the authors do, as art). To borrow the words of Ricoeur (1981), 'historical knowledge' seemed to be 'painfully missing' from existing ethnographies about young people and, indeed, from the sociology of youth more
generally. What was 'missing' in this case was a methodological engagement with the role of *historical knowledge* in the making of contemporary
representations of young people, particularly as inspired by photographic

and media images and associated written accounts (see Felman, 2000). Previous work by youth subcultural theorists had considered the importance of history (however loosely) in partially framing the nature of youth subcultural formations (Cohen, 1997), as had some feminist historians and historical sociologists before the second half of the twentieth century. But sociologists of young people in the late twentieth century seemed largely oblivious to history, concentrating instead on the present as an isolated temporal period (see also Dillabough, 2008).

As a partial response to this recognition, we undertook preliminary archival research in each urban site where contemporary ethnographic data pertaining to young people were to be collected. Through this process, we came across many striking visual and documentary sources from the public record representing young people across the course of the twentieth century. But what to do with this material? Neither of us had been trained as historians nor did we have much experience in historical method. Instead, the following methodological challenge emerged: How, through methodological intervention, should we confront the past as we undertook a sociology of economically disadvantaged young people in the present? How could we draw upon these images in legitimate ways, despite not being trained as 'mainstream historians'? How might we find

Figure 2.5 Children of the Ward (source: Fonds 1244, Item 8028, William James Collection. Permission Granted by the City of Toronto Archives).

ways to use the image as both a historical and a contemporary resource in the service of a cultural method that would illuminate the lives and contemporary social circumstances of working-class young people?

Our response turned once more to Ricoeur (1981: 33), and his suggestion that symbols can be understood as 'expressions of double meaning, wherein a primary meaning refers beyond itself to a second meaning which is never given directly'. This further emphasis upon symbols can also be witnessed in thinking through Ricoeur's concept of surplus meaning, an expression of young people's embodiment of 'historical time'; that is to say, past time (expressed symbolically through language and the visual) as it is crystallized and embodied in young people in the post-industrial city in the present. We therefore viewed the symbols young people drew upon in their narrative accounts and visual work as precisely this mediating structure, which not only spoke to their lives in the present but also to a past which may have been elusive to both us and them. We sought to capture, as far as it was possible, the idea of 'lost time' and an understanding of moral regulation in new ways, through an analysis of the present symbolic expressions of youth culture as it might relate to the past.

Thus, as well as asking participants to create their own images and symbols, we drew upon the historical representations we had discovered within local archives (see for example, Figures 2.6 and 2.7), asking participants to reflect upon these images, their meanings and to provide accounts of why young people might be in the situation they were or presented in the way they were presented. We solicited their thoughts on why young people from a different and deeply unfamiliar temporal moment were living in organized sites of urban poverty, and if this might be related to the temporal present in some way. Students were asked to write captions and stories about the archival photos they observed, as well as to discuss life in the city and their own neighbourhoods both in the past and the present. The results of these activities required us to think more seriously as methodologists about Ricoeur's conception of 'the problematic of the representation of the past [and the present]' (2004: xvi). Clearly, this is less a specific pragmatic approach or instrumental reconceptualization and more a general stance towards the expansion of justice through methods which might seek to embrace past and present. Here, the formal historical record may be seen not only as an 'institutional sedimentation', as the 'archiving of a social practice', but also as an analytical detour within method from late-twentieth-century emphases upon selfhood, identity politics and a reporting of its associated language forms. Instead, the use of archival materials allowed us to consider the power of moving towards a critique of institutions and practices responsible for sustaining such forms of ontological sedimentation (Ricoeur, 2004: 220). 'Considered in this way', Ricoeur suggests,

> the process of institutionalization brings to light two faces of
> the efficacy of representations: on the one hand, in terms of
> identification – the logical, classificatory function of representations;
> on the other, in terms of coercion, of constraint – the practical
> function of establishing conformity in behaviour. On the path to
> representation the institution creates identities and constraints.
>
> (Ricoeur, 2002: 290)

In contrast, then, to the persistence of benevolent myths within methodologies about a personal relationship with the 'poor youth subject' or a mechanical solidarity with the 'researched', it is important to take some analytical and methodological distance here. Ricoeur is aware that historical understanding can come only with temporal distance from our own analytical authority and, in our case, from images of young people in the city, as they are offered to us in static representations. Moving beyond a critique of the subject (however important now and in its own time) towards a vision of a once-present past as a form of social narration within methodological practice allows us to work towards such distancing. The nature of any such efforts must always lead us back to the persistence of that past as a complex narrative which must unfold, despite its material absence in the static representation, always remaining available to the appropriate institutional/methodological apparatus through which we may interpret it in the current moment.

Such distancing or distanciation may assist us in moving – as methodologists – beyond a critique of categories and the re-representation of autonomous speaking subjects who are responsible for their own destiny, towards a theatre of appearances about actors and sufferers who are always enclosed within moral interpretations and temporal locations, but who must not be cut off from the meaningful presence of others, without whom they could not have appeared in any meaningful sense. What this alerted us to was the need to draw on historical sources in more creative and expansive ways, to engage them not only analytically but also dialogically and dynamically. This implied that we needed to find ways, to take the case of the sources we found within the archives, of embedding images and meanings from the past more explicitly within ethnographies of the present, developing strategies which would allow both participants and researchers to respond directly to evocations of urban youth poverty speaking from a different time and place, but also from a setting which is immediately familiar. Here, the goal was to utilize images systematically to open a space within the narrative for a sustained temporal and generational dimension of public understanding of, for example, life in urban contexts, in which the research dialogue can be stretched across time as well as across place. In this case, confronting our connection to others

Figure 2.6 Slum – Rear of 18 William Street, 1914 (source: Series 372, Subseries 32, Item 326. Permission Granted by the City of Toronto Archives).

Figure 2.7 Slum Interior, October 1913 (source: Series 372, Subseries 32, Item 246. Permission Granted by the City of Toronto Archives).

living in the same city in past time through research practices emerged as one hermeneutic imperative for rethinking the present. It also required an expansion of ethical repertoires in our research – across all research actors – which could only be enabled through an interdisciplinary searching for that historical knowledge which continues to impact on our research practices in the present. This methodological intervention emerged as a temporal reflexivity which called upon us to 'know something about the past made present' (Kearney, 2009).

We pose questions, such as, does our method (e.g. dialogue, critical media discussions, self-portraits, talk, image critiques) embrace a notion of the 'once present' as we conduct our contemporary ethnographic research with young people, and does this help us to envision a less 'thoughtless' future which frames social conflict on a much wider scale? We concluded that such work can only be done through an interdisciplinary bridging which takes as axiomatic that narrowly defined subjects inherited from particular traditions of thought and practice – for example, sociology, gender and education, educational research methods and youth studies – are unlikely to expand the ethical dimensions of research without methodological detours into an ethical temporality in order to widen our research remits as well as our intellectual futures (Skocpol, 2005).

The Spatial

> Space is never empty: it always embodies meaning.
> Where there is space there is being.
>
> (Lefebvre, 1991: 22)

Within each research site (Toronto and Vancouver), several months were spent prior to embarking on fieldwork gathering contextual data from archives, government and policy documents, and books that had been written about the neighbourhoods in question. Such contextualization is essential for an ethnographic approach that understands both history and the governing approaches that have shaped contemporary neighbourhoods as essential elements of the present and imagined realities of lived experiences (Bourdieu & Wacquant, 1992). It is also central to a spatial and cultural geographical approach that understands both 'space and place in terms of social relations' (Massey, 1994: 2). A spatial/cultural geographical account is important for the questions and concerns that drive the research because, as feminist geographer Massey so eloquently suggests, 'the social relations of space are experienced differently, and variously interpreted, by those holding different positions as part of it' (1994: 3). Massey's emphasis on both experience and interpretations of space suggests the compatibility between the phenomenological and hermeneutic approaches described above and the necessity of a spatial approach that

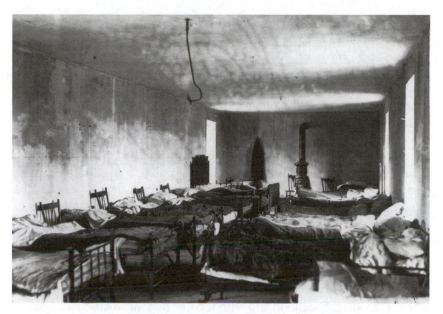

Figure 2.8 Interior January 20th, 1911 (source: Series 372, Subseries 32, Item 10. Permission granted by the City of Toronto Archives).

takes the idea that 'space is never empty: it always embodies meaning' as central to young people's lives (see, for example Figure 2.8). Like Nayak (2003a: 29), we are concerned with demonstrating that 'the changing economic geographies of places and regions are still primary landscapes upon which the cultural lives of young people are situated'.

Both of the areas in which we worked were located in sites that had been home to working-class communities since at least the nineteenth century; both had been disproportionately affected by the forces of de-industrialization and the re-organization of labour that have taken place since the rapid onset of neo-liberal scales of globalization and associated policies which were particular to the Canadian context. Each neighbourhood has likewise been the site for housing waves of migrants seeking respite from poor economic and social prospects in their countries of birth, as well as being a target for accompanying moral panics and public attention attached to perceptions of class abjection and apparently increased criminality and/or deviancy. Finally, each site rested at the edge of the urban core and had been increasingly subject to re-zoning policies and development that have resulted in substantial gentrification, and the associated rise in housing costs that typically accompanies this trend. These spatial contexts are detailed more substantially and placed within a global frame in Chapter 3.

At the level of method, we accessed young people's experiences of the spatial through project-based approaches that brought to the forefront participants' encounters with, and imaginaries of, the spaces and places through which they passed each day. For example, participants in both Toronto and Vancouver were given disposable cameras and asked to take photographs of the 'places' where they spend the most time. Participants were cautioned to take photos only of 'place' and 'space', and not of people. We developed the photos and returned them to participants so that they could organize them into booklets that would include a narrative description of the photos and an account of life for them and others in the city. This method generated an enormous range of images, including local parks, public housing projects, streets, public transport, apartment complexes and stores, with associated narratives that described the significance of that particular site to the participant. Examples are given in Figures 2.9 and 2.10.

This rich spatial method was augmented in Vancouver through the use of freely available 'Google Maps' and satellite technology. Through this Web-based tool, we printed satellite images of the local neighbourhood, and asked participants to describe various meaningful places and spaces within their neighbourhood and school contexts. This method allowed us further insight into participants' experiences of inclusion and exclusion within a local space that was both demonized and valorized, and gave us a stronger sense of where young people perceived the lines between each to be drawn.

Our spatial approach to youth research methodologies was thus deeply dependent on the phenomenological and hermeneutic appropriation of the centrality of symbolic meanings for young people in local spaces and

Figure 2.9 Student Photo-Narrative: Beacon Park, Vancouver BC.

Figure 2.10 Student Photo-Narrative: Tower Hill, Toronto, Ontario.

what these highly spatialized symbols can reveal about young people's experiences of urban transformations, moral regulation and their own everyday encounters with spatial structures of inequality.

Conclusions: Towards a Symbolic–Temporal–Spatial Ethnography of Contemporary Youth Cultures

Our epistemological approach and related methods are only useful insofar as they help reveal comparatively some elements of the often-masked relationship between social class relations, urban space and temporally reconfigured youth cultures. This chapter has described the phenomenological and hermeneutic grounding of our methodology; the role of historical and contemporary symbols as both pragmatic elicitation devices and the means by which to connect the problematics of the past with the concerns of the present; and the role of a spatial imaginary in grounding the temporal reality of a specific youth expression. In the chapters to come, we will attempt to demonstrate how this multi-faceted methodological approach, combined with an interdisciplinary theoretical frame, can help us gain a deeper understanding of the specific dilemmas, interpretations and responses of young people navigating the contemporary global city.

3
Lost Youth and Urban Landscapes
Researching the Interface of Youth Imaginaries and Urbanization

Setting the Scene

There were bars over the windows. So it kind of seemed like a prison to me […]. Couldn't wait to get out of there […]. They say it's to keep the vandals from destroying the windows but, I don't know, it felt like a prison to me.'

(Billy, 15, Tower Hill, Toronto)

Why do neighbourhoods and places have such a powerful hold over how we identify with others and the relational practices we utilize as we navigate urban spaces? Why are we often so emotionally invested – through memories of home, nostalgia, loss and attachments – in the everyday life of neighbourhood contexts? How do neighbourhoods come to constitute the cultural and moral fields of meaning and associated memories which seem to generate an outpouring of symbolic repertoires, forms of embodiment and modalities of youth practice?[1]

In this chapter, we respond to these questions by providing an overview of the two comparative sites where our study took place. In particular we offer an account of the spatial meanings and the associated contours of the urban neighbourhoods navigated by our youth participants. For our culturally grounded spatial ethnography, understanding links between abstract conceptualization of 'loss', youth cultures and the spatial divisions of each urban neighbourhood is essential if we are to describe both the parameters and patterns of new youth cultural activity, along with young people's urban spatial imaginaries.

Through detailed ethnographic description we also seek to show how the young people we encountered are living out elements of style and conflict through urban change and experiences associated with particular configurations of urban social divisions. We believe that such descriptions are particularly relevant in illuminating the scale of transformative processes at global, national and local levels, and in helping us to understand the character of the contemporary reconfiguration of social class and its attendant moral economies in Canada's large urban centres. Where possible, we develop these accounts alongside some of the images of youth and class disadvantage being portrayed in mainstream Canadian media and other sources of public record in Canada (see, for example, Figure 3.1).

For us, in understanding what we are calling the urban fringe,[2] a primary emphasis rests upon the ways in which class divisions associated with urban regeneration and degeneration are re-contextualizing the relationship between morality, youth identification and cultural activity. This emphasis allows us to see pervasive and re-emergent historical themes such as 'disgust', 'honour' and 'shame' as central to the re-organization and reclassification of working-class life, as well as in the re-ordered city. As Skeggs (2004: 5; brackets our addition) argues, attention to 'excessive, unhealthy, publicly immoral working-class [youth]' proliferates when there are also other emerging social tensions around 'propriety, and self-responsibility' in cities. From this perspective we are best able to understand the role that particular spatial landscapes and their symbolic assemblages play in framing youth groups as 'disgusting', 'superior' and/ or 'shameful'. Indeed, as we show, for many young people the urban imaginary generated some of the pivotal markers of an imagined selfhood

Figure 3.1 Jazzy, a Homeless, Pregnant Nineteen-Year-Old, Kisses the Hand of Lone Wolf, her Boyfriend of Two Weeks Who is Now her Fiance (source: © Peter Power/GetStock.com, Image Number 2083215602).

and fantasies of power, and were often drawn upon by youth groups as they performed, for example, the Gangsta, Thug or Nammer identity (see Chapter 4 for descriptions). One particularly salient marker was the role that neighbourhood imaginaries and school life played in shaping performances of masculinity and femininity, which were expressed in everyday cultural groupings. Another marker was the deeply ambivalent feelings that young people held towards the spaces in which they lived. An interview excerpt with Freddy (15), a first-generation South American living in Vancouver, highlights quite heightened degrees of urban fear and associated forms of interpellation:

INTERVIEWER: What do you think about this neighbourhood? Around the school?

FREDDY: I don't like it.

INTERVIEWER: You don't like it? How come?

FREDDY: There's too, it's too dangerous. [...] too many drugs.

INTERVIEWER: Yeah. Do you notice that a lot?

FREDDY: Yes.

INTERVIEWER: During the day around here?

FREDDY: Yeah, during the day here when I'm going to school or at lunchtime if you go out and people smoking and people drinking, doing crack.

INTERVIEWER: Near the school?

FREDDY: Near the school.

INTERVIEWER: Ah.

FREDDY: I see a lot of police officers here, a lot.

INTERVIEWER: Do you feel unsafe?

FREDDY: At times.

INTERVIEWER: Yeah? Have there been any times that you can tell me about?

FREDDY: Ah. When I have to go home. You know like in the fall when it gets dark really fast?

INTERVIEWER: Yes.

FREDDY: When I go home after like basketball practice, soccer practice, it's pretty late. The 'bums', they like start yelling or start moving a little [...].

INTERVIEWER: Makes you nervous?

FREDDY: Makes you [feel] a little unsafe.

INTERVIEWER: Mmm-hmmm.

FREDDY: And scared.

Clearly, the intersection of space and identity unfolds here as we witness Freddy's honesty about his fears of the neighbourhood and a simultaneous recognition that new 'unrecognizable neighbours' are clearly 'foe', and must therefore be re-classed or seen as distinctly shameful. For example, his expression of distaste about the local homeless population – whom he labels as 'bums' – serves to establish a degree of inter-class distinction between himself and other economically disadvantaged people in the local space. Likewise, his description of the local dangers associated with drug-use and related lawlessness mark this neighbourhood as a site of deep ambivalence for Freddy: a place that he is required to be, and yet a place where he feels distinctly uncomfortable and, at times, unsafe. McRobbie (2009) refers to this kind of ambiguity as a double entanglement where particular social-class positions – in this case economic disadvantage – are instrumentalized and new individualized constellations of social conflict begin to emerge which are associated with wider urban changes. As we demonstrate later, particular ideas about the loss of an old but reputable working-class community or the loss of nation – those myths of class origin – often reside at the centre of these entanglements and inter- and intra-class distinctions.

Another important marker turned upon racial issues. Stark contrasts between urban wealth and poverty, when set alongside novel forms of racial conflict and new sites of both settled and unsettled migration, combined to make urban space a major site for the generation of new racisms. These conflicts existed alongside longstanding, sometimes deeply sedimented conceptions of self-abjection expressed by young people, which almost always led to individual feelings of class shame and new patterns of inter-ethnic racism. These new racisms betray North American beliefs about normative race conflicts between white and black, or white colonialists and First Nations communities (although these issues remain important, as the standard and highly over-determined categories of racism). As one recently immigrated Cambodian-Canadian young woman (Chanara, also self-identified as Muslim), aged 15, commented in Beacon Park, Vancouver:

CHANARA: I think Chinese people are all so racist. When I go to China-town they stare at me and they won't treat me the same way and they'll always speak Chinese.

INTERVIEWER: To you directly or to others? [CH: yeah to other people] So tell me a bit about the Chinese people being racist.

CHANARA: Mostly it's like my whole life they've always been like that like not living in Chinatown. I used to live in Burnaby and there's a lot of people living there too and they'll always exclude me out because of my race because I'm brown skin colour.

INTERVIEWER: [...] I know the distinctions but ... when you say you're brown then how would the Chinese be classified?

CHANARA: Well, yellow.

INTERVIEWER: Ok [...] that distinction I understand. Ok so those kind of distinctions matter to the Chinese, is that what you're thinking?

CHANARA: Yeah, cause now that we live in Chinatown me and my mom we used to like go there and they used to be so rude to my mom too. Like if they have to wait in line they would be so grumpy about it and try to budge, try to push her out of the way.

Understanding how young people in both locations navigated these race relations at a highly spatialized yet local form of social distinction is critically important. Skeggs (2004: 14) writes:

Attributing negative value to the working-class is a mechanism for attributing value to the middle-class self (such as making oneself tasteful through judging others to be tasteless). So, it is not just a matter of using some aspects of the culture of the working class to enhance one's value, but also maintaining the position of judgment to attribute value, which assigns the other as immoral, repellent, abject, worthless, disgusting, even disposable.

Informed by such ethnographic observations, we wish to portray our research sites in ways which are not merely descriptive in a traditional ethnographic sense but which also expose a wider cultural repertoire of class divisions and moral values, and which therefore attach temporal meaning and significance to the spaces in which we worked. As Chanara told us:

CHANARA: Well, it's all the same. Like the houses look the same and it's really small. But one of the reasons why my parents live there is because it's hard to find other three bedroom houses for that amount. And it's better because the government helps pay a bit.

INTERVIEWER: Subsidizes and they get some support [C: Yeah] so that makes a difference in terms of their income and everything else … I forget what's the general area where your house is located?

CHANARA: [Street Name]

INTERVIEWER: So you took a picture of your room. […] Can you tell me a little bit about your room?

CHANARA: Yeah well my room is like the only place I stay in the house. I don't like to stay around my family most of the time. I just like to lock myself in my room 'cause I have everything in there too that I can just stay in there.

INTERVIEWER: What's in there … ?

CHANARA: I have a television and a computer and a phone. […] I'm ashamed to have my friends round.

In positioning descriptions such as these within a comparative context, we hope to reveal the dramatic cultural impact of spatial relations on young people's forms of identification and associated imaginaries about local spaces, and thereby to see existing theoretical notions of youth cultural activity in a new light. In the remainder of this chapter, we outline some guiding concepts for charting ethnographic spatial contexts, and then proceed to a closer description of our research sites.

Guiding Conceptual Apparatus: Interrogating the Spatial at the Level of the Ethnographic

At the outset, we wish to set the stage for distinguishing urban space from descriptive ideas of 'context'. In making this distinction, we argue that context can never be described objectively and neither can it be seen as the sole foundation for understanding why young people perform everyday cultural activities in the ways that they do. Our claim is instead that we need to move beyond the idea of context as ever truly 'local' and turn towards the idea that neighbourhood descriptions form part of urban imaginaries and symbolic authority operating in and through the lives of young people. In thinking, therefore, about issues of symbolic authority and globalizing spaces and their role in the production of youth cultures, a series of concerns emerge, challenging some of the earlier subcultural accounts of how authority is expressed through youth conflicts, and which are directly tied to associated urban divisions and trans-local elements of urban space.

Thus, while territory has always been seen as part of a neighbourhood context and shaped understandings of youth practice in earlier subcultural studies (see Clarke, 1976; Cohen, 1997; Hebdige, 1979; Willis, 1977), this kind of geographically or class-based authority can no longer be seen in straightforward terms. As cities reorganize, so too do subcultural and post-subcultural groupings and the spatial markers which authorize particular youth practices. In most contexts, young people are confronting novel youth practices which disrupt – as 'structures of feeling' – the normative conditions of a city's and youth group's collective memory. It is often within these disruptions and cultural re-alignments that young people's caged resentments or their ambivalent feelings of being 'chained to a place' emerge most starkly (Reay & Lucey, 2003). And, as cultural geographers continue to remind us, moving beyond territorial practices (although still key) and towards more nuanced understandings of place and space provide some access to those feelings as they operate on the ground. To borrow the words of Burawoy, O'Riain, Blum, George and Gille (2000), nuanced accounts of space provide a wider conceptual landscape for revealing the ways in which youth cultures 'live the global' at the level of the local. In this respect, the importance of ethnographic inquiry to reveal the global 'place making' and self-making projects young people engage in offers insight into new cultural processes operating at the borders where youth cultures and practices are reconfigured and difference is encountered (Buroway et al., 2000).

We preface our descriptions of space and locale with a brief consideration of three concepts which we have developed as elements of our theoretical and methodological lens throughout. We turn to these ideas not only as abstract theoretical markers but as expressions of an empirically grounded attempt to understand better the relationship between locale, space, youth culture and exclusion. In each case, these terms served as quite grounded principles as we witnessed young people navigate the school and city. It is with these concepts and our links to wider social and cultural theory in mind that we have attempted to elaborate more fully on our conceptual and empirical notions of urban space.

1. Space as an Authorized Relational Practice

As we set out to provide a description of each of our research spaces, we perceived them as cultural and moral fields (Bourdieu, 1999) containing within them sets of relations which can be seen to operate only, as Massey (1995) reminds us, in the context of other spatial relations and practices bound to highly classed forms of moral authority. For example, the urban school corridor was typically seen by young people as highly unregulated space or a space free from authoritarian teacher-based surveillance. Nevertheless, young people moved through the corridor in accord with particular modes of self-expression and performances which remained authorized to greater or lesser degrees by various forms of youth cultural governance and discipline. These governing practices are intimately tied to young people's place and 'positional status' within this corridor (see Bourdieu, 1999), as well as to their place in the long history of cultural legitimacy. These spaces therefore represent important sites for governing the relationship between neighbourhood, the urban imaginary and youth identification. The concept of space emerges, therefore, not only as a fluid entity but also as a materially grounded 'socioscape' (see Buroway et al., 2000) which is constantly reconfigured through authorized relational practices in the forms of, for example, sexual policing, new patterns of racialized bullying, and the authorization of particular masculinities and femininities. It is within a moral field of cultural authorization that a spatial context for understanding the emergence of what Bourdieu has identified as 'authorized language' that particular forms of identity can and do emerge (see Bourdieu, 1999).

Authorized language is defined as cultural expressions which are authorized by a powerful set of pre-existing social conditions and material relations grounded in inherited state and wider colonial classifications and which regulate youth performance in the present. Authorized language is also governed by wider social forces – new gender relations, new and emerging forms of desire, affect and resentment, new forms of power and identity – which blur fantasy and reality as young people's desires are enacted and performed in the everyday of confined spaces such as the school corridor. It is through the very practice of authorization and distinguishing friend from foe in social space that tastes are utilized by youth cultural groups to exercise a 'social vocabulary, a symbolic repertoire of membership and reference affiliations as a discourse that can be endlessly modified and renewed in the imagery and narratives of mass culture' (Clarke, 1976: 45). These vocabularies reflect a structured 'emotional geography' of classification which can be mapped onto meaningful places (e.g. the corridor, a housing project, the street, the classroom). The concept of taste necessarily moves away from an over-determined class-based understanding of youth identity and context and towards an understanding of the cultural power of urban imaginaries to enable a 'more nuanced examination of how individual identity and group dynamics are articulated, often unevenly, to a large scale cultural arena' (Stahl, 1999: 3).

At the same time, it is imperative to understand that the locality of space as part of a field of cultural forces implies that this differentiation necessarily produces deeply entrenched forms of social conflict over access to and distribution of resources at the symbolic level. How young people evaluate themselves and differentiate themselves from others – as 'legitimate' – is tied to the local impact of these authorized relations. These evaluations are bound by forms of moral governance which are always already tied to sedimented social relations (e.g. historical practices of urban zoning, drug and alcohol policies, urban housing and public retrenchment), as well as to new scales of contemporary global and transnational change (e.g. rising police presence, the devolution of municipal regional policies, transnational migration, school closures, global media).

2. Spatial Experience as Knowledge and Representations of Value and Exchange

Beyond the locality of authorized relations in a particular place, it is necessary to understand how young people make sense of the objects and events in their neighbourhoods and ultimately how they represent them in relation to the larger project of consumption, exchange and value (see Lefebvre, 1991; Skeggs, 2004). These sense-making and place-making activities often emerge as representations of a place (e.g. housing project, family house, school), a person, a moral perspective, an event or an activity. Forms of knowledge emerge in these sites which shape young people's understandings of themselves as members of that urban locale. These knowledge forms are bound to larger questions of morality and legitimacy, and classificatory practices which impact on the nature of the representations that young people both see and interpret. The social practices which take place in this space – and any associated representations (e.g. school metaphorically represented as 'ghetto' or 'warehouse', or Gangsta styles such as baggy trousers) – serve to both organize and divide the space in particular ways, and provide another referential act for the classification of oneself and others. Young people utilize this inherited cultural knowledge not only to think about themselves in relation to state and urban legitimacy but also to classify themselves and others in relation to the representations they carry as conscious and unconscious forms. Such representations are durable and inherited, as well as discontinuous and new, and form part of young people's encounters with the 'cultural ordinary' of everyday life. The cultural ordinary in this case refers to the ordinary cultural processes of 'human societies and human minds' (see Williams, 1977). It also refers to an everyday activity or cultural patterns and performances of selfhood in the broadest sense.

One way that we can witness the cultural ordinary is through, for example, the common youth practice of 'being in the know' (e.g. insider-group knowledge which serves as a form of cultural power, 'being tough', style) and the possession of 'subcultural capital' – an abundance, for example, of insider knowledge. Insider knowledge is therefore not only tied to authorized spatial relations, but is also linked to the ways in which spaces (e.g. schools or particular streets) have been represented by actors in the field, the history of that space and its symbolic order. As we show, young people draw upon the affective experiences of desire, containment and resentment as a response to these dominant representations, as well as to re-contextualize and classify their own knowledge about themselves, others and their futures. These experiences become powerful modalities of action in youth cultural communities.

3. Space as an Urban Cultural Imaginary

In speaking about any element of a neighbourhood as a youth subcultural, or post-subcultural, imaginary, we must confront the power of both new and emerging forms of social conflict as they generate desires, feelings of loss and anxieties about the changing urban landscapes which young people confront as they perceive and navigate the city. Such imaginaries (based upon authorized relations and representations) are tied in part to, for example, forms of popular culture (e.g. urban rap cultures), contemporary consumption (e.g. media adverts of young men and women, public record accounts of the neighbourhood), widening and changing patterns of migration, and feelings of belonging and security which are generating through ceaseless media outlets which penetrate and reconfigure everyday culture. These encounters with space also provide some basis for the caged resentments (Willis, 1977) and associated force behind youth interpellation, as well as young people's ongoing search for 'magical resolutions' that we have already described. When combined with the structures of envy which naturally flow from these affective forms and associated practices of interpellation, profound cultural ambiguities about selfhood and otherness in particular urban imaginaries are evident. We are particularly interested in the 'expressive form' of urban experience and their associated 'structures of feeling' in the form of youth cultural styles, perceptions, classifications and conflicts expressed between young people at a highly individualized level. However, what is most important here is that space and the symbolic elements of urban imaginary are not separated as we begin to explore the pragmatics of context, which we now address in more fundamentally practical ways.

'More than Local and Less than Global': Urban Imaginaries in Late-Modern Canada

In the same manner as we have considered the impact of wider symbolic elements of space for young people, we must now turn to consider those transnational shifts which have crystallized at the micro-level in late-modern Canadian cities striving to be 'world class'. Within the context of wider global change and the international community, Canada has often been presented as one of the last bastions of social welfare harmony, and as a public haven for the upbringing of young people and children. Indeed, as we began this work we anticipated that there would be some resonating or sedimented effects of this ideal at work, even if only as a form of symbolic language, in the lives of the young people we encountered in the field. We had expected that young people, as well as teachers, would frame their thinking at least in part in these terms. However, the shifts and turns which have taken place across the nation over the last 25 years have been so momentous that this was clearly not the case.

A key transformation in modern urban Canada concerns the ways in which urban 'regeneration', associated with neo-liberal forms of governance and devolution to cities and provinces, have changed the face of the late-modern Canadian city. No longer – particularly in these two neighbourhood sites – was the 'inner-city' the centre of concern in relation to low-income youth. The real 'centres' were quite literally moving from the centre to the inner-city fringe or periphery (and this rings true across many urban centres in Canada and across other affluent cities, with Sydney, Tokyo and New York representing some of the most obvious examples). In Vancouver, for example, the economic centre of the city has continued to move westward creating 'new cultural edges' with a much less Eurocentric centre when compared with other fringe sites in major cities such as Toronto and Montreal (Berelowitz, 2005).

The spatial movement of the urban centre to the periphery has been widely associated within globalization and urban studies literature as linked to the idea of 'the world-class city' and urban regeneration. In fact, once cities are identified as carrying the potential for 'world-class status', the city's growth is often tied to urban development that is ultimately very uneven in its focus (see Beers, 2006), drawing upon finance regimes from foreign developers and global financing companies to enhance its core attractiveness.[3]

Indeed, in accordance with wider urban-regeneration strategies, the very governance of Canadian cities had shifted, and is continuing to shift, from earlier centralized provincial and federal allocations to forms of devolved micro-management (e.g. devolved city budgets) which substantially depends upon the ambition and competitiveness of the municipality and urban neighbourhood rather than on guaranteed state support. Since there is substantial variation in resource allocation across these urban neighbourhoods, some neighbourhood municipalities must be seen as more or less able to compete for resources, and hierarchies of competition arise. Such layered pressures for municipal, national and global competition and global visibility have therefore led to substantial cuts to youth services in Canadian cities and to the crystallization of local competition within and across them in pursuit of recognition and financial support. As one study participant who provided an oral history of the Vancouver neighbourhood (Beacon Park) reported:

> it was about five years ago they cut youth outreach, they went to the hubs [...] now family services has all the outreach and they would never come to the DTES anyway [...] most of the outreach is done by youth cops [...]. It is a sad statement of our system that most of the people doing outreach are youth cops [...]. We should have had more youth outreach workers. We are not reaching out to the youth. The only support they are getting is from the cops. How much does it cost to criminalize a young person on the street? That's what living here is like [...]. It's about convictions on the streets.
> (Youth Worker, Downtown Eastside, Vancouver, BC)

As a consequence of this rising competition and urban growth, something about the very nature of the relational practices of urban cities can be seen to have undergone radical change, with local communities, neighbourhoods and community groups competing over their legitimacy rights and representation, and levels of retrenchment and community conflict both notably higher (Graham, 2007; see also Beers, 2006). Indeed, as cities have sought to 'regenerate urban spaces' so too has class conflict risen across the urban landscapes of all major Canadian cities. As Berelowitz (2005: 234) has documented in relation to Victory Square in Vancouver, this has occurred in rather negative ways:

> In recent years, with the westward shift in the city's economic centre, this part of town declined. Victory Square was virtually abandoned by Vancouver society and increasingly appropriated by more marginal people and the homeless. Faced with this situation the Park Board quietly decided to redesign the square, primarily to reduce its use by undesirables (read drug dealers and pimps), mostly through lighting and the elimination of low level vegetation that restricted the view into the square from passing police cruisers. In 2003, after a lengthy confrontation between the City and a group of homeless people who set up a squatter camp on the square to protest its gentrification, the improvements went ahead. The space has been cleaned up, shrubbery reduced, new street furniture and lighting installed. And, at least for now, the squatters are nowhere to be seen.[4]

At the same time as gentrification and so-called urban improvement were taking place, highly visible signs of urban fragmentation and class disadvantage were evident in each neighbourhood where we undertook our research (see Yoon, 2008). Indeed, the urban comforts associated with post-war social welfare reform have been eroding in all Canadian cities (Canadian Housing Observer, 2008) much faster than in many other global cities in the affluent West, even as the press continues to document the fast run to be classified in Canada as the 'new global city'. For example, growing problems such as urban homelessness, intra-urban mobility and street drug-use (Canada Social Trends, 2006) were aggravated by the substantially reduced affordability of housing in both Toronto and Vancouver (e.g. Canadian Housing Observer, 2008; City of Vancouver, 2006), with Vancouver and Toronto representing the top two most expensive housing markets in Canada.[5] As of 2005, for example, just 62% of Metro Vancouver residents lived in acceptable housing conditions, defined as 'housing in adequate condition, of suitable size and affordable' (Canadian Housing Observer, 2008).

What these statistics speak to is not the aesthetic beauty or large-scale opulence associated with new global cities but the vast and growing class divisions which were emerging between neighbourhoods. For example, in both cities upper-middle-class and lower-middle-class individuals and families were living alongside some of the most economically disadvantaged individuals, families and young people in the country (Canadian Housing Observer, 2008). The case of the now infamous

Shangri-La Hotel and Resort Development at the urban core of Vancouver is one such example of regeneration with a global twist which was designed to be housed not only in a world-class global city but also to transform the working-class face of the urban core, pushing economically disadvantaged families and individuals to the fringe.[6]

Alongside these highly visible forms of 'regeneration' in the urban core, cuts to social services were also emerging cross-nationally. Youth immigrants and their parents, for example, were no longer receiving high levels of language training for the purposes of seeking employment and achieving greater social integration (see Canadian Housing Observer, 2006). At the same time, provincial and national policies – particularly in education and social policy arenas – were converging in powerful ways to parallel wider scales of cross-national reform, particularly around moral and educational issues tied to the criminalization of young people. Consequently, by the early 1990s a convergence of policy initiatives that were symptomatic of a Victorian morality[7] and late-modern forms of surveillance was changing the atmosphere of urban Canadian centres (e.g. Open Enrolment, Safe Streets Act of Ontario, 1999; Safe Streets Act, BC, 2004). Media coverage in the late 1990s and the first years of the twenty-first century highlighted the phenomenon of young people migrating to the urban fringe of cities to avoid the close police surveillance attracted by sleeping rough in the centre or on the 'street', or being criminalized for 'squeegeeing', or for drug association (www.blogto.com/city/2007/01/squeegee_kids_get_no_quarter/).[8] The mainstream media often depicted these young people as faceless, as characterless, and as without narrative capacity. Their characteristic public image showed lost faceless bodies carrying their worldly goods in garbage bags (see Figure 3.2).

Another related shift was the micro-level crystallization of global reform practices within the urban labour market. Securing employment as a blue-collar worker or low income, working immigrant, for example, had become increasingly difficult in large Canadian cities, particularly in the aftermath of 9/11. Not unlike other Western countries, concepts of employment were shifting from an emphasis upon macro-economic activity towards micro-economic activity. The key challenges for sites such as Toronto and Vancouver were the often devolved management of such activity. Sassen (1994, 2007) identifies such structural shifts, which have accompanied intensified and varied scales of globalization within urban spaces, as particular hallmarks of the emerging global city. As Sassen (1994: 99) points out, these urban spaces are marked by three characteristics: 'the growth of an informal economy in large cities in highly developed countries; high-income commercial and residential gentrification; and the sharp rise of homelessness in rich countries'. These activities had the effect of pushing many working-class and homeless people from the urban core

Figure 3.2 Squatters Leaving 52 Division After Being Charged With Trespassing. They Collected Their Belongings from a Truck Rented by the City at the Back of the Station (source: © Jim Rankin/GetStock.com, Image Number 2083215603).

to the urban fringe. This meant that while they were still visible in the city to greater or lesser degrees, they were often pushed to parts of the city which would be less visible to tourists and those affluent groups which now lived or wished to live at the urban core.

As risk and regeneration sat side-by-side in both cities, so too did the disenfranchisement of people from regular employment in the inner-city (see Yoon, 2008). The micro-level effects of this change represented a radical discontinuity in labour practices or what has been called the 'discontinuous reinvention of workplace sites', and forced workplace mobility such that industries and associated employment structures were being moved from inner-city warehouses to the urban and suburban fringes, or, particularly since the global credit crisis in 2008 and 2009, being closed down altogether and relocated in countries where cheaper labour could be utilized. No longer, therefore, did tight employment networks exist for the parents of the young people in our study, and they commonly became victims of the new kinds of flexible production, as the following extracts show.

INTERVIEWER: What do [your parents] do now?

YENSHU: Right now my dad's in Cambodia. He's starting a new business there and he's staying there for a while just to see how it's like and my mom she's working in a factory. Yeah, a fish factory – and it's not that good.

INTERVIEWER: The fish factory – you mean her job's not that good?

YENSHU: Yeah and it's far away too so she always has to drive far [because they moved her factory to the far side of the city].

INTERVIEWER: So where abouts?

YENSHU: [name of place which is one hour's drive from the neighbourhood].

INTERVIEWER: So it's a long commute and it's factory work. Does she have to do shift work?

YENSHU: Yah. She's full-time. [She leaves] early in the morning [...]

INTERVIEWER: Does she like it?

YENSHU: No choice I guess.

[...]

INTERVIEWER: And so your dad is in construction? Does he, what kind of construction? Is it like new buildings or new developments or?

YENSHU: I'm not sure. Just do like building houses. Like do the interior and exterior.

The interview continues as Yenshu points out that her father had been made redundant and has returned to Cambodia to work. She points out that 'he has been gone since March and will be back around October'.

INTERVIEWER: OK. When your dad was here what did he do?

YENSHU: He worked with my mom and he had a second job too.

Another student in Beacon Park was living in a similar situation:

INTERVIEWER: Mmm-hmmm. And does he work for himself? Or does he work for a company?

BETTY: For a company.

INTERVIEWER: Oh, for a company. Okay. And how long has he been doing that?

BETTY: I think for, I think he moved to this one a year ago [...] He had different ones before.

[...]

INTERVIEWER: Yeah? And your mum, you said, does sewing? [...] What kind of sewing does she do?

BETTY: Like clothing.

INTERVIEWER: Okay. So it's, does she design stuff and?

BETTY: No. She doesn't design, they like give her clothing and she just sews. Like she works in a factory [but she has to keep moving to new spots].

In both cities, new patterns of work involved an increased requirement for geographical mobility which led to forms of workplace and social atomization, feelings of insecurity and ongoing isolation for young people and their families.[9] And in many cases young people were engaging in substantial childcare responsibilities while their parents completed shift work or while one of the two parents lived overseas. Childcare was a particularly striking element of life for those young people who came from single-parent households; however, it was also apparent in many two-parent families. The emergent spatial practices resolved themselves as a kind of authorized individualization driven in part by the wider effects of global material labour practices, and in part by the local cultural meanings which flowed from them. In such cases, managing for 'oneself' and making do became an imaginary form of governance in both urban neighbourhoods rather than always leading to the formation of cohesive urban networks. This left young people with the feeling that there was little in the form of social support and networks available as they dealt with increasingly complex urban arrangements and higher levels of stress.

Associated trends which are documented nationally but which resonate globally and within the modern Canadian city concern police activity. For example, a substantial amount of recent evidence has highlighted the powerful role of the police in shifting and repositioning elements of youth identification in the urban inner-city and their patterns of political engagement (see Graham, 2007; Kennelly, 2008). Much of this research tells us that wider policy changes such as zero tolerance on the street, in political communities, in particular activist communities and in schools have meant that young people felt more closely monitored, at risk, abandoned or under threat. In this case, it is not always the threat of the city as a frightening arena of radical change which poses the problems, but rather the threat of surveillance regimes which change the organization of the space that young people inhabit and the degrees to which young people felt they could be recognized under such regimes. As one young person remarked about her social housing project: 'the police don't come here any more.' Other participants remarked, conversely, on their sense that the police were omnipresent, in ways which they felt were more threatening than protective: 'They're very aggressive when you're not resisting, like, a fight or anything. They get really aggressive.'

A further significant trend was the increase in visible homelessness in all Canadian cities, but most notably in the two cities where the study was undertaken. Retrenchment began earlier in Ontario (also commonly known in Canada as the 'Common Sense Revolution')[10] than in British Columbia; however, at the time of the study both cities – Toronto and Vancouver – were facing problems associated with urban homelessness which were substantially present in each of the neighbourhoods where the study was undertaken (see the Anti-Poverty Coalition, 2004). Various efforts were in place to address these challenges, although few such efforts were concerned with augmenting social services for the working poor, workplace conditions or with increases in social housing in either city (see Graham, 2007). Arguably, one of the key effects of urban homelessness was that it served to modify the ways in which young people not only navigated their urban neighbourhoods but also how they engaged in the associated classification struggles to assess their own and others' legitimacy in the city.[11] Indeed, the tensions between pride and honour or friend and foe arguably became more apparent to young people as the global city began to fragment and divide further.

Clearly, the rise of visible social issues (e.g. increased homelessness) on young people's doorsteps also meant that their own self-evaluations as 'worthy' and legitimate were undermined by increasingly visible signs of retrenchment and substantially increased highly mobile forms of urban poverty. These urban transformations were linked to wider scales of globalization whilst simultaneously dislocating people from local forms of socialization which provided more general security. Such realities seem surprising given that Vancouver, for example, was being championed as the most liveable city in the world, as well as hosting the first established Safe Injection Site in Canada (INSITE), and serving as the location for the 2010 Winter Olympics. However, if we understand regeneration as a form of value and exchange, developed in part to be witnessed by legitimate global 'others' (e.g. large multinational companies seeking headquarter locations) yet simultaneously representing substantial loss for many others, we can better understand how the moral elements of classification associated with these wider changes were masked from young people themselves and often from members of the neighbourhood. Who were they in this new global city? How were they to respond to rising media hysteria about homelessness in modern urban Canada? And what had become of any concept of worth they might have felt themselves to possess in an earlier moment? What was the concept of the new global city masking or eliding about young people's exclusions from its very enterprise?

A final trend, evident across the entire national media, was a rise in the reporting of race and class issues, together with a mushrooming of racial profiling in the heightened hysteria of the post-9/11 context. Unfortunately, this rise in reporting often failed to describe the social and economic conditions underlying many ethnic-minority youth experiences in the city, nor did it typically point to the state's failure to respond to these conditions in positive ways (see Neumann, 2004). Rather, the media sought to target issues of race and class as an insistent moral refrain which directed the public gaze towards those young bodies marked as 'dark' and dangerous:

VANCOUVER – ... Sangra says the issue of Indo-Canadian and South Asian youth gangs is an ongoing concern in Metro Vancouver.

She says as families struggle to integrate with Canadian society, youths (sic) may lose sight of their familial or cultural identities. And, when they don't find that at home or their subculture, they're vulnerable to the allure of gangs which offer acceptance, the thrill of life on the edge and cash. It's a world where memory and tradition fade, replaced with suburban strip malls and fast food joints. It's a world where a quick cell phone call can summon 50 kids armed with knives, bats, bear mace and machetes. It's a world in which some kids struggle to reach their 25th birthday.

(Canadian Press, 2008)

Alongside these reports, of course, were real events – events which were distorted by the media about young immigrants living in Canada's urban centres, and about urban youth crime and murder. These events were heightened in intensity by a wider range of media reporting following 9/11 such as the French riots and the Australian disturbances. While of course there has always been a current of profound racism operating in Canada's inner-cities, this reporting, tainted by post-9/11 effects, has been particularly targeted at economically disadvantaged, minority ethnic youth groups. For example, many of the young people in our study, particularly in Vancouver, reported that they were referred to as 'terrorists' if they had an accent outside the range of normative Canadian accents, were visible minority youth, or if they were associated with the Middle East or other 'outlaw states' (see Simpson, 2004). In Toronto, other forms of racism were also on the rise such as inter-ethnic racisms linked to young people's commitments to wider forms of youth culture (Eminem, Slim Shady, for example). In other words, wider forms of ethnic hysteria were being crystallized as novel forms of racism directed towards these young people through that which Raymond Williams has identified as the 'cultural ordinary', so that the everyday language of racism formed the basis of targeting the new 'folk devils' of the modern Canadian city – ultimately leading to the creation of a new racial imaginary of classifications.

Post-9/11 race dynamics also played some part in how young people identified themselves and others, including denials that such racism meant anything at all (race denial sometimes seemed more prevalent than class denial). Indeed, as Parnaby (2003) has suggested, a moral language of description about young people in Canada's cities was emerging that was suggestive of a form of criminality which dated back to the late nineteenth and early twentieth centuries. This moral discourse was grounded in a long history and surplus effect of race and colonial relations, and was both reflected within, and masked by, recent wider global changes and particular urban myths of presentism. It was, however, also tied to rising class and race conflicts in both cities and associated moral panics since

9/11, and particularly from the turn of the century (see Hoerder et al., 2005). These demographic changes coincided with greater residential segregation, particularly in Vancouver, together with a phenomenon known as 'rapid replacement'. Rapid replacement is a demographic shift in urban cores 'where the rate of the decline of the non-visible minority population in a neighbourhood is greater than the median rate of the group's decline in all neighbourhoods' (see Yoon, 2008: 4; Hou & Picot, 2004). In other words, the traditional white working-class or white European immigrants were most typically being 'replaced' or displaced by visible minority or minority ethnic immigrants from both Asia and Africa. In both cities, forms of displacement were evident but these phenomena, particularly 'rapid replacement', were most apparent in the Vancouver site.

Taken together, changes in the make-up of the urban core and periphery have had a radical if uneven impact on race relations between young people in both sites, though Toronto maintained higher degrees of neighbourhood community than did Vancouver. Particularly striking was the degree of morality politics at work in both sites, and the degree to which racism was directed towards young people, often under the moral legitimization of the 'war on terror'. This meant that many acts – such as forms of civil disobedience – which might previously have been seen as innocuous, were recast in the light of forms of post-9/11 moral panic and urban political and economic reform. At the same time, a new racial imaginary contributed to the relative powerlessness of the working-class communities and individuals in shifting the discourses of abjection circulating about their neighbourhoods.

Local Landscapes: Case Study Sites

Toronto School and Neighbourhood: Tower Hill

The first inner-city site where the study took place – a quite central but still fringe neighbourhood at the edge of the urban core of Toronto – carries a long history of occupation by distinctive ethnic and class communities. Since the turn of the twentieth century, Tower Hill was the site of much Western and Southern European migration, and in the post-war period it witnessed substantial migration and chain migration from rural Portugal, Greece and Italy (Teixeira, 2007). Much of the early Southern European migration served as a response to being overrun by the effects of the Ottoman Empire. These waves of migration had particularly localized effects in Tower Hill. In 1956, for example, Toronto housed the largest Portuguese settlement in the world outside of Portugal, and in the years between 1966 to 1975 substantial chain migration took place in this neighbourhood. To date, Tower Hill and its surroundings remain home to many Portuguese, Italian and Greek families and communities.

This first-wave of migration comprised largely young, male, unskilled labourers who came to Toronto to work in factories (Novi, 1997: 121). The second wave often brought extended family members or partners, and a third post-war migration witnessed the movement of Portuguese communities from small and largely working-class villages (1955–1980) (i.e. chain migration). In the case of this latter group (which was the most heavily represented group in this case study site), Portuguese families were represented to Canadian immigration officials as 'unskilled' labourers and were admitted as residents on those terms (see Kaplan & Li, 2006). As Novi (1997: 121) documented in relation to the Portuguese community in this neighbourhood:

> The Portuguese have yet to achieve full or equal participation in this society [...] the third generation, bent on enjoying life rather than enter the dead end jobs held by previous generations, has not acquired the education or marketable skills necessary for upward mobility, and will quite possibly end up worse off than their parents.

Our youth participants were largely, although not exclusively, drawn from second- and third-generation Portuguese, Italian and Greek families. These groups were facing a substantial decline in their socio-economic standing compared to their parents' generation. The two most dominant groups in the Toronto school site were Portuguese and Italian second- and third-generation students, and the vast majority of their parents were employed in construction or blue-collar jobs. What was particularly clear in this school, and in some contrast to the Vancouver site, was the cultural boundedness of the neighbourhood or what has been called a cultural enclave (Teixeira, 2007), at least at the level of the imaginary,[12] for these young people. When compared to many other major Canadian cities, Toronto still had well-established neighbourhoods which originally began as immigration settlements such as Little Italy and Little Portugal; often within one street of any given neighbourhood, family members (e.g. cousins) or former village neighbours from their home towns still lived side-by-side. In this context, particular ideas of culture and community remained powerful even if the infrastructure associated with the twenty-first-century global economy was playing some part in individualizing and distancing these families from their immediate communities, particularly through patterns of working life and the labour market. The area did, however, maintain the feel of a former industrialized site with many empty or refurbished warehouses in the immediate vicinity and many post-war concrete buildings which were either being reclaimed or torn down. Industrialization had been the pre-war source of employment for many first- and second-generation immigrants to this Canadian neighbourhood, but this time had passed and many were instead working in factories, construction, service labour or domestic work.

When, from the late twentieth century, industrialization began to lose its dominant place as a source of employment for many working-class communities,[13] the former industrial area began to experience varying degrees of economic disadvantage and has, to greater or lesser degrees, remained disadvantaged until the present day. Currently, the area is characterized by low-cost tower apartments, together with housing which is self-owned, rented and/or subsidized by the state. In the years between 1980 and 2005, a number of important urban transformations took place. First, social support for families living in this part of the city (particularly after 1993) was cut substantially, forcing many with children to engage in full-time employment, as well as sometimes making use of their children's part-time income. Many parents of the young people in our study were sometimes working two to three contractually negotiated jobs each, or were working in factories outside the neighbourhood, usually due to the relocation or closure of businesses. This meant that not only were parents commuting extensively across the city but young people were often providing families with childcare and financial support.

Some elements of the neighbourhood itself shifted between the 1980s and the turn of the twenty-first century in accordance with zoning policies which allowed for the presence of transient forms of social housing, recently built low-cost non-state housing and state supported housing. While it is essential not to pathologize a neighbourhood dedicated to public projects, urban re-zoning nonetheless contributed to the loss of traditional local integration and to the re-shaping of the neighbourhood as a site of spatial containment (Wright, 1997). While the Southern European settlement from the early twentieth century was still in place to greater or lesser degrees, this wider urban transformation also meant that the idea of a neighbourhood of trust was no longer at the centre of the area. In the late 1990s, rental prices did in fact temporarily rise, leading to a partial gentrification of the area. So at the time of the study, there were signs of the emergence of an urban mix between those identifying themselves as lower middle-class (e.g. artists) and professionals (e.g. teachers), alongside under-employed families, the 'working poor' or families who lived in state-funded housing. However, a dramatically 'increased concentration of poor families in higher poverty neighbourhoods' was in evidence in suburban Toronto rather than the old inner-city centre. As Community Action Publishers reported:

> In 1981, there were 30 neighbourhoods identified as high poverty neighbourhoods, but 20 years later there are 120 such neighbourhoods. The study also showed the increase in higher

poverty neighbourhoods was 'especially acute' in the inner suburbs (the former cities of Scarborough, North York, Etobicoke, York and East York) where the combined total of higher poverty neighbourhoods rose from 15 in 1981 to 92 in 2001. Only one postal code area in the Greater Toronto Area surrounding the city has been identified as high poverty. In addition, the concentration of family poverty is increasing, with 43.2% of poor families living in higher poverty neighbourhoods compared with 17.8% in 1981. The study also found that since 1981 there has been a 484% increase in the poor immigrant family population living in higher poverty neighbourhoods, with immigrant families accounting for two-thirds of the total family population living in higher poverty neighbourhoods. 'The increase in poor neighbourhoods is alarming,' says Frances Lankin, president and CEO of the United Way of Greater Toronto. 'We know that the consequences of living in a poor neighbourhood are significant and long term for children and youth, for newcomers to our country, for the entire community. Toronto is losing ground faster than almost all other urban centres in Canada,' regarding poverty levels and the greater number of poor neighbourhoods.

(Community Action Publishers, 2004: 1)

In other words, class disadvantage was being pushed to the sometimes invisible urban fringe and in some cases to the suburbs (see Yoon, 2008). Cumulatively, what is most significant about this area is that it was widely seen by many young people in the study as a site of abandonment by government, the city officials and others.

Schools which are located in the inner-city fringe neighbourhoods are substantially affected by such broader economic shifts, particularly in terms of educational choice policy and the publication of league tables.[14] If schools appear, particularly when they are seen to be residing at the edge of the urban core, as 'demonized', then many parents who live in surrounding areas of the school (e.g. 'regenerated' or mixed neighbourhoods) increasingly 'choose' to send their children to other 'higher-performing' settings, thus creating both competition between schools across class communities and what some young people in the urban school context referred to as a 'ghetto' or 'warehousing effect'. This school stratification effect was compounded by larger global trends which were manifested locally. For example, in 1996, the Ontario Ministry of Education instituted a Literacy Test for all secondary schools. Students were obliged to take this test regardless of their schooling history or their domestic language situation, and literacy support was crucial but absent. School success was rendered more difficult as the conditions for learning had been undermined by programme cuts which would traditionally have supported young people with English as a second language or other learning challenges. Teachers reported that funds designed to enhance literacy among various communities of youth had dissipated through programme cuts. In this context, teachers themselves, many of whom had not been trained in ESL practices, were being asked to do literacy training.

At the same time, the student population was becoming increasingly transient, with many young people forced to move out of public housing complexes that were overcrowded and, in some cases, being forced to change schools. Students lived both with the burden of the stigmas attaching to 'failure' and to the adverse effects of urban transformation. While participants did not discuss these stigmas in the language of neo-liberalism, it was eminently clear that they understood the role that related educational (e.g. increased testing) and social reforms were playing in their lives. And there were times too when students also took the responsibility of blame upon themselves. The constant reminders, operating through heightened forms of individualization in educational rhetoric, that they were not truly deserving students when compared to middle-class pupils meant that the levels of anxiety associated with neo-liberal regimes of testing, coupled with urban transformations, were particularly acutely felt.

Vancouver School and Neighbourhood Site: Beacon Park

The second ethnographic case study site within the city of Vancouver can be seen as a microcosm of global forms of stratification and unprecedented social change taking place across post-industrial urban concentrations. Particularly marked was the degree to which the city had been transformed by widespread migration, largely from Asian and South Asian source countries. Indeed, such migration patterns are one of the defining characteristics of a 'global city', where low-income migrant workers increasingly constitute the majority of employees in expanding urban service industries (Sassen, 1994, 2007).

Since the late 1980s, 31,000 immigrants have entered Vancouver each year, making up 38% of its population in 2001. Between 1991 and 2001, 51% of Vancouver's immigrants had Asian origins; as of 2001, one in five Vancouverites was a recent immigrant and nearly two-thirds were either immigrants themselves or the children of immigrants (Heisz, 2006). This is particularly relevant for young people living within the city: about one in four children under 17 is an immigrant or the Canadian-born child of recent immigrants (Heisz, 2006).

Equally marked is the degree to which the city has been the site of increased economic stratification, largely divided along lines of migration history, race and neighbourhood. For example, between 1980 and 2000 the gap between the affluent and economically disadvantaged groups

Figure 3.3 Vancouver's Chinatown (source: Jacqueline Kennelly, Permission granted by Jacqueline Kennelly).

increased substantially within Vancouver: those in the tenth percentile saw their earnings fall by 25% while those in the ninetieth percentile saw a rise of 5.3% (Heisz, 2006). The drop in earnings was felt most acutely by young workers aged 25 to 34 as they saw their pay fall by 11.7%; earning drops were larger for high-school-educated workers than the university educated (Heisz, 2006).

Increasing stratification was apparent and can be found within housing data collected over the last 15 to 20 years. Based on census data between 1991 and 2001, Aboriginal, female lone parents, seniors living alone and recent immigrant households were identified as groups with high housing needs in Vancouver (Engeland, Lewis, Ehrlich & Che, 2005). In particular, recent immigrant and Aboriginal households were identified as living in overcrowded dwellings and in need of major repairs (Engeland et al., 2005). As housing becomes increasingly unaffordable within the urban core (a more traditional site in Vancouver for the working class), families with children, and low-income service industry workers, were being pushed out of Vancouver into the surrounding fringe neighbourhoods and suburbs (Lee, Villagomez, Gurstein, Eby & Wyly, 2008). And those who were living in low-cost hotel dwellings in the urban core were often seen wandering and sleeping on the streets in the neighbourhood adjacent to Beacon Park because of rising hotel prices and welfare reductions.[15] The degree to which Vancouver residents face income inequality and related forms of substantial economic disadvantage is strongly linked to migration and race. Almost half (46%) of Vancouver's visible minority households lived under the low income cut-off level in 2001, and the earnings of Canadian-born visible minorities were consistently less than Canadian-born European descendants in the period between 1971 and 2001 (Hoerder et al., 2005; Pendakur & Pendakur, 2004).

As the Canadian economy shifts from industrialized labour to a so-called 'knowledge-based economy' (colloquially referred to as the shift from 'bricks' to 'clicks'), economic disadvantages for recent immigrants have increased (Hoerder et al., 2005: 30).[16] The percentage of recent immigrants with low incomes increased from 25% in 1980 to 36% in 2000, while the likelihood that they would be low income in comparison to comparable Canadian workers increased from 1.4 times in 1980 to 2.3 times in 2000 (Hoerder et al., 2005; Smith, 2004). Between 1980 and 2000, Vancouver saw the largest increase in low-income rates of all major cities in Canada; this increase was found to be particularly concentrated amongst recent immigrants, of whom 37.2% were low-income. Aboriginal people were also highly disadvantaged, with 40.9% falling within the low-income bracket. This is in contrast with the rest of Vancouverites, of whom only 19.4% were categorized as low-income (Heisz, 2006).

Despite the apparent increase in stratification for specific groups within Vancouver, the city continues to attract high rankings variously as the first, second and third most attractive city in the world to live, reflecting the degree to which the city's affluent image has overtaken the realities of urban displacement and impoverishment. Such rankings overlook the fact that Vancouver contains an urban area that has been deemed the poorest neighbourhood in Canada (Downtown Eastside Community Monitoring Report (DECMR), 2000). This area of the city has been assigned various derogatory labels, being referred to, for example, as 'the only open air institution' in Canada (see Graham, 2007). As an area of highly concentrated poverty, it stands in stark contrast to the so-called 'liveability' of greater Vancouver and its associated, growing affluence. Over 45% of adults in the city's urban east side possess no educational qualifications of any kind, 75% of young people in the area are from ethnic-minority groups and less than 12% progress to post-secondary education. The area also contains the highest percentage of public or subsidized housing units, urban hotel dwellings and youth homelessness in BC (DECMR, 2000). This neighbourhood, referred to as the Downtown Eastside (or DTES, see Figure 3.4), also contains a highly visible proportion of Aboriginal residents; in 2001, 10% self-identified as Aboriginal, compared to 3% in

Vancouver (City of Vancouver, 2006). The broader trends of gentrification and loss of low-income housing within the city of Vancouver were undeniably intensified within the DTES, where low-income rental buildings and single-residence occupancy buildings (or SROs) were being rapidly converted into high-end condominiums (Lee et al., 2008). This has resulted in an enormous increase in visible homelessness and

Figure 3.4 'Living Rough' on the Streets of the Downtown Eastside (source: Jacqueline Kennelly, Permission granted by Jacqueline Kennelly).

displacement, both within the area and in adjacent neighbourhoods, as the most vulnerable residents are forced on to the street (Lee et al., 2008; Eby & Misura, 2006).

The school where our ethnography was undertaken resides near the Downtown Eastside. The school and neighbourhood has a strong working-class history, particularly by comparison with the west side of Vancouver. The pressures of gentrification have been increasing in recent years, with subsequent housing-cost rises and a proliferation of condominium townhouse and high-rise buildings. Nonetheless, the area still remains a relatively low-income neighbourhood. Although the median household income rose from \$26,539 in 1996 to \$35,342 in 2006, it remains substantially below the Vancouver-wide median household income of \$47,299 (Community Statistics Census Data, 2008). Likewise, the percentage of low-income households in the neighbourhood (35.7%) is significantly higher than the city-wide average (26.6%) (Community Statistics Census Data, 2008). The neighbourhood has historically been the site of widespread Aboriginal residency, beginning as the traditional lands of the Musqueam and Squamish peoples, and continuing into the present day. In the 1990s, it was documented that one in six households in the neighbourhood was inhabited by Aboriginal people (Tupechka et al., 1997). British immigrants first arrived in this specific Vancouver

Figure 3.5 Neighbourhood Street, Vancouver site (source: Jacqueline Kennelly, Permission granted by Jacqueline Kennelly).

neighbourhood in the early 1900s, and were followed by Italians and East Europeans in the 1920s and 1950s. Asian immigrants (largely Chinese and Indian) arrived from the 1960s onwards (Buchan, 1985).

Many of the associated activities of the district (e.g. panhandling, squeegeeing, drug-dealing, homelessness) were heavily influenced by those who were either trapped in, or were being pushed out of, the DTES. Indeed, the combined effects of urban restructuring, policy change and municipal retrenchment have meant that many DTES dwellers were either living rough or spending their day-time hours on the main street adjacent to the school that participants attended. This highly visible element of social change presented immediate challenges for young people who experienced constant reminders that they were inheriting a deprived urban core and were to some degrees implicated in its pathologized identity. Many project participants would pass through areas of the DTES to get to school each day, and many reported being approached each morning about whether or not they wanted to buy drugs. This urban imaginary, which included the daily experience of attending school in a lower socio-economic neighbourhood which butted up against the most demonized area of the city, played a major role in shaping young people's conceptions of their own and others' legitimacy (including their own experiences of shame and honour), and their associated classification struggles. Most importantly, the neighbourhood itself was being constantly demonized

Figure 3.6 Student Photo-Narrative.

and pathologized in the media, and such representations of abjection in the public record clearly played some part in shaping young people's urban imaginaries (another photo narrative sample can be seen in Figure 3.6).

Conclusions

This chapter has offered an in-depth examination of the multiple ways in which space and place are implicated – as both real and imaginary – in our comparative ethnography of low-income young people residing within the specific spatial locus of the global city. We began with an extensive theoretical investigation of the meanings with which space is imbued, and its intricate connections to such wide-reaching conceptual terms as authorized language, exchange value and cultural imaginaries. Our argument here is that space cannot be understood in isolation from the interdisciplinary theoretical frame that informs our analysis; rather, it can be understood as one important facet in a multi-faceted framework, whereby each element informs and influences the other. As Bourdieu (1999: 126) notes:

> Because social space is inscribed at once in spatial structures and in the mental structures that are partly produced by the incorporation of these structures, space is one of the sites where power is asserted and exercised, and, no doubt in its subtlest form, as symbolic violence that goes unperceived as violence.

In other words, space must be understood as more than the mere site of occupation within which young people are situated. Rather, it is one important element amongst a multitude of elements that carries with it a constellation of cultural symbols and imaginaries with associated practical implications, many of which remain unseen without careful analysis. Indeed, we are able to witness fragments and pathways of imperialism even as they are re-contextualized in new patterns and urban labyrinths of the present.

We have also outlined, with the help of historical and contemporary data, the specific micro-sociological spatial contexts in which our study took place. We offer this description not by way of explanation for the actions and views of our youth participants, but rather as one mode of insight into the very specific spatial and temporal realities with which these young people must negotiate daily. What they then do with these realities is as varied as the individuals themselves; and yet always they encounter the boundedness, the borders and the fringes of their specific historical and spatial location within these global cities. Their creative responses, and the subcultural and post-subcultural resources they mobilize from within these locales, constitute the main focus for the remainder of the book.

Part II: Young People's Urban Imaginaries in the Global City

Utopian Fantasies and Classification Struggles

In the first part of the book, we sought to explore a number of issues in relation to the young people and youth cultures in our comparative contexts. In particular, we sought to highlight the novel dilemmas and contradictions that young people face as they navigate new urban social spaces at the turn of the twenty-first century, specifically when considered within comparative scales of globalizing change and the embedded moral structures and forms of surveillance which serve to constitute these sites. A key aim was to provide a socio-political context for understanding the interface between the notable rise of moralizing discourses about young people as a specific condition of late-modernity and young people's experiences and performances of youth culture. A consideration of these contexts has provided another layer of ethnographic interpretation for understanding the impact of both liberal and neo-liberal modern state power formations on young people's expressions and narrations of selfhood.

Second, we offered an overview of key theoretical debates and impasses surrounding the contemporary study of urban youth cultures, and have wrestled with these impasses, particularly through the traditions of cultural phenomenology and wider debates about youth selfhood in social and cultural thought. In seeking to extend our interdisciplinary thinking we have followed in particular the studies and readings of history and social change offered through the work of Paul Ricoeur, with a focus upon the ideas of 'narrative identity' and 'social imaginaries' as they pertain to young people and urban space. Ricoeur writes that the 'creative conflict in interpretations is inevitable [...]. The myth of absolute reason must always be resisted in favour of a plurality of critical debates and detours'. We therefore wish to remain open to a variety of interlocutors in social and cultural theory and put forward the case that the 'shortest route from self to self is through the other' (cited in Kearney, 2004: 4). To put this point more straightforwardly, it is through an engagement with a wide body of theory – those theoretical others – that we are best able to return to the narrative accounts of youth and youth culture anew and shed new horizons of understanding on their actions, relations and performances.

We might also recognize the idea of interdisciplinarity and Ricoeur's concept of the 'detour' as a critical and reflexive form of distanciation that is capable of undermining the techniques of theoretical formalism and paradigmatic dominance as we seek to reveal the hidden meanings underlying symbolic narratives of youth culture. For example, we have embraced theoretical tools which challenge the idea of youth cultures as only a technique of subjectification, as individualized and self-choosing, or, conversely, as directly controlled only through the techniques of governmentality. These kinds of challenges and associated horizons of theorizing which emerge have provided us with some partial conceptual understanding that points to the following idea adapted from Ricoeur's oeuvre: the social imaginary of youth culture(s) must necessarily operate in the spaces between memory, tradition and new horizons of the symbolic order: 'insofar as we remain aware of this gap, it can remind us that any representation of oneself remains an open process' (Kearney, 2004: 4).

Last, we outlined the potential methodological contributions of our spatial ethnography, with a particular focus on the bridging of phenomenology, youth cultural theory and cultural geography. We also offered the beginnings of some potentially new and revised conceptual terms which evolved out of our relationship to theory in a wide sense and our own cultural immersion in the ethnographic sites. We have placed substantial emphases upon visual sociology and cultural historiography as key methodological innovations for better understanding contemporary youth cultures in comparative contexts. These 'innovations' are seen as intricately tied to the very purpose of understanding the 'phenomenologies of meaning' young people draw upon as they express notions of selfhood, particularly as they struggle to classify and reclassify themselves and others to make sense of the micro-spatial landscapes of the global city. Finally, we offered extended descriptions of the socio-spatial contexts within which our ethnographies were conducted, reflecting particularly on the scaled effects of global change in local settings.

In this part of the book, we introduce our readers to the young people who inhabit the local schools and neighbourhoods of our two global cities: the 'Ginos' and 'Ginas', the 'Rockers', the 'Thugs', the 'Real Asians', and those young people who do not easily or comfortably identify with any of these forms of narrativization or who utilize them as cultural resources when necessary and attempt to discard them when they imagine themselves as choice-making and freed from subcultural affiliation.

In conceptualizing these chapters, we sought to highlight both the comparative and authentic aspects of each locale as they might relate to wider forms of urban change. Consistent with cultural geography's insights about the importance of space and place, and their mediating effects on youth cultural practice, Chapter 4 focuses primarily on the Toronto neighbourhood and school. It reveals in particular the sedimented gender and class subcultural performances of peer rivalry between the two dominant subcultural groups in this relatively homogenous first-, second- and third-generation Portuguese and Italian working-class community and mixed fringe neighbourhood – the Gangsta Girls and Boys and the Ginas and Ginos.

Chapter 5 moves forward to explore the dialectics of urban spatial arrangements, young people's feelings of belonging and their urban imaginaries as they move at the edges of uncertain and continuously changing fringe neighbourhoods in two quite different parts of the country. Chapter 6 focuses primarily on comparative data emerging from the Vancouver site (Beacon Park), where the impact of micro-scales of globalizing migratory flows, micro-nationalisms and quite new forms of the diaspora have created a multi-ethnic site that constitutes a more persuasively 'post-subcultural' space, with a particular focus on new patterns of race relations. Chapter 7 assesses the relationship between youth cultural practice, individualization, and young people's narratives of citizenship and state legitimacy.

A pervasive theme throughout is the impact of moral regulation, and the moral claims that flow from the collision of particular spatial and historical relations within the political realities of the present. Rather than theorizing morality and power – emerging as the resurgence of moral panics across time – as somehow existing in isolation from the socio-historical geographies of youth cultures, we see them both (moral discourse and power formations) as crystallized representations and ideologies which circulate in spatial and temporal contexts, riding the waves of persistent and re-contextualized anxieties about 'the stranger', 'the foreign other', or twenty-first-century accounts of the foe (see Honig, 2001). The forms of power that we witnessed in operation in our comparative sites therefore stretched across geographical distances and spatial domains. Here we wish to argue that the state, in isolation, did not serve as a point of origin for the performance of youth cultures. Nor were the symbolic elements of power which were expressed by young people the end node of power in a traditional system of state exclusion which could be witnessed objectively as young people engaged in the everyday and the cultural ordinary (see Miller and Rose, 2008). Rather, alongside elements of traditional state discourses were late-modern ideas concerning expertise, choice and freedom which were woven into the very fabric of youth cultures in particular spaces and places, as well as in the very structure of the two urban neighbourhoods within which we worked. These ideas were not tied to anything particularly visible, objective or expert-like in a professional sense, but instead represented examples of what Miller and Rose (2008) have called 'minor' expertises, emerging as part of a sometimes quite organized system of cultural protection and symbolic orders. Here we witnessed how young people created an 'empire' through particular forms of surplus meaning, self-crafting and 'alliance-building' as they worked towards transforming themselves into formidable and highly visible cultural forces. We could also witness how expertise, insider knowledge or being 'in the know' among group members were formed, symbolic fronts established (Gangsta clothes, for example), recruitments offered and alliances across members were built. It is because of these very empires and the linkages between *place and self-making* projects young people engaged in that, following Miller and Rose (2008), we view this work, at least in part, as micro-cultural analyses of the 'kinds of persons' young people imagine themselves to be and how these imaginaries are translated into cultural narratives of selfhood and identity.

While we have organized the chapters in part to reveal distinctions between youth cultural expressions reflecting subcultural or post-subcultural effects, or a combination of tradition and the new, it is important to reiterate here that any over-reliance on either subcultural or post-subcultural theory cannot do justice to the complexity of the symbolic narratives young people expressed as part of the ethnographic encounter. Indeed, as Ricoeur (1981) has persistently reminded us, myth and tradition, and truth and fiction, come together to form powerful social imaginaries in the present. Young people's social imaginaries and indeed youth cultures cannot therefore exist without the symbolic and surplus powers of narrative. For example, the sedimented effects of historical class, race and colonial relations did indeed collide with novel attempts made by young people to 'make oneself over' in a new and imagined skin, or to 'make the best of a bad situation' with an emphasis on one's individual responsibility to become suitably self-perfecting (*pace* Harris and 'the can do' girl). This meant that, unlike Willis' 'Lads' and McRobbie's 'bedroom girl cultures', our youth participants were doubly entangled; they still of course sought to magically resolve the cultural impact of economic stratification in highly unfavourable circumstances, whilst simultaneously taking on the reflexive burden of 'making their own selves anew' without the recourse to humour and friendship that seemed so striking amongst Willis' 'Lads' in an earlier time.

In each of the forthcoming chapters, we attempt to highlight the manner in which the spatial and the temporal appear within youthful rituals and cultures, whether it is through the intensification of gendered peer rivalries and forms of female masculinity (Chapter 4), the dialectics of space, youth identity and interpellation (Chapter 5), the symbolic racialization of rival groups (Chapter 6) or the individualized 'front' and classification of friend and foe through the language of the citizen within the neo-liberal state, and alongside the forms of classed rhetoric (e.g. disgust) that are associated with moral authority of a highly individualized late-modern political landscape (Chapter 7). Within each of these spaces, we find our young participants working out their 'place' and 'legitimacy' within urban arrangements that are, at their best, residual spaces of surplus meaning pointing to previous forms of intense working-class resilience and, at their limits and edges, late-modern sites of diasporic memory alongside elements of state abandonment. It is not the diaspora that is a problem or its memory (as all urban spaces, one way or another, retain elements of a diasporic memory). What is at stake is the reality of loss and abandonment at the edge of the global city. This is not a 'lost youth' but rather a group of young people who have been lost to the negative and endlessly moralizing imperatives of what Bourdieu (2006) has named the 'right hand of the state' – a state which no longer wishes, Bourdieu (2006) argues, to know what the left hand is doing. It is in this very gap that the concept of loss emerges most powerfully. Importantly, though, these spaces never remain static nor outside the realm of changing social relations.

The concluding chapter offers reflections on the novel aspects of social life governing youth cultures of the present, as well as identifying those elements which are continuous with tradition, ritual and the power of past time as it is narrated by young people in the present. This bridging of past, present and future has led us towards some theoretical transformation in how we conceptualized youth cultures and urban exclusion. For us, it did not require a theory of youth subjectification (*pace* Foucault) or its deconstruction (*pace* Derrida) since such theories, on their own, might mask the very processes which enabled young people to position themselves in a 'theatre of the urban' (see Gallagher, 2007). As Miller and Rose (2008: 8; brackets our addition) write:

> instead of writing the history of the self or of subjectivity, we [would] study the history of the individuals' relations with themselves and with others, the practices which both were their correlate and condition of possibility, and enabled these relations to be acted upon. Not who they were, but who they thought [and imagined] they were, what they wanted to be, the languages and norms according to which they judged themselves and were judged by others, the actions they took upon themselves and that others might take, in light of those understandings.

4

Warehousing 'Ginos', 'Thugs' and 'Gangstas' in Urban Canadian Schools
Gender Rivalries and Subcultural Defences in Late-Modernity

Setting the Ethnographic Scene

To understand what happens in places like 'projects' or 'housing developments' or certain kinds of schools, places which bring together people who have nothing in common and force them to live together, either in mutual ignorance and incomprehension or else in latent or open conflict – with all the mutual suffering this entails is not enough to explain each point of view separately. All of them must be brought together as they are in reality, not to relativize them into an infinite number of cross-cutting images, but, quite to the contrary, through simple juxtaposition, to bring everything that results when different or antagonistic visions of the world confront each other – that is, in certain cases, the tragic consequences of making incompatible points of view confront each other, where no concession or compromise is possible because each one of them is equally founded in social reason.

(Bourdieu, 2006: 3)

In this chapter, we make our first extended foray into the ethnographic data gathered in our two 'global cities', with a particular focus here on the Toronto case study (Tower Hill). In line with the theoretical and methodological frameworks elaborated in the first part of the book, our primary aim is to examine young people's accounts of peer rivalry, their subcultural affiliations and gendered experiences of urban exclusion. In so doing, we seek to reveal how economically-disadvantaged male and female youth comprehend the everyday tensions and contradictions inherent in urban schooling and urban space more generally, tensions which shape their conceptions of themselves, their gender relations and their social futures, all of which can be seen as 'tied to the geography' of urban cities and school life (Reay & Lucey, 2003).

Here, we view 'peer rivalry' as constituted within, and governed by, new patterns of gender and wider cultural relations (Miller & Rose, 2008) which, while varying across generation and place, also retain unifying temporal and moral traces of tradition and ritual. These are characteristics which are much less evident at surface levels in diasporic, hybridized or post-subcultural groupings. These traces can sometimes emerge as a moral register and set of conventions which young people expect cultural foes to conform to in what Clarke (1976) has called a 'defensively organized collective'. Brown (1995: 24; brackets our addition) writes: 'moralism would appear to be a kind of temporal trace, a remnant of a trace, a remnant of a discourse whose heritage and legitimacy it claims [in everyday culture] while in fact inverting that discourse's sense and sensibility.'

In this respect, a unifying theme which bridges the cultural politics of peer rivalry and youth subcultural practice is the moralizing and strategic role of identity as an imaginative and utopian liberal ideal. Indeed it is the imaginary nucleus of identity and the ongoing need, as Clarke (1976) reminds us, to challenge those who carry liberal pretensions of superiority which still underpin young people's 'classification struggles' in their urban quest for symbolic territory. We are therefore able to renounce, at least in part, the notion of an endlessly new youth culture which is thought to exist only in the present – that is, the 'cult of the new as an end in itself' (see Kearney, 2004: 134). As our Toronto case study shows, peer rivalry still remains faithful in part to the latent and surplus manifestation of heritage discourses through the performance of a masterful identity. At the fringe of the twenty-first-century global city, however, peer rivalry is not always or only inherited cultural or class conflict operating as a result of unequal power formations. Rather, both new and more traditional 'rules' and highly sexualized 'territorial' discourses converge and are articulated in new ways through the cultural practices young people engage with in their struggle to be recognized as both moral and moralizing subjects. These moralizing practices and discourses do not and cannot be spoken and acted upon everywhere; rather, they are *authorized* in particular urban spatial arrangements. In this sense, peer rivalry may be seen as a highly moralizing 'place-making' and 'self-making' project tied to both tradition and the present (see Buroway et al., 2000) where intense identity work and ideological subcultural engagement are undertaken. As Kearney (2004: 25) writes: 'symbolic language means to designate possible modes of existence which surpass the limits of any given, present situation. [...] Language itself, as a signifying milieu, must be referred to existence.'

In our attempts to reveal the meaningful existence of subcultures through peer rivalry, we might envision peer conflict as forming part of the symbolic order of wider youth cultural conflict, often articulated as moral conflicts over style and gender identity. Within this order, young people draw upon elements of peer rivalry to obtain 'subcultural capital' within school and to exercise mastery over the urban spaces to which they are tied both practically and emotionally.[1] Thus Thornton (1997) writes that:

> subcultural capital [...] accords reasonably well with Bourdieu's system of thought ... subcultural capital confers status on its owner in the eyes of the relevant beholder ... subcultural capital is embodied in the form of being in the know.

Amongst the young people in Tower Hill, particularly those identifying as Ginos and Ginas and Gangsta Boys and Gangsta Girls, subcultural capital represented a fantasy of power that fed into their desires for a recognizable high-status identity. This powerful identity is best understood as a form of subcultural capital, typically performed as 'being in the know', and which draws upon particular stylistic gestures such as Gangsta Boys with shaved heads, the wearing of Rapper baseball caps and expensive name-brand baggy trousers inherited from Black Slick and Hip Hop bands such as EAZE-E.[2]

The accompanying fantasies of selfhood that young people carried with them as they performed a slick version of 'being in the know' served paradoxically to both unify and divide subcultural membership, particularly in relation to gender, style and territory. As Rodriguez (14 years old, first-generation Portuguese-Canadian boy), a lead member of the Gangsta Boys, tells us:

> RODRIGUEZ: I don't know where they got the [idea of the] Thug [also Gangsta]. I don't even know how I got classified as Thug [the lead Thug]. For me it's a music and look thing [...]. I don't know what it's like [...] you know like probably all the other Thugs in the school. It's like you get to know each other. One thing you don't want to be part of is like the gang, right which they try to drag you into [...]. They try to drag me into a gang and it's, I just keep saying no. I prefer to stay away from it [...] There's a whole lot of gang rivalry in the school [...] Lots of fights.
>
> INTERVIEWER: What's that about do you think?
>
> RODRIGUEZ: I just think it's about territory [...]. Like who wants to own the school, wants to be the main authority around here [...]. Mostly boys [...]

As Rodriguez alludes to, insider knowledge in such groups can also lead to social divisions to the extent that any one individual might exercise particular elements of 'choice', 'reflection' or apparently liberal freedoms in sometimes challenging or transgressing identity norms or rules of power, or in attempts to redefine aggressive masculinities both within or beyond the group. As Rodriguez goes on to say:

> Some people are trying to act like [the boss], like carrying a pipe in their pants of pepper spray. [...] I don't see the point of it cause I mean carrying a weapon is like saying well you're like the wussy of the fight [...]. Like people are saying you gotta be mighty, you gotta win, yet they pull out pipes and weapons. I think how can you prove you are a man by using a weapon? [...] Like I remember one time I got into a fight. [...] Here (pointing to a photo-narrative he made as part of the project) outside of the school with someone from the school who got suspended. He wanted to fight and he pulled out a pipe.

These choice practices and gender transgressions did, paradoxically, turn 'individual choice' into an instrument of regulation over others that operated by apparently distinguishing itself as an authentic style tied to the language of freedom ('not real men'), yet still 'bearing tactics from the power and regime it decried' (Brown, 2001: 25). As Rodriguez continues:

> I told him if you want to be a real man put down the pipe and fight with your hands, but it turned out he just ended up walking away so it kept me out of trouble. [...] If he didn't put it down I was gonna back off [...]. Yeah, I was gonna walk away, show him I was the bigger man [...]. I didn't need to fight with him to prove anything. Better to walk away and prove they're not strong enough [...]. Yeah and that's another thing, [...] they're all big at the elbow; their friends come and everything. That's another point proving that they're not [real men] [...]. Yeah, they bring in their pals and all that to show how big they are ...

As we show later in the chapter, these paradoxical tensions between rule-bound membership, wider gender relations and 'individual choice' served as powerful cultural mediators of both traditional and new forms of class conflict among youth groups, as well as in mediating still necessarily defensive subcultural practices.

Key Arguments: The Symbolic Imagination and Youth Rivalry

In our efforts to understand modes of youth subcultural identification and any associated transgressions, we wish to put forward two key arguments. First, we argue that a broad constellation of competing and contradictory cultural processes is at work in re-contextualizing female and male youth subcultural narratives and pre-figuring post-subcultural practice (see Chapters 6 and 7). Some of the most significant of these processes are: the global scales of inner-city re-organization, retrenchment and regeneration at the level of the local urban fringe space and school; the sedimented effects of historically shaped gender, race and class relations, alongside the impact of both historical and more recent diasporic movements and colonial imaginaries (see Ahmed, 2003); contrasts between young people's family experience of a first-modernity migration and a second- or late-modernity migration biography (see Sheilbelhofer, 2009); the material symbols within popular and global cultures which are appropriated and re-appropriated by those who inhabit local spaces;[3] and the impact of converging neo-liberal educational and social policy agendas which have led to, for example, the practices of open enrolment and the devolution of provincial policies to municipal decision-making, favouring the private sector more generally. These processes are further compounded by young people's localized positioning within 'demonized schools' in newly redrawn urban arrangements (Reay & Lucey, 2003).

Second, we argue that contemporary youth subcultural narratives and any emergent post-subcultural effects are substantially founded upon the often covert and sometimes invisible relationships between global and localized narratives and scales of 'symbolic domination' (see Bourdieu, 2001) operating in urban schools and cities. These relationships are shaped by powerful modernizing forces such as consumption, rising late-twentieth-century class conflict and diasporic migration biographies. Taken together, these forces have converged in highly complex ways and have resulted in a profound social distancing of disadvantaged urban youth from established 'cultures of success' within an increasingly stratified educational market.[4] Yet this social distancing has not eliminated the pressure to perform class insults and engage in transgressive class fantasies which are grounded in the drive for social status in relation to a wide-ranging set of gender identity narratives about possible youth cultural styles. As Mandy (aged 15, Cambodian-Canadian, Beacon Park) reminds us in the following excerpt captured at the Vancouver site, a competitive and culturally specific array of gendered norms and associated conflicts are manifest within subcultural and post-subcultural performances at the fringe of the global city:

M: Usually nowadays girls have to look a certain way, like how they have to be fit and in style [...] in clothing ...

INTERVIEWER: So, physically fit in?

M: Yeah.

INTERVIEWER: And what style and stuff? What's the certain look? Can you describe it for me?

M: Just a type of clothing. Like most of the girls now buy those really expensive clothing [because of the city life]. Like only one sweater's just a hundred [dollars] or something.

INTERVIEWER: Like name brand?

M: Yeah. And [...] some people name them by the type they are. Like if they're Vietnamese or something, they call them the 'nammers' because they wear this kind of spandex [...]. Have you seen those?

INTERVIEWER: No I haven't. I'm learning a lot talking to you. So they call them the 'nammers'? Is that the clothes or is that...

M: No, type of people, 'Nammers'. Vietnamese with like blonde hair and eyebrows and lots of make-up.

INTERVIEWER: Tell me, is that girls or boys or both?

M: Oh, they're girls.

INTERVIEWER: Girls [...] and they wear spandex.

M: Yeah, like really tight clothing

Mandy is here describing the subcultural style associated with the diasporic Asian girls' subculture (with some post-subcultural effects) identified as the 'Nammers'. It consists chiefly of spandex clothing, bleached blonde hair and heavy make-up with distinctive 1970s dark black Mod-like eyeliner. The Nammers reside on the upper-scale of the working-class Vietnamese-Canadian class ladder and were often merging their own subcultural performances with Japanese and Western styles possessing high levels of technological capital such as cell phones, iPhones, and with immediate access to global networks of power. Mandy's account offers a brief but important insight into some of the ways in which young people are expected to respond to wider regimes of gender and global style, used both as resources and as gender capital in the subcultural process of differentiating friend from foe, and as a yard-stick against which to measure one's own imagined success in the urban school. Mandy's account also illustrates how local forms of gender, race and intra-class conflict are tied to trans-local fantasies and gender norms, contingent largely upon inter-ethnic Asian conflict in the neighbourhood and some of the wider diasporic movements in Beacon Park with highly differentiated and emergent post-subcultural youth effects (see Chapters 6 and 7). Like McLeod and Yates (2006), we are therefore reluctant to assume that modernization in the forms articulated by scholars such as Ulrich Beck (1992, 1999) impacts on all young people in the same way. Rather, inherited ethnic conflicts, alongside spatial arrangements and divisions at the fringe of the urban core,[5] continue to impinge strongly upon young people's subcultural narratives and, where visible, such as in the blonde Nammers, the emergence of post-subcultural identifications.

In Defence of Subcultural Practice at Tower Hill: Gender, Ritual and Tradition

In Tower Hill, the Toronto neighbourhood, which we now move forward to showcase for the remainder of this chapter, youth cultural practice was most often performed as 'being in the know' and manifested as intense gender rivalry between young people who shared similar class positions. These conflicts reflected that trace of a history which was tied to young people's sometimes displaced responses to longstanding social relationships of class differentiation and to earlier, inherited ethnic, cultural and migration conflicts which began elsewhere (i.e. Southern Europe) but which re-emerged in new forms in Tower Hill (e.g. Italian and Portuguese families). Hence, many of the cultural strategies young people drew upon resembled sedimented forms of cultural tradition and, in Walkerdine and Lucey's (1989) terms, 'objectified discourses' of a heteronormative gender order. These discourses appeared even when new forms of domination emerged at the symbolic level, such as girl toughness, the late-modern version of the Gangsta Girl or the techno-obsessive Gino boy.[6]

In this sense, 'being in the know' as a member of a youth culture was best understood both as a cultural modality of class conflict and a narrative identity which remained grounded in the wider symbolic gender order and in the cultural traditions of place and migration biographies. Being 'in the know' also represented a historical element of gender relations amongst isolated youth subjects – subjects who often 'claim membership in an identity-based community [such as the Gina, Thug or Gangsta Girl] but rarely experience themselves as concretely sustained or protected by actual communities of solidarity' (Brown, 2001: 38; brackets our addition). To the extent that these young people were institutionalized into the dual logics of an entrenched and radically urbanizing city seeking 'world-class' status and discourses of apparent 'freedom', they were intensely vulnerable to the deeply problematic ethos of the empty and de-politicizing liberalism by which such cities are consumed.

In the following analysis, we focus upon class and territorial contexts, and their interplay with re-contextualized forms of masculinity and femininity within the Toronto pre-9/11 case study site.[7] We are concerned here with offering a window of illumination on how dominant forms of (hetero)normativity and particular cultural traditions emerged as powerful modalities of youth subcultural surveillance within schools, organized in Tower Hill according to traditional systems of territorial space. Narrative authority is the form used by the young people as they express the continuous process of meaning-creation through the performance of a narrative identity or a storied self. As we demonstrate, these narratives are heavily shaped by the 'authorized language' (as discussed in Chapter 3) and ideological paradigms of particular school and neighbourhood spaces. Indeed, young people were constantly searching for a narrative which could 'elevate their own suffering and identity to action' and their presence into visibility (see Kearney, 2004). Importantly, these narratives also served as a partial response to their own family's historical suffering but they also represented a border or fringe narrative that led to forms of cultural alienation (anomie) that made their neighbours and some fellow school-mates into 'strangers' and 'foes'. Following the work of Paul Ricoeur (1981), we refer to this process – the intersection of space, action, suffering, authority and meaning – as youth narrativization and 'phenomenologies of meaning-making'.

Sexualized School Territories and Urban 'Corridors of Power': Peer Rivalry, Space and Regimes of Gendered Governance

Here we focus upon gender and other elements of social positioning as key categories of analysis in illuminating young people's 'phenomenologies of meaning', their forms of subcultural capital and 'being in the know'. Here, the weighty signifiers of dominant gender narratives mean that the 'subjective work' (Reay & Lucey, 2003) involved in accommodating 'gender ideals of the "perfect girl" or "perfect boy"' remains a focus for intense struggle among young people. Such subjective work combines the exercise of particular kinds of class advantage and fantasy enactments of power, particularly in the form of heterosexual masculinities, with the standardized and artificially narrow definition of student success experienced within schools. However, the character of power associated with the liberal re-contextualization of moralizing gender relations is not transparently expressed and is therefore not easily identified as power. Instead, gendered peer rivalries represent 'symptoms of a certain fragmentation of suffering, and of suffering lived as identity' (for example, a Gangsta Girl who re-represents the language of equality or female freedoms as girl toughness or female bullying) but, as we learn, for these young people, this 'suffering [cannot] be resolved at the identitarian level' (Brown, 2001: 39; brackets our addition). The result is considerable anxiety for young people as they pursue deeply conflicted social and personal objectives in their neighbourhoods and schools.

In Tower Hill, wider symbolic discourses of the gender order and territoriality were often exploited by young people to gain 'symbolic control' (Cohen, 1997) over both their educational and urban landscapes. Following Cohen, we define territoriality as a spatial dimension of the 'classification struggles' (Bourdieu, 2001; see also Foucault, 1977) young people must undertake to establish their social status and gain visibility within a peer group. Cohen (1999: 66) writes:

The function of territoriality is [...] to [...] provide a material basis for a system of positional rules which preserve the boundaries of the loose knit peer group network, and assigns the entire youthful population, big and little, boy and girl, to a place which cuts across these distinctions ... Friend or Foe.

Like Cohen, this seeking out of friend or foe in a loose-knit peer group – sometimes operating within the parameters of more traditional class, race and gender conflict – is one of the key mechanisms for the formation of a gendered front (or a fantasy of gender identity) which results in particularly symbolic (here a symbol, as somehow beyond discourse, emerges as surveillance) forms of gendered surveillance in schools. It also lays the foundation for re-contextualized intra-class and racial conflicts between young people pushed to the margins through spatial divisions at the urban core and fringe. Peer rivalry thus emerged in Tower Hill as the paramount location for the official and unofficial classification struggles that young people undertook in their efforts to reclaim meaningful spatial territory in their lives. It also served as a survival strategy and a form of subcultural protection in which students persistently referred to the school as the 'Ghetto' and the 'Warehouse'. This symbolic territory – the corridor – constituted a 'horizon of action' (see Bourdieu, 1999) – for the defence of strongly drawn youth identifications through the gendered acquisition of subcultural capital. At the same time, elements of strong group identification or rule-bound practices were sometimes seen as a threat to a certain notion of liberal authenticity which, despite all constraints, continued to hold out the future promise of becoming any kind of person at any time. As Rodriguez, a key member of the Gangsta Boys, remarked:

INTERVIEWER: So who do you hang with? How would you classify yourself? I hear about the Thugs, there's Rockers, and there's Ginos.
RODRIGUEZ: Oh yeah. There is a whole bunch of people.
INTERVIEWER: So how do you classify yourself?
RODRIGUEZ: I'm myself.
INTERVIEWER: So you're not any one of those things?
RODRIGUEZ: Well yes, I could be all of them, well no not really ...
INTERVIEWER: So you listen to rap music?
RODRIGUEZ: Yeah.
INTERVIEWER: And you say that you are kind of 'Gangster' like?
RODRIGUEZ: Yeah, and I don't like Rock Music and [that is, I am NOT a Rocker] The school is filled with Ginos.

In under-resourced schools located on the fringes of the inner-city, each element of school life imposes its own meaning sets, positional rules and regulatory functions. Young people are therefore bound together, as

Rodriguez tells us, as much by similarities and shared allegiances (e.g. the position of Portuguese and Italian families in the Canadian labour class, Ginos, for example) as by perceived radical differences (*Thugs don't like Ginos*). This meant that, while some young people strived for some relative autonomy or individuality ('I'm myself', or 'I could be all of them really'), if we are to use the language of late-modern social theory in matters of subcultural style, the interplay between economic disadvantage, family migration biographies and the neo-liberal structures operating in this demonized urban school remained deeply embedded in highly sexualized youth subcultural classifications. This was further compounded by the fact that tightly bound Portuguese and Italian communities still lived side-by-side in the local neighbourhood, and remained marked by the historical legacies of migration patterns and associated cultural struggles both between and within these two communities (see Kaplan & Li, 2006).

Hence, young people's subcultural classifications – as a repository for feelings of personal security and for daily life – remained prominent features of young people's own narrations, whether they saw themselves as firmly entrenched as an insider or as someone striving for authentic self-definitions. In drawing boundaries around such classifications, elements of pop culture often served as key positional markers. As one First Nations boy of 16, who saw himself as a relative outsider to these communities, remarked:

R: Like Rockers [the boys] usually stay together and listen to rock music basically [e.g. Nickelback, Our Lady Piece]. Ginos are Italian [and Portuguese] kids that listen to like Techno-type music [...]. And a Thug [Gangsta] is just a guy who belongs to a gang that listens to rap music basically [...]. They basically stay in their own groups ...

INTERVIEWER: And what about the girls? Do they all belong to these groups too?

R: Nah [...]. I notice there is not much black girls in the school so they really stick together ....

INTERVIEWER: So what about you? [...]

R: I just hang around with anyone, well not anyone [...] I'm just saying I'm not into these group things.

A related account is offered by Tony, another Portuguese-Canadian Gangsta Boy (aged 15) who is attempting to redefine himself through the imaginative force of redescription:

TONY: Before I used to hang out with people related to me (Portuguese boys). Now I hang out with all kinds of people, like Rockers.

INTERVIEWER: What's a Rocker?

TONY: Listen to Rock music, which I usually don't like but now I'm getting fully into it [...]. The Rockers are happy with that, me getting into it [...]. Most people classify me as a Thug because they call me Sun [Slim] Shady,[8] you know, Eminem. They mostly classify me as that 'cause I listen to rap and all that [and I had my head shaved and dyed blonde at the base].

INTERVIEWER: Okay.

TONY: But they said that I'm slowly starting to turn [...] I eventually hope to get out of that, like to be my own self, by next year. [...] Stop looking like [...]. Like this year I was trying to impress people by trying to look like them, get all the new fashions but I've learned. I've had my fun so next year I'll be dressing the way I feel like. Yeah, then [those others] they'll be on their own [...]. If they can't accept me for who I am then it's their own fault [...]. Oh yeah [and just so you know], mainly being a Thug, you gotta listen to Rap. You've got mainly to have your own records of getting into trouble.

Beyond the more spectacular iconographic markers underlying claims to subcultural identity or the emerging contradictions in its denial, the key locus at which these identities encountered the heavy weight of symbolic power and modes of surveillance in the 'demonized school' converged in the space of the school corridor. Thus, within the corridor, boys and girls moved in groups of three to four, both as strategies of self-protection but also to mark a defined school area as a primary site for the enactment of sexualized power and a 'revolt into style' (see Cohen, 1997). Young people therefore utilized the corridor as a site for the performance of both gendered and racialized forms of youth subcultural style, authorized through language games and physical gestures of power, and as a highly visible – and equally dangerous – setting for territorial competition. As Danny, a 14-year-old Gino boy, remarked: 'some of the Gangsta Boys have pepper spray in their locker and they show it off every now and again.' And another suggested: 'Ginos just run away in the corridor because they're femmy.'

Such struggles were much less noticeable in classroom contexts, particularly because students often reported being reprimanded for engaging in what was regarded by some teachers as deeply problematic 'working-class' behaviour. Consequently, the corridor presented itself as a 'free' space beyond the formal regulation of the school, where intra-class alienation and symbolic regulation through youth subcultural style could find its expression. We were therefore able to comprehend the corridor as fundamentally 'an emblematic class related place' (Massey, 1995, 1999) where gendered regulation and mutual surveillance could be exercised in reaction to wider cultural conflicts.

Fieldnotes and interviews often indicated the high degrees of disciplining in which young people participated in support of their own subcultural status and narrative. For example, disciplining often took place through racialized and sexualized slurs, derived from wider derogatory discourses (i.e. 'easy girls', 'spoonies', 'whores', 'sluts', 'black hoes'), and were a common currency in defining the identity negotiations for which the corridor was an open site. The idea of the corridor as a dangerous space was more commonly remarked upon by young women, and more particularly by minority ethnic girls. As one 14-year-old Filipino-Canadian girl illustrated in remarking upon the language characteristically used to describe the visible minority teenage girls in the school corridor:

A: They'll [the Gangsta Girls] use this language [...]. They don't care [...]. Every kind of bad word [...]. Slut [...] I don't know [...]. Mother-fucker. [...] I don't know ...

INTERVIEWER: So why these names, slut, whore, what's this all about?

A: Probably that's the only way they can get their anger out.

These terms, as highly charged class signifiers of sexual humiliation and disgust, circulated at every classroom break (and often at the back of the classroom during lessons), typically with the 'tough' (Gangsta) girls physically positioned face-to-face with Ginas in an attempt to dramatize tension or physical threat.

How did these dramatizations and the dominant phenomenologies of meaning associated with peer rivalries play out within these corridors of power? The most striking turned upon representations aligned with 'tough girl' or 'bad girl' metaphors (see also Kelly et al., 2005), as well as towards the enforcement of more traditional conceptions of working-class femininity. The 'tough' girls situated themselves as belonging to the Gangsta culture (girls characteristically referenced Rap, 'girl on girl' bullying and Thug culture, baggy trousers (no skirts), dossing on homework and playing 'hard'; boys' symbolic referencing was chiefly to baggy trousers, slick hair-cuts, references to black rappers and violent musical forms, the wearing of chains and the carrying of cell phones, and affiliation with brand-name clothing).

By contrast, the so-called 'soft, more geeky' girls who needed 'roughing up' or 'sorting out' were identified by the Gangsta Girls as the 'Ginas'. Ginas often objectified their cultural self-understandings as tied to contemporary Techno dance music, snug clothing, attempts to complete homework, partial allegiances to Southern European forms of emphasized femininity and to popular European cultural expressions which rejected the 'Gangsta' culture (such as high heels, skirts and heavy make-up).[9]

For Gangsta Girls, it was essential to conform – through various modalities of representation – to notions of the 'tough girl' whilst simultaneously ensuring that particular notions of femininity remained intact – in short, 'look tough, be tough, be rough and still be sexy'. In this respect, the Gangsta Girls share much in common with Willis' and McRobbie's earlier accounts of determined 'working-class' resistance to acceptable gender norms of middle-class behaviour. However, at the same time, a new, more modern and assertive cultural account of female gender identity free to behave, as one girl suggested, 'like the boys', was enacted to challenge officially sanctioned, traditional gender norms of the aspiring working-class 'good girl' or the 'nice girl' which remained entrenched within local class and community cultures.

Simultaneously, in displays of deeply paradoxical gender behaviour, some of the 'tough girls' also encouraged the surveillance of traditional forms of femininity such that Gina girls became the objects and targets for the enforcement of established forms of working-class femininity and compulsory heterosexuality (e.g. such as demanding Ginas wear short skirts whilst at the same time referring to them as 'sluts', 'spoonies', 'whores' and 'easy-sleezy'). Much of this surveillance began with dramatizations of physical hardness displayed by the Gangsta Girls. As Zoe (an Italian-Canadian Gina) remarked:

> every time we passed by these girls, they'd see us, they'd come and push us out of the way so one time one of my friends stood up for herself and it started a whole fight. They were yelling and screaming and all that [...]. The way they were treating us, they think they are all big and bad. Here you have to be a tough girl. A tough girl doesn't take anything from anyone. Like no kind of bullshit.

Paradoxically, these demands also led in particular ethnographic contexts (e.g. self portraits and images of the future) to the sanctioning of identities (at the level of the imaginary) within an inherited symbolic system of the domestic private sphere (see Candy's image of her future, Figure 4.1).

Clearly the symbolic legacy of domesticity is far from new in the framing of subcultural practice. It remains closely tied to the spaces where gender surveillance is practised as 'incessant confrontations' forming the cultural system and moral fields of these spaces. The magnitude and cultural force of this surveillance that was immanent in the space of the corridor, whilst apparently new in its expanding range of possible performances and narrations of femininities and masculinities (e.g. tough Gangsta or Rapper girl, or Gino Techno Boy) did, however, remain confined within traditional heterosexual gender narratives. It was through 'incessant [gender] confrontations' (being told to 'wear

In the future I'm not yet sure what I will be doing. like what job I'll be having but I do no that I will be living here becaus I don't really plan on mouving. But I am sure that when I'm married and have children of my own, I will have a good proffession so that I can be able to help support my family.

Me in the Future...

Figure 4.1 Student Self-Portrait of a Gina Girl's Future: Tower Hill, Toronto, Ontario.

short skirts', 'get roughed up', wear make-up, show cleavage, have sex) which transformed young people's subcultural identities on one level but which ultimately reinforced tradition (e.g. compulsory heterosexuality) through 'inversions' of it on another level (such as, the liberal freedom to be 'tough', to be equal to the tough boys; to be 'like the boys'). The consequence was that the overwhelming support for traditional gender relations in the corridor led to what Michel Foucault named the formation of cultural 'hegemonies' (Foucault, 1977) of gender, such as the demand for emphasized femininity, girl scraps, learning to be 'tough' and 'boyfriend' wars, effected through the laws of the corridor. It was in the constant reclaiming of narratives of gender identity through the authorized language of particular school spaces that we witnessed the appropriation of apparently new gender regimes, alongside the persistence of more traditional gender norms.

Seen in these terms, it makes little sense to identify a target in the form of one central subcultural group (i.e. Gangsta Girls) or female bully, a group or leader who organizes some hegemonic sub-powers and sets loose fantasies of identity that merely regulate other identities. There is, however, an inherited set of subcultural politics which frame power relations in the corridor; although these politics are necessarily embedded in a wider macro-history and in a re-contextualized set of localized relations that can only be authorized with particular spatial and historical imaginaries operating on the ground. As Tina, a 15-year-old Italian-Canadian Gina, remarked: 'the Thugs are supposed to be tougher and rougher and you're supposed to act tough.' Another girl describing herself as a Gino said: 'I listen to Gino beats, soft rock. [...] A Gina is someone who wears really tight clothes and listens to Gino Beats, goes clubbing all the time.' 'They [the Gangstas] call us "sluts and bitches"'. And in Rodriguez's own words about 'girl scraps': 'They slap [over boys and boyfriends][...] and mostly they scream but they slap.'

Gender Regulation, Class Territories and Young People's Utopian Fantasies of the Future

Forms of power which, on the surface, appear to rest in the hands of particular subcultural groups – in this case the Gangsta Girls – are not only linked to the symbolic manifestations of the wider gender order. They are intrinsic to wider economic processes (e.g. public housing versus owning your own home), to the knowledge of what it means to be a girl or boy in urban neighbourhoods (Gangsta Girls gained more symbolic power when paired up with Gangsta Boys, for example), to wider social and cultural systems and to migration biographies which are inherited from past time. More importantly, the oppositional tensions between apparent oppressor (i.e. the Gangsta Girls) and the apparently subordinated (Ginas) are also illusory. This is because subcultural power cannot in reality be directed from one 'place' to another or from one group to another (it is a form of historical relations operating in the present), particularly since the Gangsta Girls in this particular neighbourhood lived with higher degrees of economic disadvantage (e.g. more commonly living in social housing) when compared to the Ginas (who most commonly lived in privately owned homes which were purchased by their families after post-war slum clearances and renewed migration settlement agreements in Tower Hill).

While the direction or force of power, in Foucault's words, 'can .. .never be entirely intentional, never entirely objective' (1977: 123), objectifying the performance of perceived power and class fantasies was a central project of youth subcultural members. For example, for the Gangsta Girls who practised it, objectifying the ideological discourse of 'girl toughness' brought the advantages of a utopian form of agency, particularly as they struggled to manage often conflicting gender relations operating in the school, the city and in their families. Such demonstrations of girl toughness were, however, always riven by ambivalence. Indeed, when such young women imagined themselves in the future, modes of representations tied to their families, their working-class histories and traditional forms of

In 10 years this I what I'm going to look like. In 10years I'm going to be a hairdresser, and cutting, designing peoples hair. I am going to be a hard working person and trying my best to cut the hair. I like to cut hair because It's fun and I also enjoy colouring hair.

I have a Cousin who is also a hairdresser, she tells me It's a hard job, but It's not really easy to cut hair. She teaches me how to cut hair on a wig and when she says you did a great job I get happy when She says that. I will start working when I am 24 years old. I am going to be living with my future husband In Brampton, and have 2 children In the Future.

Figure 4.2 Self-Portrait of Sherry's Future (a 'Gangsta' Girl), a Tower Hill Participant, Toronto, Ontario.

employment (and gender relations) tended to dominate the consciousness of both the Ginas and the Gangstas (see Figure 4.2).

In an attempt to interpret the cultural text that Sherry presents, we cite one of Cohen's youth participants (1997: 368) in a much earlier study on youth cultures:

Jane was going to be a hairdresser. She was the most definite and confident member of the group when it came to plans for leaving school. Indeed her disinterest in school stemmed from the strength of her commitment to what she saw as her career. But then she had already made the transition to work, at home. She had, as she put it, grown up with hairdressing. It was in her family: her mother, her aunt ... And from these sources she had picked up a wealth of knowledge about styles ... cultural capital she fully intended to cash in on.

Cohen's description, alongside Sherry's image of her future, highlights the symbolic power of imagining one's future in a constrained social world.[10] Both also highlight how any modality of agency is limited by a complex gender order which positions women as free and equal to men on the one hand, and, on the other, as subjects of reproduction in the 'domestic register' of social life (see Cohen, 1990). The symbolic narrative of the private in this tightly woven working-class community was clearly significant in the re-contextualization of existing class and gender relations. As Becky, a Portuguese Gangsta Girl who sometimes hung out with the Ginas, remarked about marriage and her future: 'I am getting married early. Really early. As soon as I get out of school.'

Indeed, a second modernity where female freedoms surpassed the effects of subcultural politics remained a largely unavailable attainment for many of the girls and most of the boys in Tower Hill. Here we are able to witness the power of Ricoeur's notion of symbolic narratives and their surplus effects. Ricoeur suggests that individuals must narrate themselves into a possible world based upon their own historically informed imagination of the future: 'what is proposed in the text is the proposing of a world that I might [or can] inhabit and into which I might project my own powers' (Kearney, 2004: 53). It is therefore in both Sherry's and Jane's narrations, then, that we are able to witness their imagination as 'redescription, as a reference through traces' (Kearney, 2004: 54). This imagination both opens and constrains future actions, but it is in no way an individual narrative of legitimate sovereignty, high individualization or liberal freedoms. For young people, it is precisely their narrative imagination that provides a context for action and is one key factor, as Kearney (2004: 57) argues, for the 'refiguring of the world of action under the sign of the plot'. The collective stories and unique histories of the neighbourhood need not bear the authorship or autonomy of any one person, even as they exercised a formative influence on young people's symbolic accounts of who they imagined they'd become (see Figures 4.3 and 4.4): 'This is what Ricoeur calls the social imaginary. And this social function of imagination is constitutive of reality itself' (Kearney, 2004: 37).

In Tower Hill, such forms of imagination about one's future could be seen precisely as the creation of a working-class utopia, the horizon of a young persons' future value, transcending the limits of contemporary

Figure 4.3 Student Self-Portrait of the Future: Tower Hill, Toronto, Ontario.

Figure 4.4 Self-Portrait of a Gina Boy's Future: Tower Hill, Toronto, Ontario.

social class relations by way of a structure of feeling about one's future which has been inherited, in part, from a spatially located past.

Let us explore some of these emergent themes in more detail within young people's phenomenological meaning by looking more closely at the case of Lola, self-identifying as a Gina, who reported being both verbally and physically harassed by a group of Gangsta Girls (to whom she refers as 'bullies'). The Gangsta Girls had frequently reprimanded Lola to the effect that her uniform skirt was far too long for the other girls and boys in the school to tolerate.

INTERVIEWER: [you mentioned that] Some kids [Gangsta Girls] are bullies, do you think the majority?

LOLA: I think most are bullies and the others, you know ...

INTERVIEWER: Have you had any experience with that?

LOLA: Well I have once cause I had my skirt too long, my kilt and they're calling me (spoon), they would tease me well roll up your kilt or they'd push me around.

INTERVIEWER: Ah-hah.

LOLA: So ...

INTERVIEWER: Physically push you?

LOLA: Yeah.

INTERVIEWER: Girls or boys?

LOLA: Some kind of girls/boys, but now I'm used to it. I just roll up my kilt now.

INTERVIEWER: So they wanted it to be shorter?

LOLA: Yeah.

INTERVIEWER: Not longer? Right. Why? Why do you think?

LOLA: Cause they thought I was geeky and nerdy and all that [stuff].

INTERVIEWER: To wear it too long?

LOLA: Yeah.

Randy, a young man who referred to himself as a Thug (a signifier of Gangsta subcultures) also confirmed in an interview that Lola was the target of much sexualized disciplining:

RANDY: One of the girls gets picked on.

INTERVIEWER: Why does she get picked on?

RANDY: I dunno, they say it's cause she fingers herself with a spoon. Whatever, so they call her spoony and stuff.

How do we understand Lola's experience? How do we understand the actions of her peers? One interpretation (beyond the more obvious forms of embedded gender domination at play) is that Lola represents a symbolic trace of a narrative of an earlier time, indeed a class and cultural foe, a re-contextualized expression of the primary class conflict between the

Gangsta Girls and the Ginas. In part we may understand this in Bourdieu's terms as a gendered or sexualized 'habitus', a heightened sense of apparently approved and appropriate gender behaviour which has evolved dialectically over time as a classed form of gender conflict. Hence, class insults and sexualized disciplining asserted by the Gangsta Girls were fed by intra-class gender conflicts which ultimately regulated the conditions of acceptable femininity in the school. This allowed the Gangsta Girls to define the gendered 'foe' and 'class enemy' – that is, to practice, enable and police certain forms of classed femininity. Here, 'being in the know', possessing subcultural capital, meant learning – through habitus formations and incessant conflicts which governed gender behaviour – the correct mode of feminine representation in the classification of oneself as powerful. Within the same subcultural grouping, however, some of the Ginas engaged in their own gendered regulation which served as a reaction to wider gender politics in the corridor. As Naomi, a 15-year-old Italian-Canadian Gina remarked:

> There was one time when I used to come to the school and hang out with these other two [Gina] friends. And for some reason [I wore a kilt] they went to some of the [Gangsta Girls] and said I was easy. She said that the girls that wear a kilt are hoes […]. I don't [even] like wearing kilts but I never say anything about it […] or about girls that do. Then they'll say you're a hoe and a slut.

Paradoxically, heterosexual domination – at the level of the symbolic signifiers of local male culture – served as a form of invisible pedagogy or as a set of restricted social codes through which girls exercised their attempts to claim and redefine their class and gender position. In this way, the forms of disciplining that took place sometimes served as a regulatory instrument of classed heteronormativity and as a more general representation of heightened intra-class conflict. One way of escaping the disciplinary process – of being exempted from being 'tough' – was to seek status through exploiting channels of personal consumption which connected with identities founded upon globalizing cultural references. This strategy afforded some mediation of the class wars waged by other young women in the school context. The seizing of these global–local micro-channels of meaning offered some access to the very basis of acceptable gendered behaviour for girls (see Ahmed, 1999, 2003). As Renissa reflected on the pressure to 'fit in' by drawing upon the image of the 'tough girl':

RENISSA: At recess you'd always have to go and pick on a kid and make his life like hell.

INTERVIEWER: So do people put pressure on you to do that?

RENISSA: Yeah, to fit in, to be cool but I never did it 'cause [I had brand name clothing so they left me alone].

In other words, class advantage provided one avenue for escaping substantial gender regulation and sometimes overrode the potential for social conflict.

Another form of spatial authority was assumed by a group of Gangsta Girls who followed other girls in the school corridors and outdoors at recess and lunch breaks. Much of this gender regulation served as the basis for positional competition over male 'boyfriends' and was often referred to as the 'boyfriend wars'. Often the direction of the conflict seemed manifested in the Gangsta Girls' understanding of themselves as 'being in the know' about sex and sexuality in the Gangsta world and about 'correct' sexual behaviour, and therefore determining which girls were allowed to have boyfriends or talk to other boys. This 'being in the know' almost always functioned as a more severe form of gender disciplining when the targeted group of young women was racialized in particular ways (as 'Black'). As Wanda, an Afro-Caribbean Canadian student, reports:

INTERVIEWER: Anything that happened to you at school?

WANDA: I don't know, they'd just follow me (in the corridor) and they'd just start going why mess with my man, bitch? Dah, dah, dah and I asked whose your man? It'd be like well you don't know. It's like, no, shut up and leave me alone.

INTERVIEWER: So you were upset, you had a boyfriend. What was going on there you think?

WANDA: If it were true (that I was messin' round) they would say the boyfriend's name and they would say the friend's name and they would know things about me but they don't know nothing, so they were trying to scare me. [...]

What is important about Wanda's narrative is its deeply symbolic elements. In this case, girls, such as Wanda, do not choose to be consumed by such boyfriend wars or the associated class insults as understood within the cultural laws of this Toronto school. Rather, they embody such ideals as a form of cultural inheritance in a pre-existing gender order with very powerful local and spatial resonances. In this order, such symbols as 'bitch', or 'messin' round', speak to the inherited traces of an enduring class narrative which frames working-class girls as essentially promiscuous. The 'foe', therefore, could be identified as in some degree beyond the field of such resonances. That is, the 'foe' could be associated with the racialized female immigrant – that 'dark' phantom foreigner (see also Chapter 6) who has stolen another young woman's man. When this happens, the young woman is caught up in the wider social relations of peer rivalry, and serves as the 'scapegoat of all the tensions circulating in the seesaw of person-to-person perceptions' (Cohen, 1997: 68). She ultimately becomes the target for the enhanced policing and exclusionary pressures which are associated with historical patterns of gender, class and colonial relations (Douzinas, 2007; Gilroy, 2004).

Here is another account by Sarah, a 15-year-old, second-generation Portuguese-Canadian girl self-identifying as a member of the Ginas:

INTERVIEWER: Nobody ever pushed you round or anything like that?
SARAH: Yeah.
INTERVIEWER: What happened, how did you handle it?
SARAH: I would just be like don't touch me [...]. I wouldn't do anything. I'm not the type to swear or I'm not the type to be brave 'cause I don't wanna get my ass kicked.

The primary problem for some Ginas is that, whilst identified as 'working-class', they appear to have landed on the wrong side of femininity when faced with competition from the Gangsta Girls. Here we see how McRobbie's (1982) conception of 'tough' femininity becomes a high-status form of subcultural capital that provides powerful symbolic leverage in the gender order whilst ultimately serving as an appropriation of compulsory heterosexuality. This was why Gangsta Girls often referred to young men (typically Gangsta Boys) as their closest allies in the struggle against the Ginas. The social texts circulating about 'being tough' and female–male partnerships therefore provided the material premise which made the reproductive elements of the gender order possible. At the same time, however, such texts also subsumed these young women into a category of gender which ultimately subordinated them to men. McNay's (2000: 5) argument about the durability of the gender order for particular groups of girls and women is very illuminating in this context. She writes: 'gender identities are not free floating: they involve deeply rooted investments on the part of individuals and historically sedimented practices which severely limit their transferability and transformability.' Yet, at the same time, understanding the objectified discourse of 'toughness' in the mode of the Gangsta Girl means understanding the gendered elements of change for girls themselves. With the shifting registers of gender as a social category, the discourse of toughness (when attributed to girls) as a form of female freedom was clearly under less official and moral scrutiny and played a more active role in shaping young girls' peer rivalries. In this way, we can begin to see the localized and temporalized significance of the 'Gangsta Girl'. She can be configured as fundamentally 'new' but also locally familiar.

When we shift our gaze to the context of masculinity, we witness the deeply sedimented ways in which particular forms of femininity, particularly when linked to working-class masculinities, is conflated with class deviance. It also becomes clear why particular masculine ideals emerge as visual and cultural markers for determining one's place as insider or outsider, friend or foe. Here, Randy's words give some clues as to how masculinity emerges as a point of mediation between education and social class:

INTERVIEWER: You don't like rock music?

RANDY: No.

INTERVIEWER: Alright, what about the Gino stuff?

RANDY: No I hate that.

INTERVIEWER: What's wrong with the Ginos?

RANDY: I don't know, their clothes, their hair.

INTERVIEWER: Yeah, but what's wrong with it? [...]

RANDY: It's too girlish ...

INTERVIEWER: It's too girlish?

RANDY: Yes, it's girlish.

INTERVIEWER: So what's wrong with being girlish? Is there a problem with that?

RANDY: Well if you're a guy ... you can't be girlish, the school is filled with Ginos.

INTERVIEWER: Are they the ones that do well in school too, the Ginos?

RANDY: Yeah, but they're the greasy people.

INTERVIEWER: But you know they might get a good job.

RANDY: It's not worth it for me [...]. Guys are *just too cool* for school.

The multi-layered expression of this account has relatively little to do with Randy's understanding (as a Thug or Gangsta Boy) of what may be going on here in terms of gender domination. Rather, what Randy is doing is using his own experience to account for the power of masculinity for boys who know they are on the economic fringes of a wider global city. It would seem, therefore, that any rituals of resistance and their associated classification struggles can only be established by a set of underlying spatial phenomenologies of meaning. Such meanings are not only historical. They are deeply rooted in the present because they imply that any rupture of classed masculinities is not only risky business but potentially humiliating, at least at the surface level of peer rivalry.

Randy's remarks can be read through the corridors of power, but their real origins lie outside the school. The symbolic logic of becoming somebody, of being in the know, of redeeming recognition as a male actor who remains part of a powerful narrative plot, reflects a claim for legitimacy through the assertion of a heteronormative masculinity authorized in school and validated by the traditions of history and the local space where Randy must live out his life. Within the corridor, the Gangsta or Thug identity is tied up – as a positional rule – with contesting the Gino mentality, perceived as a feminine artefact which is not only classed but constructed as a form of weak, diminished masculinity. As

Cohen writes:

> Maturity and masculinity are both linked to a paradigm of physical
> hardness and where consequently the display of emotion becomes
> the despised attribute of the weaker sex, to be a baby or a fairy [or
> girlish] are about the worst insults that can be levelled.
>
> (1997: 73; brackets our addition)

Randy's gendered account is also positional to the extent that it exposes
the moral – good or right – position of a Gangsta Boy within the spatial
division of labour and within particularly segregated and entrenched
migration histories particularly, but not exclusively, from Southern
Europe. As Cohen (1997: 74) goes on to argue:

> In working-class cultures, recognition is always of a difference, either
> one that is shared [i.e. Gangstas] or one that isn't [i.e. Ginos]. If such
> rituals also involve a misrecognition, it is because these differences
> are regarded as contingent qualities emanating from – and hidden
> – inside individuals, rather than what they are: the structural
> properties of a system of relations governed by positional rules. It is
> a misrecognition of the grounds of identity.

These inherited rules associated with masculinity and femininity were
closely tied to forms of value exchange, class protection and gender learning in environments where surviving the demonized schools still constituted a basic condition of daily life (see Skeggs, 2004). As Joseph, another
Portuguese-Canadian boy (aged 15) stated:

> Thugs [Gangsta Boys] are pretty tough. I was always the strongest
> one in my school, like I look small but I'm strong for my height [...].
> You gotta learn how to fight and be very big because since you're
> small, people are gonna try and take advantage of that, right? So
> you do it to protect yourself. Like since I'm six years old in schools, I
> learned to be a [Gangsta] and my sister said flex your muscles and I
> did like.

When young people engage in a 'classification struggle' they are
attempting to master their environment, be it in the school corridor or in
the city, in ways which are objectified through highly sexualized, cultural
narratives of identity. The embodiment of particular forms of masculinity
and femininity therefore become important exercises in self-protection
and in the maintenance of group membership and visibility – in 'gaining
closure such that a boundary can be created between those who are out to
get you and those who are not' (Cohen, 1997: 45). Noteworthy, then, is
that metaphorical references to 'Gangstas' and 'Ginos' in Tower Hill represent a form of self-protection, a stylistic gesture of class warfare and

associated class insults and, to greater or lesser degrees, as class reproduction, highly consistent with earlier accounts of subcultural practice offered in the past (e.g. Hebdige, Clark, Willis). As Willis (2003: 394) writes:

> although resistant cultures continue to be condemned in schools with teachers and administrators seeing them as pathological, they actually show some clear sign of rationality [...]. These resistant cultures supply cultural forms and shields from stigma to blunt the cruel edge of individualism and meritocracy in capitalist societies.

Against this, it is therefore by no means clear that Beck's classed notion of the de-ritualized self or Redhead's (1997) post-subcultural self – at least in the localized setting of Tower Hill – bears much relation to groups of working-class young people, who live at the hard edge of the global city. For such groups, conceptions of the gender order – symbolically organized within locally defined histories and similarly constrained futures – remain very strong. At the narrative heart of the modes of youth culture which bear these histories and promise these futures stands the highly spatialized culture of the school, and particularly the symbolic authority of the corridor.

Conclusions

Since the publication of Paul Willis' (1977) seminal work *Learning to Labour*, and the creative work of many other members of the Birmingham school (e.g. Clark, Hall, Hebdige, Nayak, McRobbie, Griffin, McDonald, Shildrick, Pilkington), sociologists of education and cultural studies scholars have debated over whether schools are still profoundly implicated in the cultural re-making of economic disadvantage and gender subordination. Willis, however, was not primarily concerned with questions of urban space, and nor are those contemporary sociologists, such as Beck, who see individualization and class mobility as the dominant elements shaping youth identity in late-modernity.

In contrast to Beck's individualization thesis, then, evidence from Tower Hill suggests that particular groups of economically disadvantaged youth remain tied, as they were in the past, to deeply 'sedimented' and moralizing forms of gender relations. These practices are authorized in particular spatial locations and through subcultural affiliations, yet still shaped by the narratives of the heterosexual family and of kinship communities and migration conflicts which form part of a first- and second-modernity of working-class labour migration, starting first from the turn of the twentieth century and emanating primarily, in the case of Tower Hill, from Southern Europe in the post-war period. In other words, geography, migration and space play a substantial authorizing role in the performance of identity and traditional subcultural forms of peer rivalry rather than providing a landscape of possibilities for the performance of post-subcultural identification or heightened individualization in every instance. We should not be surprised, then, that we continue to witness forms of noise generated by youth through particular subcultural identifications and defences, alongside emergent and sometimes quite subtle signs of a post-subcultural identification and/or forms of individualization (Portuguese Rappers, or being 'me'), especially those associated with style, the struggle for gendered authenticity and liberal discourses of freedom in the making of the self. Forms of style and rivalry also emerged as local and global adaptations, playing some part in new social divisions, particularly through heightened intra-class conflicts. We have argued that these conflicts are linked to young people's social location in 'geographical arrangements of power' in urban schools and cities. These struggles are an outcome of both inheriting and challenging – often through liberal discourses of the freedom to be tough – a related set of classed, gendered, cultural and spatial positions in the city which are historically significant. This local inheritance does not function as it might have done (or was theorized to do) in the past – to simply determine and reinforce class positions – but rather regulates the ways in which young people re-contextualize a utopian image of themselves and others, creating perhaps more (rather than less) anxiety about their ability to perfect themselves for an imagined future in 'new' times.

In bridging spatial arrangements with a cultural analysis of youth cultures in schools, we have also demonstrated that links made between neo-liberal school cultures and the spatial elements of social exclusion should be reconsidered in light of the symbolic power of ritual and territoriality. This return to a focus on territory (seen here as a spatial form of power which is not only driven by class and perhaps never was) and the heightened need for security in particular spaces is significant, as most late-modern accounts of youth identity imply that young people are less and less tied to ritualistic cultural practices. However, arguably in particular geographical arrangements, young people remain tied in part by classed codes of cultural inheritance such as the Gangsta ideal of school territory as a form of power ('like whose the main authority'). These marked elements of space represent vehicles of social meaning for young people, emerging as part of the cultural logic of power and social reason in the moral fields of the school corridor, and, as such, in Bourdieu's terms, play a signifying role in young people's embodiment of domination, anxiety and engagement with peer rivalry.

At the same time, these young people are also actors who struggle daily to move beyond such embodiment. One must be clear, however, that the range of youth subcultural expressions and forms of identification available is substantially narrowed by symbolic economies of social exclusion and migration biographies operating on a far broader scale. As Clara reported when talking about the Ginos and their futures as compared to her own: 'the [Ginos] are geeks and they study too hard. Like I can't do that. There is always a book in their face. It's like you look at them and you're like, my god, they don't have a life.' She goes on to say: 'I'm gonna feel excluded at university because I'm gonna see all these people with high marks and like they know a lot of stuff and I'm gonna be like lost.' Undoubtedly, in this particular neighbourhood, theories of de-traditionalization have exaggerated the degree to which cultural norms have been reconfigured, even if self-making and discourses of freedom mediate the subcultural narratives of tradition. In this sense, individualization theorists have, at least in particular places, grossly inflated the real freedoms now thought to be generally available to economically disadvantaged youth.

At the level of geographical space, it may also be the case that post-subcultural theorists have sometimes exaggerated the extent to which the formation of fluid and highly mobile global identifications are possible. We do not wish to argue that such global identifications or global–local forms of identification are non-existent, but rather, that different youth communities have differential access to the freedoms associated with 'post-subcultural' identification and the material and historical conditions under which such fluidity becomes possible. Hence, in subsequent chapters we outline the ethnographic significance of both subcultural and post-subcultural identification as ultimately grounded in the practical and highly classed elements of a social and cultural geography of power influencing youth practices, as opposed to the imposition of theoretical formalism(s) which carry hagiographical status in defining youth identity in late-modernity.

In summary, then, a phenomenology of meaning-making among young people is symbolically located in the local formation of youth culture itself (and its global narratives and cultural connections) and impacts upon the material conditions underwriting young people's social circumstances and, very likely, upon their future destinies. We cannot therefore assume that young people are a product of their own making or that they are determined, as some sociological accounts might have us believe, by their 'class'. We need instead to view young people as responding to contested trans-local histories as they confront contemporary social change. Such a position will allow us to understand young people's complex phenomenologies of meaning as emerging from a reconfigured history of marginalization 'set in motion' in the present.

In the next chapter, we offer an account of how young people draw upon a symbolic and spatial imagination of their neighbourhoods as one means for evaluating their social positioning in the global city. A particular focus rests upon young people's conceptions of security, belonging and home in urban neighbourhoods. Our aim is to reveal empirically the ways in which spatial imaginaries are drawn upon by young people as an indirect mechanism for deciphering meaning about themselves and their futures.

5

Urban Imaginaries and Youth Geographies of Emotion
Ambivalence, Anxiety and Class Fantasies of Home

Things are always going on in the bad streets. I don't feel safe in the street … It's people talking bad about other people, lots of fighting, across the streets, close to the park.

(Carrie, aged 14)

The capability of neighbourhoods to produce contexts (within which their very localizing activities acquire meaning and historical potential) and to produce local subjects is profoundly affected by the locality-producing capabilities of larger-scale formations (nation-states, kingdoms, missionary empires, and trading cartels) to determine the general shape of all the neighbourhoods within the reach of their powers.

(Cohen, 1972: 54)

As Cohen's (1972) now seminal youth subcultural work in traditional white working-class communities and Nayak's (2003b) more recent work on Chavs and Real Geordies in globalizing regions of the UK suggest, the neighbourhood remains a powerful metaphor and practical site for the organization of youth practices, highlighting connections between the ever-changing nature of geographical areas, the physical structures young people encounter and the various affective attachments for those who inhabit such spaces. Such linkages between neighbourhood, physical structures and affect therefore still exist as powerful cultural contexts for the making of youthful symbolic orders, where meaningful activity is enacted and embodied in everyday life. Importantly, however, the corridor on its own seems a rather limited space for understanding young people's expressions of the 'cultural ordinary' and youthful symbolic orders. Clearly, some of the complex geographies and performances of neighbourhood life and young people's associated affective investments lie outside

135

the range of schooling or the more obvious forms of subcultural peer rivalry associated with the authorized spatial power of the school corridor.

In this chapter, we therefore turn away from the corridors of power in urban schools and turn towards the local spatial contours of urban neighbourhoods and young people's imaginations of city space. In this turn towards the imaginative elements of urban space, we seek to explore, at the level of affect, young people's imaginaries of their fringe neighbourhood in the global city, the lived 'cartographies of power' and associated contradictions which they must struggle to apprehend. We are most interested in the 'structures of feeling' young people express about neighbourhoods which have been transformed by forms of retrenchment and regeneration simultaneously. As we show, young people who live daily with substantial economic disadvantage and vast scales of urban regeneration often experience their neighbourhood 'as deeply ambivalent understandings of their social context' (Reay & Lucey, 2003: 121), particularly in relation to feelings of home, belonging and security. Here we witness the power of urban social-class relations to be resignified as individualized human emotion. As Leo, a 14-year-old Italian-Canadian, remarked in Tower Hill:

LEO: My apartment is not safe 'cause there's ways to get in the building, like through the steps, [...] and everything is always unlocked and in my area of [Tower Hill] there's a lot of dumb people [...] [coming in and out of the building].

INTERVIEWER: How do you feel about that?

LEO: Not really [too bad], 'cause my brother's usually home 'cause he's still young right, but when he gets older and you see all these kids together [...]. So I think they do drugs [...]. And there's always a problem.

In Vancouver (Beacon Park), similar sentiments were expressed by young people about their locale, particularly as they were being persistently confronted with new communities of low-income and/or homeless groups sleeping rough and who had been pushed out of the inner-city as a consequence of new urban legislation (e.g. Safe Streets Act) and radical regeneration strategies in operation at the urban core (Sarah, Beacon Park):

We had a problem with substitutes or student teachers 'cause they won't want to come [...] – 'they are young hooligans, they are starting their life of drug addiction' – I find it very insulting because [...] my teachers have showed frustration [...] because they would not be able to get a substitute. It's hard for the kids, it feels like 'what did we do?' When I tell somebody I go to [name of school], they'll say you are like a gangster chick. It's labelling. It's a stereotype.

These examples offered by young people provide some insight into how one might begin to link concepts of youth narrativization, disciplining categories of the classed person (e.g. 'Gangsta chick'), and spaces of representation which ultimately include the imaginative, dialectical and productive elements of collectively experienced spaces: 'These include symbolic differentiations and collective fantasies around space, the resistances to the dominant practices and resulting forms of individual and collective transgression' (Stahl, 1999: 52). It is with these ideas in mind that we examine the imaginative force of space in young people's lives and how they attempt to resolve some of the conflicts, dilemmas and exclusions they experience as members of their neighbourhood and locale.

We focus indirectly throughout on the concepts of 'ambivalent modes of knowing', 'space invaders' and 'trespassing' as part of young people's spatial experience whereby they experience substantial unease in urban mobility operating primarily through their representations of place. In so doing, we reveal young people's imaginary relationship to real space which often leads to what Jameson (cited in Ross, 2000) has identified as 'existential bewilderment' in highly moralizing fringe sites (see Roy & Al-Sayad, 2004). In the following sections, we explore two conceptual themes concerned with young people's conceptions of their neighbourhood: the affective force of notions of home and space invaders in urban sites of abjection; and class strategies for coping with cultural aliens in fringe neighbourhoods.

Warehousing Young People in the Space of the City and the Affective Confines of Home: Space Invaders in Urban Sites of Abjection

Is there still a living choice between Necropolis and Utopia: the possibility of building a new kind of city that will, freed of inner contradictions, positively enrich and further human development?

(Mumford, 1922; cited in Wilson, 1995: 146)

Cities are always too complex to be captured in axioms ... The close relationship between space and society, between cities and history ... [results not in] the coherent spatial form of an overwhelming social logic ... but [in] the tortured and disorderly, yet beautiful patchwork of human creation and suffering.

(Manuel Castells, 1978; cited in Wilson, 1995: 146)

As some globalization theorists and cultural geographers have suggested (see, e.g., Appadurai, Buroway, Castells, Jameson), there has been a return to the idea of the imagination of city space as operating as a container or place-holder for weighty emotions such as loss, nostalgia and hope. As Appadurai (1996) argues, these affective dimensions of urban experience have multiple functions which provoke the potential for some collective urban experience (e.g. feeling safe in a space). Alternatively, the affective may take the form of denial or revulsion if the space is represented as pathological or as stigmatized and does not offer the promise of autonomy or any potential for individual freedoms (see Bettie, 2003). City spaces are therefore emblematic of precisely the forms of classification which are seen to operate most substantially in moral fields of social practice associated with wider social class relations. Appadurai (1996: 53) writes:

> the imagination has become an organized field of social practices, a form of work (in the sense of both labour and culturally organized practice), and a form of negotiation between sites of agency (individuals) and globally defined fields of possibility.

How do young people who are confined to low-income globalizing neighbourhoods or city spaces that are pathologized by the wider public imaginary experience their neighbourhood as an organized field of social practices during times of substantial retrenchment? How do they respond to such social stigmas and what are the forms of alienation and interpellation they draw upon to survive? How do young people fuse different and contesting social-class horizons as one mechanism for resolving the ambiguities and contradictions present in urban concentrations of poverty?

In both Tower Hill (Toronto) and Beacon Park (Vancouver), the social confinement of young people to particular places can be seen to contribute to what one young person referred to as 'warehousing kids' and what Bourdieu identifies as being 'chained to a place' (Bourdieu, 2001; see also Reay & Lucey, 2003). This chaining effect was not visible in any obvious or objective way. More typically, it was expressed through a geography of emotions or what might loosely be referred to as a 'Prisoner's Cinema'[1] which left young people feeling paralysed, in the dark or *lost* about urban and academic mobility, and carrying highly ambivalent emotions about the neighbourhoods in which they lived. It was either through the interpellation of others as against oneself (e.g. 'lots of dumb people') or through contradiction ('don't really like it here but don't want to go anywhere else') that a structure of feeling about place – especially in response to questions about *home* – emerged. To put this another way, the feelings of what Wright (1997) has referred to as both spatial confinement and displacement were often manifest in young people's conceptualizations of urban space, even as they sought to create class fantasies of a perfect domestic home life in their everyday lives. As a poetics of fantasy and imagination, such creations were most evident in the visual projects young people participated in as part of the ethnographic study (such as the photo-narrative seen in Figure 5.1). This attitude towards neighbourhood – as both confining and as 'home' – is evident in the following interview and photo-narrative project completed with Clara, a 14-year-old girl who had recently arrived as a refugee from West Africa:

CLARA: [Referring to photo narratives] What I would like about this place is it's very quiet and lovely.

INTERVIEWER: Is it very quiet?

CLARA: Yeah, it's very quiet.

INTERVIEWER: And no problems on the street or anything?

CLARA: No.

INTERVIEWER: So you live there with your family [sister]?

CLARA: Yeah. [...] She doesn't have a job right now. My building [...] someone got killed there. Yeah, in the elevator.

INTERVIEWER: Oh, what happened?

CLARA: [...] I'm not really sure but I heard this guy got killed inside the elevator. I went there, I seen, yeah, and the guy got killed inside the elevator cause he ... I think he was dealing with drugs or something.

In the photograph to which Clara is referring in this interview, stands one of the tower apartments common to this urban fringe neighborhood; above it, Clara has written 'Home Sweet Home'.

The message which is hidden but immanent in this narrative account is that of an injury over which Clara has no control. Indeed, the progressively worsening cuts in social support and public housing subsidies for economically disadvantaged young people living in urban fringe sites in Ontario from the early 1990s onward have led to a rise in crime in urban housing projects in Canadian cities (see Campaign, 2000). Such cuts to social welfare support have meant that many people who live on the urban fringe of economic disadvantage must deny their reality to gain a sense of place or to avoid the experience of shame. Class fantasies therefore emerge as powerful forms of denial about the safety of place. In this case, we witness a 'state of injury' (see Brown, 1995) but this is not an individual state. Rather, it is a class creation that becomes necessary as one seeks to overcome an abjection that can never be registered as either individual or as human.

In the absence of a clear sense of place, and to avoid what Frederic Jameson refers to as 'existential bewilderment' (see Ross, 1988: 7), young people often resorted to fierce assertions of identity alongside the expression of a deeply ambivalent sense of place. These reactions emerged partly as a response to a constellation of distinct social forces (e.g. reduced policing in particular housing projects, heightened racial conflicts outside

Figure 5.1 Clara's Photo-Narrative: Tower Hill, Toronto, Ontario.

the school and in the neighbourhood) impacting upon the integrity of the urban communities in both sites and their ability to remain cohesive. This became increasingly evident as NGOs and social services in both neighbourhoods began to compete for municipal resources, and youth and social workers were cut substantially in both Tower Hill and Beacon Park. Clara's spatial imaginary was, then, intimately related to the temporal configurations of social change and neo-liberal assaults on her urban neighbourhood, as well as to her ambivalent feelings about an under-resourced public housing project on the edge of the urban core. In understanding her spatial location in the urban city, she bore the 'weight of the world' (Bourdieu, 2006) and carried with her intensely utopian fantasies of 'home'. A similar account of home and place is offered by Georgina, a Filipino-Canadian girl from Tower Hill (aged 15):

Some people may describe this place as bad but I don't think so because I feel safe [...]. Well I don't feel safe but like I'm used to it so

I can say that I know the place so I can go anywhere and I won't get lost [...]. But there is lots of crime.

Similar sentiments and class fantasies about security and danger emerged in Beacon Park, the fringe site in Vancouver. Here Mandy (aged 16), a Cambodian-Canadian, provides a window of illumination into her spatial imaginary. While there is less ambivalence in Mandy's account when compared to Clara's (Mandy, for example, lives in a low rise which is better funded and closer to the urban core), young people were persistently struggling to find comfortable metaphors for their neighbourhoods without feeling shame or experiencing disorientation:

INTERVIEWER: Do you like the neighbourhood?

MANDY: No! (laughing)

INTERVIEWER: Tell me more about that.

MANDY: It's kind of dangerous, well scary 'cause I live near [street name] in the project area.

[...]

INTERVIEWER: Are you living in the project?

MANDY: Yeah.

INTERVIEWER: Oh, what's it called? You don't have to tell me the name of it. Is it high-rise or low-rise? Subsidised housing, in other words, some of it's paid for by the government?

MANDY: Yeah.

INTERVIEWER: Can you say a little bit more about that?

MANDY: Yeah like prostitutes are around the corner and sometimes I'm embarrassed to tell people where I live too.

[...]

MANDY: But it's ok because quite a few of my friends live around there too.

INTERVIEWER: Right from school, from (name of school).

MANDY: Yeah.

INTERVIEWER: So one of the things you're saying about the area is that you feel like it might be a bit dangerous.

MANDY: Yeah.

INTERVIEWER: And that there's some prostitution.

MANDY: Yeah.

INTERVIEWER: Right in your building?

MANDY: No, just on the street and it's just dangerous to walk around at night but during daytime it's alright.

[...]

INTERVIEWER: Inside your building would you say it's safe?

MANDY: They are different houses backed together.

INTERVIEWER: So separate independent houses?

MANDY: Yeah.

[...]

INTERVIEWER: Anything else that goes on there? Anything that you want to share about the projects and the people. How would you describe the people who are living there?

MANDY: Most of them are pretty friendly 'cause they have like group gatherings too sometimes. Programmes and they help you to like, if you're 15–18, they help you get a job, a summer job. So it's pretty supporting.

INTERVIEWER: If you could live somewhere else any idea where [you'd live]?

MANDY: A rich place. A nicer place.

INTERVIEWER: Tell me what that would be.

MANDY: A nice clean area that is quiet, and 'cause around my area is lots of noise too and it's disturbing.

INTERVIEWER: Do you know parts of the city that you think would be better? Have you been in any?

MANDY: Yeah, sometimes I hear that if it's too quiet then that's where the most dangers happen, 'cause like kidnapping and stuff.

Mandy's words convey how, as Massey puts it, 'space is constituted through social relations and material social practices' (1994: 337). These relations and practices are not outside the imaginary young people carry with them as they seek recognition or engage in the project of self-making in the city. In this complex spatial terrain, young people must necessarily fantasize about being something else, as a fantasy narrative that exists beyond their working-class category and any associated forms of revulsion, abjection or disgust ('a rich place, a nice place'). To return to Lawler (2005: 429) once more:

> What was at issue for Orwell was less literal (real or imagined) than what smell signifies – the alterity, for the middle classes, of working class existence. [Being disgusted] is at the very core of their subjectivity: their very selves are produced in opposition to the low and the low cannot do anything but repulse them.

To put this another way, the classed dimensions of social space cannot exist without an abject identity as its spectacular material and cultural backdrop (see Figure 5.2 as a photo-narrative of such a space in Tower Hill).

At the same time, young people must also read their lives and notions of legitimate selfhood as a reaction to the apparent 'invader' (the 'prostitute', the 'bums'), to aliens or to trespassers of their space (such as a new group of homeless people or a visible minority group who have not yet learned English) in an effort to make 'noise' and re-classify oneself and others as a

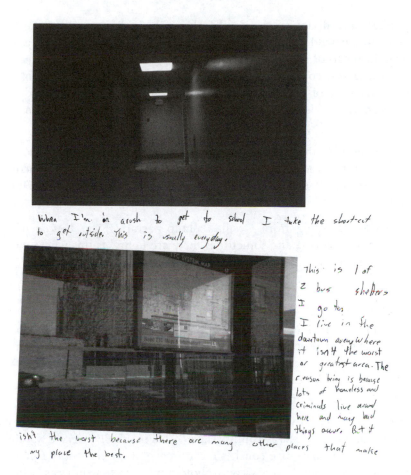

When I'm in a rush to get to school I take the short-cut to get inside. This is usually everyday.

This is 1 of 2 bus shelters I go to. I live in the downtown area, where it isn't the worst or greatest area. The reason being is because lots of homeless and criminals live around here and many bad things occur. But it

isn't the worst because there are many other places that make my place the best.

Figure 5.2 Student Photo-Narrative: Tower Hill, Toronto, Ontario.

response to a 'semantic disorder' which operates in and through the split character of a stigmatized site (see Hebdige, 1979). Hence, young people imagine urban space as a fusing of class horizons which bridge 'being affected by the past [inherited class conditions] and our imaginative projection of a history yet to be made' (Kearney, 2004: 60). Deviations from these fused horizons and expected narrative plots regarding one's legitimacy and future in this place, regardless of the desire a young person may have to move out of this space, are likely to have very disorienting outcomes. These experiences of disorientation occur not only in Canada. As Jameson writes (cited in Ross, 1988: 7):

What is striking about the new essembles around Paris […] is that there is absolutely no perspective at all. Not only has the street disappeared (that was already the task of modernism) but all profiles have disappeared as well. This is bewildering, and I use existential bewilderment in the new post-modern space to make a final diagnosis of the loss of our ability to position ourselves within this space and cognitively map it. This is then projected back on the emergence of a global, multinational culture that is decentered and cannot be visualized, a culture in which one cannot position oneself.

This decentring, this feeling of a lack of vision, also led to highly disorienting accounts of neighbourhood safety in both Tower Hill and Beacon Park. As Cecilia, a Portuguese-Canadian living on the fringe of Tower Hill, remarks:

INTERVIEWER: [Reading from Cecilia's photo-narrative] 'So this is just where people hang and sometimes there are fights.' Is this where you got into some of your fights, too, in that neighbourhood?

CECILIA: Yup.

INTERVIEWER: Yeah. Would you rather live some place else or are you happy there?

CECILIA: I'm kind of happy but my mom just had a baby so I don't think it's the proper neighbourhood for the baby to grow up in. Right?

INTERVIEWER: [...] What are you gonna do?

CECILIA: My mom's trying to move out of there.

In her photo narratives, Cecilia documents the 'shortcut' that she uses to get to school when she is running late ('This is usually every day,' she notes). Her photo-narrative consists of an image of a long empty tunnel that leads underground. In a second photograph, she has showcased the local bus shelter, which she identifies as one of two that she uses. Her written piece accompanying this photograph contains the following comments: 'I live in the downtown area which isn't the worst or greatest area. The reason being is because lots of homeless and criminals live in this area and many bad things occur. But it isn't the worst because there are many other places that make my place the best' (see also Figure 5.2, p. 143).

Louis, a 15-year-old, first-generation immigrant from El Salvador living in Vancouver, represented similarly ambivalent spatial imaginaries in his account of Beacon Park. In his photo-narrative he wrote: '[name of street] is like a second home to me because I see it everyday. When I go to school I pass by it and when I visit it I see my friends at work.' In his next photo (see Figure 5.3), he wrote the following in relation to the same neighbourhood street: 'As you can see this is what I see every day on my way to school. Most people on the [street name] try to sell weed to me and I always say no. After a while it gets annoying.'

Figure 5.3 Louis's Photo-Narrative: Beacon Park, Vancouver, BC.

Another student from Tower Hill in Toronto reported that 'people on the street are always screaming at each other'.

This personal struggle between recognizing 'place' as a symbolic marker of multiple dangers, yet striving to reconfigure it as one that 'isn't the worst', 'as a second home' or 'there are lots of things that make my place the best' indicates the degree of affective ambivalence emerging from the pressures contingent upon middle-class assertions of urban space and one's own recognition of a shameful or abject identity associated with such spaces (see Binnie & Skeggs, 2004). Such structures of feeling point to the effects of class conflict on the urban fringe whilst other middle-class neighbourhoods are permitted by wider social-class relations to define their own borders and communities or keep others from trespassing. For many young people, it means they have indeed lost a meaningful and coherent sense of place or are unable to position themselves within it, and if they attempt to gain mobility they often express feelings of being out of place or as trespassing and as therefore unrecognizable.

The symbolic force of the concept of 'home' was also applied by young people to others who were sometimes deemed as foes or as abject in some ways, such that they represented even greater feelings of loss and nostalgia for those who were classifying them. They often applied these expressions of abjection towards groups of homeless young people in the past and the present which the youth participants studied in our classroom lessons. Even though many of our participants in both sites had learned through classroom lessons that youth homelessness and panhandling had recently become a criminal offence (hence young people's forced mobility to the edge of the city, a forced invisibility facilitated by legislation such as the Safe Streets Acts in both BC and Ontario), class denial, class insult and sameness remained at the centre of their explanations for why homeless youth were forced to sleep rough far from the urban core. In captioning a media account of Squeegee kids sleeping rough outside a Toronto sports stadium, the SkyDome, Marty, a 15-year-old from Vancouver wrote:

> People of all ages come here when they have no place to go. Here nobody is different. Everyone is alike here. Homeless. Kids and adults and troubled teens all come here when there is nowhere else to go. Here others might think it's hell or it's a dump. But to these people it is a home and to others a home away from home. They get a good night's sleep here.

Another student wrote: 'they sleep here because they are lazy.' And another wrote: 'They shouldn't be here in our neighbourhood.'

Louis Althusser, Stuart Hall and Raymond Williams, often forgotten in contemporary cultural theory, remind us that tensions between home and displacement must not be read as a personal or individualized feeling, expressed here as trespassing. Instead one can read these tensions as a deeply classed form of interpellation and a spatialization of emotion necessary for coping with the realities of living in a highly stigmatized neighbourhood witnessing increasing levels of homelessness, degeneration and regeneration simultaneously. These scales of change might explain, at least in part, why such fantasies of home emerge as they do – often tied to young people's utopian dreams of a middle-class life where the concept of home is imagined as safe and carries with it the 'exegesis of narrative comfort' (see Steedman, 1995) without the moral traces and classed projections of disorder, disgust or shame. Such class fantasies necessarily emerged as a social symptom of powerlessness and as a form of existential loss or as a redress to it.

Importantly, too, these class fantasies and spatial imaginaries cannot be understood beyond the socio-spatial or material relations young people were experiencing. Rather, structures of feeling bound by fear, denial and interpellation must be understood as symptomatic of the unfolding of widening class relations, a long history of middle-class projections about working-class neighbourhoods, and transnational forms of urban regeneration which are refracting themselves through the specificities of local spaces which constantly negotiate between the centre, margins and the periphery in highly complex ways. We therefore return to the question with which we opened this section, as posed by Lewis Mumford: 'Is there still a living choice between Necropolis and Utopia: the possibility of building a new kind of city that will, freed of inner contradictions, positively enrich and further human development?'

Class Strategies, Cultural Aliens and the Urban Imaginary: Representing and Resolving Dangers in the City

It is one thing to imagine your place in the city and altogether a different matter to seek resolutions to both real and symbolic forms of danger encountered in urban space. How do young people living at the edge of the inner-city resolve urban conflicts at a highly individualized level? What strategies do they draw upon to survive trans-local imaginaries which are both familiar and strange, safe and dangerous, friendly and hostile?

In attempting to answer these questions, we consider the power of imaginative contexts, of classifying contexts and of territorial contexts (see Lefebvre, 1991). In so doing we have come to understand the power of geography to shape young people's feelings of security and urban belonging, particularly through vivid phenomenological descriptions of space or, in geographical terms, what could be called an urban imaginary. We also witness the linkage of urban spaces and wider social relations which carry with them multiple, historical layers of cultural understanding which serve to constitute such spaces. These include class fantasies about the space, as well as differentiated conceptions of it which point to the necessary strategies young people must draw upon to assess the real social conditions underwriting their experiences. These strategies provide some context for understanding how it is that young people ultimately form horizons of identity which are constrained by their horizons of possibility in any given space. These possibilities form part of young people's imaginary but not in the conditions of their own making, and any strategies for confronting space are not free 'choices' but are instead tied to symbolic distinctions and classifying histories of space itself.

Young people in both Beacon Park and Tower Hill mentioned strategies they drew upon to increase their sense of safety within neighbourhoods objectified as dangerous, and often experienced as such. Strategies included saying 'Hi' to an imaginary person in a doorway, in order to suggest to any potential nearby predators that they were being observed and cared for by another responsible adult. Many witnessed regular and overt drug use on the streets and in the school, increasing their sense of their local neighbourhood as dangerous. Young people also reported strategies such as 'street crossing' and other related urban strategies for avoiding 'dealers' and 'bums'. Many young people felt that many criminal activities were taking place with impunity or that they had been effectively abandoned, with no police presence or the wrong kind of police presence to curb them.[2] Such accounts provide insight into a 'structure of feeling' founded upon circulating social fears of abandonment and exclusion. As Vicki (aged 15) writes about her public housing project in Tower Hill:

nothing bad has happened for the past two years [...] but before that someone got killed. And then someone got abducted on the street nearby [But my building is pretty much safe] [...]. The police are never on my street. Never. They are dealing just outside my door.

These structures of feeling are not located inside the marked bodies of economically disadvantaged individuals who are sometimes seen to own such feelings as free liberal subjects in the new 'global city'. Nor do young people possess the degree of autonomy they imagine in the 'risk society' even if such imagined freedom emerges as a response to heightened individualization operating in the early twenty-first century. Rather, their feelings are better read as attempts to make sense of their lives – to find what Hebdige refers to as a 'magical solution' (1977) – in light of deeply contradictory social messages and experiences about the very spaces they inhabit.

On the one hand, young people living at the turn of the twenty-first century are expected to absorb the dominant belief that their situations are theirs to make the best of ('we are not what we are but what we make of ourselves'; see Giddens, 1991: 75), and that they are limited only by their own skills and willingness to persevere. On the other hand, within the context of socio-spatial relations, young people daily confront circumstances which are wholly beyond their control, largely the products of differentiated scales of neo-liberal restructuring of urban cities, new migration patterns and schools targeted as 'demonized' and often thought to be in need of middle-class interests and imaginaries (e.g. specialist choice schools). This lack of control was often resolved in forms of denial and ambivalence and, when possible, resilience.

Wider forms of ambivalence often extended beyond students' urban location to their families' working situation, where young people consistently affirmed that their situation was tolerable, was 'okay', even after sharing family experiences which appeared objectively as deeply challenging. As Hayden, a 15-year-old Portuguese boy living with his mother, remarks:

HAYDEN: Like my mom goes to work in the morning at like six till, like four o'clock. Then she goes to work at five till nine, till 10, I think.
INTERVIEWER: Somewhere else?
HAYDEN: Yeah.
INTERVIEWER: At another place? So she's got two jobs?
HAYDEN: Yeah.
INTERVIEWER: Alright. So one factory in the daytime.
HAYDEN: And then cleaning an office building in the night.

When asked the question, 'What's the ideal situation? Would you prefer your mother to be in a different situation or for you to be in a different situation?' Hayden went on to respond that:

HAYDEN: No, everything's okay for me.
INTERVIEWER: Yeah?
HAYDEN: Yeah.

This pattern re-emerged in interview after interview. Another participant, who had been forced to flee Haiti in the wake of an impending political crisis, was living in public housing with her sister and two nieces. This young woman, aged 15, was responsible for a large part of the care of her sister's children. Nonetheless, when asked by the researcher, 'And are you finding it tough at home with the money and the [care] situation or is it working out okay?' [bracket our addition], the participant responded, 'It's working out okay.'

There are myriad ways in which young people's structures of feeling may be theorized. For example, Reay and Lucey (2000, 2003) describe ambivalence as a form of working-class resilience or refusal, a manner of seeing things as bearable, 'even OK', in order not to be overwhelmed. In bearing the weight of their worlds, they argue that young people are engaging in the dual process of refusal and 'reclassification'. Reclassification is one action young people undertake to cope in uncertain worlds and to negotiate the class conflicts between home, unfamiliarity and risk. Another more spatially oriented interpretation we might offer is that when a place (such as public housing) does not belong to the individual but, rather, the individual must belong to it, ambivalent readings, associated class fantasies and the search for magical resolutions (now thought also to be dead) should not be unexpected (see Wright, 1997). Indeed, feelings of placelessness or even displacement as a form of positional suffering may dominate the consciousness of those who are not choosing a place called 'home' or a 'demonized' school. Clearly, it is in the very relation of the classes and urban spaces to each other that abjection and shame about one's place must necessarily exist. Most middle-class youth have substantially more spatial resources. They are often driven home in cars, live in property owned by their families or walk home through leafy neighbourhoods and have little cause to worry about the 'dangers' of inner-city life. Such early degrees of spatial mobility reinforce social advantages accorded to those who live in privileged areas of the city.

Against the knowledge of such mobility, the experience of economic disadvantage and 'failing schools' confirms economically disadvantaged young people's distinctiveness to others and to themselves as abject non-citizens. Young people are, to borrow from Bourdieu (1984), obliged to navigate the path of a particular distinction but this navigation always requires a double consciousness. This double consciousness represents itself in the dual forms of potential anxiety both in deviating from a place called home and in the recognition of being chained to a place. In this way, place and youth cultural identity are closely intertwined. As Bourdieu reminds us, the urban city and the 'demonized' school – now celebrated as sites of world-class opportunity in the affluent 'West' – persist in the transnational world as a kind of spatially organized, permeable container for 'potential outcasts', who experience them as both contradictions and as forms of shame

> associated with the type of education that is an end in itself [...]. All one can do is to try and prolong the period of time in the state of uncertainty that itself keeps him/her from mastering that period of time.
>
> (Cited in Reid, 2002: 351)

Finally, if we are to return to the very core of class conflict as we read young people's accounts of space, then we are enabled to visualize and witness the very symbolic power of the imaginary in the making of identities.

Yet such claims are not supportive of a derivative class account of the urban imaginary. As we have shown, there are also signs of change in how diverse groups of economically disadvantaged youth think about their futures in relation to urban space and contemporary school life which would serve to contest any straightforward form of class reproduction. First, unlike working-class youth in earlier studies, such as those portrayed in early British cultural studies research, male and female youth at Tower Hill (Toronto site) and Beacon Park (Vancouver site) showed strong desires to break their own class ranks, did not carry working-class pride and sought to escape their feelings of spatial entrapment. Paradoxically, however, these desires were themselves often trapped in a political economy of urban constraints and 'structures of feeling' that young people held towards the spaces and urban schools in which they were confined. The outcome was deep ambivalence towards the spaces they inhabited, as well as towards any one person's ability to provide them with security under the dynamics of neo-liberal retrenchment. Yet, class conflicts associated with the abandonment of such spaces, with a lack of social recognition, or with late-modern forms of social or academic mobility seemed to signal an impossible future for many of these young people, even as class fantasies persisted in powerful ways.

Given such a situation, what appeared important, but was seemingly absent from young people's understanding, was the possession of a 'cognitive map' of the present (Jameson, 1991), one that could provide young people with an understanding of the space's real historicity, with some acknowledgement of why they must bear the burden of shame for a space which they themselves have not made (Jameson, cited in Durham & Kellner, 2001). Jameson provides some explanation for why these feelings might exist. He writes:

> In a classic work, *The Image of the City*, Kevin Lynch taught us that the alienated city is above all a space in which people are unable to map (in their minds) either their own positions or the urban totality in which they find themselves: grids such as those of Jersey City, in which none of the traditional markers (monuments, nodes, natural boundaries, built perspectives) obtain, are the most obvious examples.
>
> (Jameson, cited in Durham & Kellner, 2001: 584)

The notion, then, of an urban imaginary enables 'a situational representation on the part of the individual subject to that vaster and properly unrepresentable totality which is the ensemble of society's structures as a whole' (Jameson, cited in Ross, 2000: 51). But, importantly, in these imaginaries young people are not relating centre to periphery unless they are operating solely on a metaphorical description of their neighbourhoods (i.e. as 'ghettos', prisons or as 'warehouses'). Nor are their representations of the city grounded in pride of place, a class pride or a set of well-known monuments and historic sites. Rather, their representations provide a cartography of emotion which in part remains outside the realm of language or any twenty-first-century form of cosmopolitanism. As Althusser's conception of Lacanian ideology necessarily reminds us: 'the representation of the subject's Imaginary relationship to his or her Real conditions of existence' (Jameson, cited in Ross, 2000: 51) provides a context for ambivalent modes of knowing and interpellation. Importantly, though, the 'Real conditions of existence' remain, for these young people, beyond the present. History, in this case, therefore functions as an 'absent cause', insofar as it remains unspeakable as a foundation for class imaginaries that lead to feelings of shame or even denial. As Jameson (cited in Durham & Kellner, 2001) reminds us, we may never get beyond the challenge of a multitude of ideological contradictions operating as layers of complex emotion and cultural antagonisms in the urban landscape; however, as he asserts, it is crucial, nonetheless, to acknowledge that these emotions and antagonisms are, in fact, driving young people's fantasy constructions and play some part in the very making of youth cultures.

In the next chapter, we move away from a focused concentration on conceptions of urban space towards a more substantial framing of youth cultural belonging associated with new patterns of race relations in youth cultures at the urban fringe. In so doing, we seek to reveal how new urban social divisions are shaping the ways in which young people conceptualize race relations and new youth cultures, as well as the role that symbolic elements of a highly moralizing post-9/11 racial order play in reshaping young people's experience of the city and school.

6

Impossible Citizens in the Global Metropolis
Race, Landscapes of Power and the New 'Emotional Geographies' of the City

I would like to give you a few words about becoming a citizen. Well from my point of view a good citizen should be someone that doesn't hang out with gangsters because they give you bad influences. And I would recommend you to respect others because that way they would also respect you. I should also say that you should hang out with people who are friendly because that way you can learn more from them than from gangsters, and trust me, gangsters ain't cool. And you <u>MUST</u> show everyone even that if you are an immigrant that you can do everything that us Canadians can do! By that I mean you should be working harder than other people. Lastly there shouldn't be any racism. That's all the advice I can give you. Hope you enjoy Canada.

(Shing Lu, Chinese-Canadian, 14, Beacon Park)

Shing Lu, an immigrant girl from China, offers a window of illumination into some of the social relations which frame youth classifications of the legitimate and illegitimate subject in the late-modern Canadian city. The means by which these classifications are reasserted, reclaimed and maintained are through the forms of bricolage or pastiche young people piece together where signifiers from the margins (e.g. the 'immigrant') are incorporated into elements of a dominant national narrative (e.g. respect, hard work) which function to evade the wider problematic of race in relation to youth legitimacy and belonging. In this chapter, we look more closely at some of the hidden dimensions of racialization which unfold and overlap in the form of moral claims constantly circulating in the cultural ordinary of youth subcultural and post-subcultural practice.

In the previous chapter, we sought to reveal how reconfigurations of spatiality and young people's urban imaginaries both in and out of school impact upon social relations and the associated 'psychic costs' at the level of youth cultural practice. A close ethnographic encounter with these social relations exposed the power of gender, home and spatiality – as particularly weighty class signifiers – to modify the ways in which young people performed their cultural activities, engaged in peer rivalry and narrated their experiences of exclusion. These narrations appear to be tied to the ways that social class and race relations are linked to tastes, style and forms of gendered affiliation, all part of a wider classification system upon which young people draw in the justification of cultural actions and in the attribution of meaning to particular youth groupings. In particular, such attributions can be seen to be authorized through the operation of language games and the re-appropriation of compulsory heterosexuality in and through the spaces where young people reside. Against this background, the corridor and the neighbourhood emerged – not unsurprisingly – as a site 'fraught with competition, negotiation and accommodation occurring on multiple and intersecting planes' (Stahl, 1999: 3). In the authorization of particular ideas of selfhood in the corridor as well as on the street, we can witness both traditional and new youth cultural patterns co-existing. But in both cases – the established and the novel – the youth subcultural dimension of positionality, symbolic power and class protection retained a dominating presence. Subcultural style is always designed in part to make 'noise' essential to the success of the group, most often through a discourse of gender and social class, with the racial categories of Thug and Gangsta expressing the post-war 'phantom history of race relations' (Hebdige, 1979).

Here then we move beyond the authorized language of city streets to showcase the ways in which new patterns of race relations emerge and are 'deposited' upon what Stahl (1999) has called the already 'loaded surface' of working-class youth cultures living at the urban fringe, in circumstances of unprecedented national security and moral anxiety directed particularly towards low-income young people. Intimations of the scale and direction of these anxieties may be seen in their dissemination through the agencies of an increasingly sophisticated and globalized visual, electronic and print media (e.g. Levi & Wall, 2004; Lyon, 2004; Mason, 2004). The folk 'agents' of the accelerating threat which is presumed to be levelled at the 'West' in this moment are portrayed as typically living on the fringe – both literally and metaphorically – of global cities.

It is with the complex currents of this late-modern context in mind that we now move forward to address wider questions about youth cultures, particularly as they interface with late-modern forms of politically driven morality associated with migration patterns and circulating perceptions of the 'global city'. The questions we ask here are: How have wider media discourses of terror associated with low income groups shifted the character of everyday youth racism, and impinged upon daily patterns of youth cultural activity? How might we understand the character, as well as the dimensions, of the consuming combination of suspicion and dread seen to be posed by post-9/11 low-income urban youth? How might we begin to comprehend, at the level of the everyday, the new geographies of difference and the novel strategies by which young people endeavour to respond to such anxieties in terms of youth subcultural and post-subcultural practice? And how do patterns of race relations, inherited through distinctive migration patterns in particular spaces, influence the expression of the complex concerns of the contemporary urban city? In effect, these key questions speak to the pervasive issue that informs the entire book, which is to say: How might we witness, through the lens of youth culture itself, the social construction of difference, both in and through place? The primary empirical reference point for this chapter is the Vancouver site (Beacon Park), as the research here was undertaken in a post-9/11 context. By contrast, the Toronto work, begun in 1999 and not completed until the immediate aftermath of 9/11, will serve as a point of temporal and spatial comparison with the Vancouver setting.

Rethinking Moral Panic, Regulation and the New Folk Devils of the Twenty-First-Century City: Enduring Conceptual Themes and New Directions

As discussed in the Introduction to the book, the seminal notion of moral panic – albeit reconfigured for the twenty-first century – with all its intimations of social paranoia and urban decline, generalized decay and impending crisis, can certainly be seen as retaining some of its original conceptual power. It also continues to afford an important conceptual strategy through which to address the contemporary problems experienced by excluded, low-income youth impacted by large-scale migratory flows, and by the vast scale of changes that are emerging between nations and cities. Here, the threat of those constructed as youthful twenty-first-century 'folk devils' provides the symbolic focus for the localized expression of a globalized, highly mobile social perception of uncertainty, loss and anxiety. In the new times of the twenty-first century, however, the basis for moral panic no longer consists only in localized class threats – such as those issued by the Mods and Rockers battling on the beach at Clacton, or by the early Hip Hop and Latino gangs of Los Angeles.[1] Rather, the new moral registers of change available to excluded urban youth must be seen as involving behaviours, practices and strategies which are now global as well as local and national, and which can be referred to as trans-local. In the light of such changes, we have sought to travel beyond the school and towards young people's more general accounts of schooling, of the city, and of the wider processes of racialization as they impinge upon new class conflicts operating at the fringe of a radically reconfigured urban core.

Again we return to the work of Paul Ricoeur, to Wendy Brown and youth cultural theorists to explore the ways in which the historically sedimented category of 'race' and its associated moral economies have become deeply implicated in the production of cultural exclusion. Here, we uncover the operation of new youth classification processes which are linked to wider transformations in the relationship between race, the scale of urbanization in the city and wider national and global imaginaries which not only operate locally but are mobile in young people's inherited memories of home and nation. In so doing, we show how forms of nationalism (both micro and macro), as inherited forms of ethnic and class conflict centring upon home and place, together with the burdens and pleasures of their personal, family and migrant histories, reconfigure classification struggles and racialized conflicts within the urban landscapes in which young people are obliged to live.

We trace three key themes which pertain to race, class, and wider moral claims which circulate about the good and legitimate young person. First, we critique recent interventions by cultural studies theorists that focus solely on concepts such as 'hybridity' (the new 'cultural hybrid') and cultural identity (McCrae, 2006). While offering important insights into young people's contemporary experiences of race, these approaches may sometimes fail to capture the complexity of the production of race as a 'structure of feeling', and as new patterns of racial classification within particular urban contexts (see Kennelly & Dillabough, 2008). This complexity can be understood by exploring the interpretive meanings of race that are produced within the sphere of youth cultural activity at a phenomenological, affective, temporal and spatial level – that is to say, at the level of interpretation in specific locations and particular times. The meanings which are generated through young people's attempts to classify others and themselves in relation to race are never singularly tied to the moment of contemporary experience. Rather, they are inflected with the traces of the past, and are enacted by young people as an affective form of highly spatialized performance. As Hebdige (1979) writes:

> The succession of white subcultural forms can be read as a series of deep structural adaptations which symbolically accommodate or expunge the black presence from the host community. It is on the plane of aesthetics [...] in the whole rhetoric of style, that we find the dialogue between black and white most subtly and comprehensively recorded in code.

However, despite our shared focus on the symbolic codes of race, we cannot – as Hebdige might have in the past – rely upon racial binaries to understand the production of race among youth cultural groups. Instead we need to turn to both Hall's (1997) and Williams' (1977) powerful expressions – culture is a utopian happening or even a utopian dream – to begin to understand how new racial classifications persist as crystallizations of moral anxiety at the level of class, and as historical burdens tied to the experiences of entrenchment in wider national imaginaries. For young people, these expressions characteristically serve as an imaginary community 'in which human relations are organized more perfectly than in their [own] community' (Cohen 1997: 45), representing a place in which a home or a 'perfect utopia' might be sought but which ultimately comes to represent exclusion in a new urban world order. Modalities of youth representation here speak to the manner in which symbolic expressions of race may reflect a 'feeling' or a class-based anxiety derived from urban membership within a symbolic history and from residual forms of surplus meaning. Some of these feelings emerging in the present – such as race and class denial, along with forms of disgust or class harms – may be conventionally seen as constituting highly problematic behaviour. However, the real power of these experiences lies in their capacity to show us how late-modern structures play a framing role in the cultural formation of young people's utopian fantasies, and in feelings of community loss for past times and places that they may imagine once belonged to them and/or their families. These experiences are significant for their resonances with the geographies of migration, and urban change, and for their capacity to shape the ways in which anxieties may re-emerge as a mode of cultural performance in all spheres of social life.

The second theme centres upon the notion that race is not a 'thing' or an entity which is easily or even *consciously* observed; following E.P. Thompson (1982), we might say that race is rather a happening, a performance and a production. In this way, we are forced to move beyond identity politics – as a liberal project of 'tolerance', a multicultural identity, or in fact as a denial – and towards an understanding of how race is produced through space. In this way, we might argue that divided cities inhabit and live through us spatially, and that any transformation in racial categories or the eradication of racism requires not only a change in how young people come to think about racial classifications but also how they think about and imagine urban space.

The third major theme concerns the role played by 'historical time' in shaping the subcultural and post-subcultural identifications that young people engage in across contexts, and how these remain linked to some of the sedimented and classic subcultural ideas such as the symbolic control of territory, alongside new urban geographies of difference. We might identify this idea of historical time as a form of subcultural representation that functions to some degree as historicized moral anxiety. Here we draw upon Ricoeur's hermeneutic approach which suggests that history and temporality are integral elements of the interpretive struggles undertaken by young people to make sense of their 'positional status' in the urban city. We show how modalities of youth subcultural and post-subcultural representation sometimes emerge from the intersection of circulating panics over race and widening class anxieties which are both new and inherited. Modes of youth representation can therefore be seen as 'human temporality ... concretely lived and described' (see Ricoeur, 1989: 64). Young people are not, by virtue and necessity, constantly reinventing themselves as wholly new 'individuals', as late-twentieth-century discourses of high liberalism and theories of late-modernity might suggest. Rather, as we show, young people are expressing, alongside the cultural force of liberalism(s) and the trajectories of colonialism in everyday life, cultural modalities which remain bound by their specific symbolic inheritances as they navigate new urban boundaries of legitimacy. As we demonstrate, the symbolic power of the relationship between enduring colonial forms, new micro-nationalisms operating at the urban fringe and more recent racialized discourses of terror should not be understated in understanding the local production of race and the racialized transformation of urban youth cultures.

We might perhaps summarize the goals of this chapter by turning to Julie Bettie's injunction to 'think class' with a clarity that will enable us to read the politics of race differently. Bettie (2000) writes:

> Beyond the invisibility of gender, there is also a failure to think class with much clarity. On the Oprah Show, white is middle class, is suburban; black is lower class, is urban. But a slippage occurs where the class references are dropped off and white stands in for [middle class], or where suburban stands in for white and urban for black [...]. There are overly simplified identity categories offered but they do not reflect the complexity of life.

In following this lead, we seek to avoid becoming trapped in the categories of race or class.[2] We therefore move towards an identification of the processes which underlie the production of race and the associated racial/national/global scripts which young people draw upon as they classify themselves and others in the city.[3]

In Search of New Skin: Eminem, Twenty-First-Century 'Boxer Boys' and Wannabe and Official Hardcore Asians

As McDonald (1999: 21) argues, 'in a decentered world social actors face the challenge of forming some sort of unity from their experience in a context where the logics of action are not necessarily coherent.' Here, the self is seen to emerge as a larger social metaphor embedded in meaning, and as an interpretive metaphor of wider social struggles. Rather than always resting within the highly demarcated racial and ethnic categories of times past, or within the more recent post-modern hybridized self, young people find themselves facing new challenges of self-definition in deeply divided urban settings. Obliged to navigate both the hidden class dimensions of ostensibly meritocratic school environments and the apparently obvious racial divisions within schools and neighbourhoods, they are developing new strategies for marking who can be considered friend or foe. These divisions, while often overtly racialized, defy simple racial categories, indicating a complex mix of class, race and gender as the sources of young people's interpretive repertoires. These support the production of particular elements of subcultural practice alongside spatially contingent post-subcultural effects. They also draw upon gendered representations of the 'tough guy', where masculine displays of violence and physical prowess remain a highly desirable attribute that young men can draw upon in their racialized struggles to belong.

Andy, a first-generation Chinese-Canadian boy whose working-class parents migrated from China, and who attends school in Beacon Park, offers a glimpse into some of the new patterns of race relations and their links to tough masculinities within urban youth cultures. Here he discusses a subcultural group of young men with whom he has some indirect affiliation in the neighbourhood:

ANDY: There are some white people being Asian right now. Like I know a guy who is like super white and now he is officially Asian.[4]

INTERVIEWER: So how does that happen? What do you mean he's officially Asian?

ANDY: Like. I don't know. I don't know how it happened. There's like a group of like hardcore Asians who go around like, beating people up and stuff like that, and some look mean and stuff like that. I don't know. He joined their group and now he's like officially Asian.

INTERVIEWER: So what did he do to join their group? He started doing the things they were doing and then they kind of … ?

ANDY: Yeah. I guess. Yeah.

INTERVIEWER: And is he the only non-Asian in that group?

ANDY: Yeah. [laughs] It's like what is he doing? Like before, like before he'd get beaten up for like being a *wannabe* and stuff like that but now he's like official. [laughs]

INTERVIEWER: And so he doesn't get beat up any more?

ANDY: No.

[…]

INTERVIEWER: Did he have to do anything to prove that he was part of that group besides the, let's say smoking or ... ?

ANDY: Mmm. Not really. I don't know. *It's just like if you have your friends and like you have to support them and back them up.*

In this example, the Hardcore Asians appear to be substantially concerned with class protection, over and above the recognition of 'sameness' along essentialized racial categories. It was (after some rather difficult *wannabe* struggles), however, ultimately possible for a 'super white' young man to become a 'Hardcore Asian', assuming he conformed to the subcultural stipulation that he perform aggressive masculinity and 'support [his friends]'. To put this differently, group membership still required a commitment to the positional rules, but the forms of identification within such communities had widened in response to the local migration patterns and micro-nationalism(s) which were moving into this neighbourhood from Asian and most particularly Chinese settings.[5] In such contexts, we witnessed affective shifts in young people's desires for belonging and security, their desires for a spatially contingent form of recognition and fantasies of cultural affiliation, as well as in the affiliational strategies involved in their search for power. By recognizing urban space as one precondition for the recognition of a desired selfhood (Skeggs, 2004), we might understand how young people's affiliations and classifications may shift in line with wider urban changes.

Other similar accounts reflected the fracturing of essential subcultural groupings in the same moment that essentializing elements remained strong. Here, for example, is Cynthia, a white working-class girl living on the fringe of Vancouver's Downtown East Side, a site known as the 'poorest postal code in Canada', and grounded in high levels of spatial and economic inequality that remains entrenched in colonial distinctions and classifications:

> There are quite a few different groups in our school, we got the white people group, and they are a group of white Europeans who hang out together, then you get these Asian guy gangs, they are pretty much gangs, technically gangs are the ones that get arrested for bringing pipes or chains to school, they are going to fight after school, they listen to Rap music and almost WANTED TO BE [Black] yet they are Asian. It's like people are having an identity crisis at this time of their life, can't you just accept your own culture, you have a great culture.
>
> (Cynthia, white working-class, Beacon Park, aged 16)

We see in Cynthia's account the place that liberalism and multiculturalism occupy in governing the politics of selfhood (the paradoxically essentialized idea that 'you have a great culture'), alongside the simultaneous yet subtle operation of a post-subcultural effect where she reports on the 'Asian guy gangs' who want to be black. If the powerful group in the neighbourhood is no longer aggressive white working-class males, then any fracturing of group identity emerges as the drive for power which is tied to the scales of micro-nationalism(s) and multicultural discourses at play in a particular space, even as certain social conditions remain constant.

Hence we witness a 'difference', but that difference cannot eliminate the power of racial essentialisms or of racism itself. Rather, the reconfiguration of neighbourhoods and migration memories, alongside an increasing need for self-recognition, becomes one process in driving young people to re-classify 'race' and associated forms of membership in subcultural communities. But this reclassification may not necessarily be sufficiently strong to modify the stratified position of the actor or the positional rules of the subcultural formation. Recall Tony's story from Chapter 4: a Portuguese-Canadian boy who was struggling to determine where he belonged amongst his Toronto school's subcultures in Tower Hill. As he noted, he was beginning to hang out with the 'Rockers', a traditionally white working-class culture, but had previously been identified with the Thug/Gangsta culture, to which he was still drawn:

TONY: Most people classify me as a Thug because they call me Slim Shady, you know Eminem. They mostly classify me as that 'cause I listen to rap and all that' and [I shaved my head, see Figure 6.1].

INTERVIEWER: Okay …

TONY: But they said that I'm slowly starting to turn.

INTERVIEWER: Yeah.

TONY: I eventually hope to get out of that, like to be my own self, by next year. [...] Stop looking like, like this year I was trying to impress people by trying to look like them, get all the new fashions [...] but I've learned, I've had my fun so next year I'll be dressing the way I feel like [...]. Yeah, then [those others] they'll be on their own [...]. If they can't accept me for who I am [...] then it's their own fault.

Tony's narrative provides yet another example of the power of racialized imagery, tough masculinity, wannabe struggles and the effects of prominent liberal discourses of multiculturalism. They also indicate the potential for an imagined form of individualization resulting in a desire for an imagined self – 'inside a new skin' as it were, or the 'real me'. It is apparent, therefore, that elements of subcultural practice remain intact to greater or lesser degrees; in Tony's case, his options for subcultural affiliation lie between three working-class subcultures, the largely Portuguese and white working class Rockers, the Gangstas and/or the Italian and Portuguese

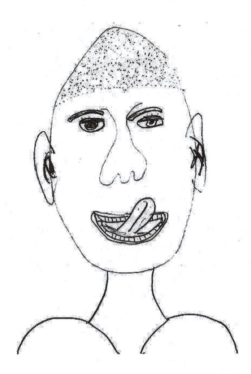

Figure 6.1 Tony's Self-Portrait of the Present: Tower Hill, Toronto, Ontario.

Ginos. Yet he posits a fourth possibility, 'to be my own self', a future happening that he views as desirable even if not immediately achievable.

Here we are witnessing elements of liberalism – the idea of the autonomous self who can be who (s)he wants to be – ultimately disembedding Tony from his traditional place in a bounded subcultural context. Simultaneously, however, we also witness the racialized metaphor of the 'white' working-class hero who forms part of Tony's narrative identity, even if the hidden meaning underlying the insignia of Eminem (himself a white rap artist) could represent elements of *Wannabe* associated with the desire to be black (see Nayak, 2003a), not unlike Cynthia's account of Asian youth cultures in Beacon Park. This is particularly so when, as Tony suggested during the interview, powerful media images are everywhere, emphasizing the need for young boys to 'be black', a racialized albeit deeply colonial subjectivity that they equate with being tough and masculine. Figure 6.1 is a representation of Eminem that Tony drew as his self-portrait, a self-representation that might be derisively labelled by some scholars as 'cultural appropriation'. Instead, we suggest seeing this image as an appropriation of wider-circulating discourses of powerful, racialized, masculinity which, while masking deeply colonial codes, still interrupts Tony's narrative of origin and provides new possibilities for his own need for recognition. In other words, it is a twenty-first-century magical resolution. It becomes a cultural necessity within the geographical landscapes of youth cultural practice.

Tony's perceptions of his place amongst the local subcultures shed some light on the ideas of MacDonald and Ricoeur in relation to the self as social metaphor or the idea of 'oneself as another'. Unlike earlier accounts of youth subcultural membership, Tony's boundedness, as a Portuguese Torontonian, to the group or the subculture seems at times, at least at surface levels, more ambiguous. This is largely because wider individualized discourses of the subject and 'self' lead to a plurality of conflicted positions about the nature of that which we imagine ourselves to be at this or that moment in history. As Ricoeur tells us: 'So here we do not close the circle to centralize or totalize knowledge, but to keep open the irreducibility and plurality of knowledge/discourse' (cited in Kearney, 2004: 35). As Ricoeur's work on narrative identity suggests, young people's subjectivities are ultimately divested in practice from their own intentions to represent – as a self – the origin of their family's or nation's intended cultural meanings (such as, for example, the Portuguese Gino). Indeed, subjectivity:

> is a goal to be reached after the intersubjective detour of interpretation. In the process, of course, the very concept of subjectivity is radically altered. For as Ricoeur never tires of reminding us, it is only by means of distancing oneself from its original ego that the interpreter can hope to recover a new sense of subjectivity: enlarged, decentred and open to novel possibilities of interpretation.
>
> (Kearney, 2004: 32)

In order to enlarge and move beyond these very origins, and at an even more complex level, one could argue that Tony is in fact *appropriating* a wider social metaphor which responds to the central narrative of a mastery text, a hero, a potential affiliate and friend. At the same time he is also reinventing his Portuguese history and the Gangsta image by imaginatively reliving the story or the world represented by the honorary 'black' figure of Eminem (even though Eminem himself is not black). And in so doing, he is (in his imagination) disassociated for that moment in time from received assumptions about his Portuguese history and its futures. In this dialectical movement between imagining one's 'real' place, distancing oneself from its origins, and appropriating the symbols of other urban cultures, what is ultimately revealed are 'possible worlds'.

In the encounter between Tony's 'old world' and Eminem's new world, a new horizon of experience is widened because of the very existence of rap culture and the rappers. Within this 'identity' encounter, there can be little doubt that the characteristics of being male, working class and Portuguese have been transformed. But the transformation does not result in a sovereign powerful male self (even if Tony imagines this to be so) or the emergence of a true or pure representation of twenty-first-century individualism. This is largely because youth subculture in this particular place – a tightly woven neighbourhood carrying three generations of working-class Portuguese and Southern Europeans who are still struggling to access the kinds of global mobility that middle-class groups in the same city have already acquired – can never be completely unleashed from the structural inequalities and colonial discourses which shape the very rules of performance associated with aggressive masculinity. Indeed, in this neighbourhood, male narratives of class protection remain largely stable – at least as a narrative identity – and form a prominent part of Tony's collective memory, even if a new racialized desire and horizon of selfhood does emerge.

Ultimately, in his constrained world, as Tony plays with the possibilities for selfhood, he is engaging in a form of semantic innovation – and performing a 'structure of feeling' – through the subtle production of new racial meaning(s) in old clothing: the 'nearly black' working-class male hero. We can best understand this using Ricoeur's language, as a symbol of state power and as an expression of surplus meaning still bound in part by tradition:

> every historical narrative borrows from the imaginative power of re-description since 'as a reference through traces', the 'past can only be reconstructed by the imagination'. But it is clearly in fictional narrative that the productive power of human imagination to configure and reconfigure human time is dramatically evident ... For the human being 'in-the-world' in its most everyday sense – as 'Kant and Heidegger' realized – involves a process of temporalization which makes our present actions meaningful by interpreting them in terms of a recollected past and a projected future.
>
> (Kearney, 2004: 54)

In this case, the ambivalence and contradictions associated with subcultural urban belonging need not be seen as marking some 'post-subcultural' moment or fluid effect, or indicating that identity has become indelibly hybridized (indeed, perhaps in some degree, it has always been hybridized in various underground forms but without sufficient legitimacy and visibility, depending on the temporal period and place). Rather, they could be better read as highlighting some of the symbolic creativity (Willis, 1977), recuperative appropriations or forms of 'passing' to which Sarah Ahmed (1999) refers in circumstances where wide-ranging migration patterns produce and govern a spatial geography of difference. These geographies might ultimately be understood through Bourdieu's notion of a moral 'field' where the appropriation of powerful symbols for a particular audience is a necessary element of subcultural survival. The space and its active audiences thus come to represent one of many landscapes of possibility in an urban imaginary, even as they mask the 'dark phantom' of race relations or folks devils from an earlier time. But this space can never be seen as a simple space. It is a site of conflict structured by existing histories and arrangements, feelings of loss and nostalgia, struggles to recuperate power, and subject to the forms of urban mobility and re-arrangement which characterize the fringe of the global city. And this space is always and necessarily imbued with collective memory (even as it fragments), particular fantasies and new desires for recognition, which persist even as young people attempt to re-invent themselves through cultural narratives that allow those who live on the margins to forge 'affective alliances and networks of empowerment' (Stahl, 1999: 26).

Racialized Identities and Historical Time: Oneself as Another in 'the Colonial Present'

Within the complexity of contemporary urban spatial arrangements, young people are not only encountering far greater ethnic diversity than was the case in the past in urban Canada. They are also navigating their own racial marginalization both against, and sometimes alongside, others who are also marginalized by race, class, ethnicity and/or religious affiliations. Here we draw on Ricoeur's phenomenological approach that views time and history as integral elements of the interpretive struggles undertaken by young people to 'make sense' of their place in the world. This frame assumes that no individual narrative of legitimacy – or a narrative of others' legitimacy – is ever completely displaced from the past. Indeed, young people necessarily bear the mark of time as they manage their feelings of belonging and security in the present. To borrow from Ricoeur, all contemporary performances 'possess and repossess a past'.

In the case of our study sites, young people navigated specific constellations of Canadian history – national, local and urban – as they imagined themselves within stratified working-class neighbourhoods. The historical relationship in Canada between people of British descent and Aboriginal peoples, as well as those coming from Asia and Africa, has been marked by exclusion, discrimination, and intensely racist policies designed to denigrate and deny the legitimacy of people of non-white (and, in particular, British) ancestry. Although such overtly racist ideologies have been more or less eliminated from policy,[6] to be replaced by discourses of multiculturalism and 'tolerance', the traces of this virulently racist past are nonetheless strongly present in Canada's contemporary cities. Young people in the Vancouver site experienced these traces through, for example, repeated references to the social marginalization of First Nations students within their school:

INTERVIEWER: There's fighting. Yeah? Do you notice in particular who fights? Or no?

BRIAN: First Nations.

INTERVIEWER: Okay. With?

BRIAN: Themselves.

INTERVIEWER: Themselves. Okay. Do you see a lot of that?

BRIAN: Yeah.

From a different student:

SHARLEE: That's what other people say. That the reputation of Beacon Park is not that great. They say there's mostly First Nations here.

And from another:

ERIC: Kind of on and off for the First Nations people.

INTERVIEWER: Okay.

ERIC: There's a lot of them here, so.

INTERVIEWER: And for you, is that a good thing or a bad thing?

ERIC: Bad thing. Because, not to be any racial thing, but First Nations is probably the race that gets picked on the most.

INTERVIEWER: It gets picked on the most?

ERIC: Yeah.

INTERVIEWER: Why do you think that is?

ERIC: The reputations about booze and stuff like that.

INTERVIEWER: Do you think it's all their own fault?

ERIC: I don't know if it's their fault, but it's just the way that it is. First Nations is probably the race that gets picked on the most.

INTERVIEWER: Okay. Do you notice that?

ERIC: Yeah. At school there's a lot of exclusion for them. It's why most kids drop out. Because I think the rate of First Nations graduating is really low. So they like [leave school to go to] work after a year.

The colonial history that has contributed to the ongoing exclusion of First Nations students is largely invisible to the young people commenting above, who witness the marginalization of their Aboriginal peers but who have little access to in-depth historical analyses of the conditions that underwrite this exclusion. The label used to describe Aboriginal students by a member of the Hardcore Asians is 'Jugs', which apparently represents the visual metaphor of the 'boozer' quaffing from a jug. These imaginary subsystems are also the very workings of spatial exclusion, for such meaning systems result in the exclusion of First Nations youth from the neighbourhood in the most visible of the subcultural communities. The material effects of these symbolic exclusions were apparent in the Vancouver classroom that we observed for several months. In that time, the three Aboriginal students who were supposed to be in class barely attended; when they were present, they sat apart from the other students, and were almost always completely silent.

Another significant group in Beacon Park comprises second-generation immigrant youth of Asian ancestry. Vancouver, as a city located on the Pacific Rim of North America, has been a port of entry for Asian migrants seeking economic improvement from the turn of the twentieth century, when Asian workers arrived as cheap labour for the Canadian nation-building project of the trans-continental railway. Like other West Coast North American cities, Vancouver was the site of anti-Asian riots in the early twentieth century, and, after the need for immigrant labour abated, the Canadian parliament felt able to pass the Asian Exclusion Act which specifically excluded migration from Asiatic countries such as China and Japan for 23 years (Stanley, 2003).

More recently, Asian countries have become the target of a kind of economic courtship by national and provincial governments, seeking to capitalize on the expanding markets and vast populations of countries such as China. Alongside national immigration rules that have made it increasingly difficult for people of lower economic means to come to Canada, and combined with the return of Hong Kong from British rule to China in 1996, Vancouver has more recently become one of the destinations of choice for affluent Asian migrants. These migrants are often, although not exclusively, from Hong Kong, and typically live in the well-heeled West Side of the city or the developing affluent suburb of Richmond (Edgington, Goldberg & Hutton, 2003).

This particular combination of historical and more recent Asian migration, alongside the colonial treatment of Aboriginal peoples in Canada, led to new class conflicts in Beacon Park, appearing on the surface to involve classifications premised exclusively on 'race'. Rather than restricting our assessment of the subcultural conflicts documented below to an exclusively race-based analysis, we suggest that the incorporation of both social class and the sedimented role of historical relationships and associated ethnic conflicts better reveals the constellation of forces influencing young people's actions within sites of urban stratification. Here Andy provides some insight into the complexity of these forces in Beacon Park:

ANDY: I don't know. Like there's some people because there's like a lot of Asians here because this school is by Chinatown.

INTERVIEWER: Mmm-hmmm.

ANDY: And stuff like that. They call us chinks and stuff like that.

INTERVIEWER: Who's they? Who does the calling usually? When you say 'They call us chinks'?

ANDY: Native people.

INTERVIEWER: The First Nations people?

ANDY: Yeah.

INTERVIEWER: Yeah.

ANDY: They're like 'get off our land' and stuff. And it's like, they're like, 'there's too many of you' and stuff. You know, we go call them a racist word for a Native.

INTERVIEWER: What do you call them?

ANDY: Jugs.

We need to apply a multi-layered analytical lens to better understand the complexity of this account. In so doing, we find of particular use Cohen's concept of territoriality and more contemporary ideas about spatial contexts and the role they play for working-class young people formulating their own resolutions to class-based conflicts within deeply divided urban spaces. Also centrally important is Ricoeur's assertion that the present always comes with its own burden of history; in other words, these young people are in fact engaging in peer conflicts and racial classifications which exceed the frontiers of the present. In short, it is impossible to apprehend a conflict between Asian and First Nations students at the same school through a straightforward race analysis where the default position is the juxtaposition of 'white' and 'black', or as a binary of categorical distinctions. Instead, we see the ways in which the deeply symbolic role of both history and spatiality begin to emerge within Andy's account. The conflict his words illuminate, in many ways unique to the specific context of Vancouver's urban East Side, echoes with past histories of colonialism, Asian migration, and the construction of the 'other' encountered by both Aboriginal peoples and Asian communities within the (British) white-dominant imaginary of the Canadian nation-state. It also reverberates with the record of Aboriginal resistance to colonialism, upon which the First Nations student draws in ordering Andy to 'get off our land', as well as with the racism experienced by Chinese migrants ('chinks') to this Pacific coastal city. At this level, therefore, we see the continuing 'effects' of history as they are expressed by young people in this fringe neighbourhood in the global city.

Yet, to leave the account at the level of history alone would be to undermine the integral part played by new social-class relations within this conflict. Andy comes from a working-class immigrant history, as do his 'gang' of Asian friends. The Aboriginal students at the school are also economically marginalized and come from communities with working-class urban and rural histories – again, a result of histories of colonialism and forced migration mobilities (to reservations, for example; or to deprived neighbourhoods with weekly hotel dwellings within cities when work can't be found in rural contexts).

Through the incorporation of class analysis, deeper levels of complexity emerge within a story of what appears on the surface to be a more straightforward conflict between two 'racial' groups. Andy himself is trying to apprehend this conflict through the language of race – the resources which are most readily available in the contemporary moment (see also Bettie, 2003). But this language can provide only a partial explanation for the conflicts he encounters in the school-yard. As Ricoeur reminds us: 'the subject is not a centralizing master but rather a disciple or auditor of language larger than itself' (Kearney, 2004: 172). From a phenomenological vantage point, then, youth subcultural identification and race relations are not straightforwardly reproduced and neither are they solely class-based. Understanding the role of historical memory in the reconfiguration of youth subcultural identification recognizes its power in the circumstances of the present: 'to give people a memory is not to give them back their past but to give them a future' (Kearney, 2004: 137). Modalities of youth culture therefore tell us as much about social change as they do about economic entrapment and the history of colonization and its ongoing racialized effects. They also illuminate the ways in which place, space and the urban landscape remain central to the very operation of youth cultures. These operations can therefore never be truly classified as ultimately subcultural or post-subcultural as so much of their evidence and visibility is contingent upon 'history, memory, and forgetting' across space.

Interview data provided multiple examples of symbolic classifications that appeared exclusively bound to race but which are actually better understood as the multivalent expression of post-industrial class conflicts within global cities. Indeed, the classifications young people applied to each other reflected this reality, together with the wider circulating discourses of race and racism that continue to position those who are not white-skinned and fluent English-speakers as inferior within the Canadian nation-state. Several participants in Beacon Park, for example, referenced two specific sub-groups within the school: the 'FOBs' (an acronym drawn from the derogatory term 'Fresh off the boat') and the 'Hongers' (referring to people from Hong Kong). The following came from Shareen, the daughter of working-class Cambodian refugees:

INTERVIEWER: Ok, who are the 'FOBs'?
SHAREEN: The people who just came from China and they don't speak English and all they do is play little card games. They're mostly just

the Chinese people and they don't associate with anyone else – just their own group.

INTERVIEWER: And what about their school work?

SHAREEN: I guess they're all in 'ESL' (English as Second Language Classes) – I don't know 'cause I don't associate with them.

INTERVIEWER: Who are the other ones – you gave me another group – preppies, Fobs and …

SHAREEN: The Hongers? (laughter) sorry! […] They're also the Chinese people but they know how to speak English too but they're still also in their own little group.

INTERVIEWER: And how would they be characterized, are they studious and all that? Do they study hard?

SHAREEN: Yeah.

Shareen's description highlights the varying degrees of cultural capital accumulated by the two groups she identifies: the 'FOBS', with their limited English and subsequent inability to socialize outside their language group, and the 'Hongers', with their apparent relative ease and success within school. Her classification of each revolves around racialized terms, but they also each contain hidden classed meanings which are elided by the racial classifications. Due to the highly visible presence of affluent Hong Kong migrants to Vancouver prior to the transfer of Hong Kong back to Chinese rule in 1996, the designation 'the Hongers' is implicated in a class-based assessment of affluence and ease within the global city. Although such migration has dropped substantially since this period, and the likely destination of any current affluent Hong Kong migrants within Vancouver would be far from this working-class neighbourhood (Edgington et al., 2003), nonetheless a historical sediment and class trace of race lives on through the very category of the 'Hongers'. Whether or not the young people that Shareen is describing are, in fact, from Hong Kong, the designation 'Hongers' has emerged as shorthand for the affluence and cultural capital that symbolizes the successful and legitimate Canadian citizen (e.g. speaking English, doing well in school).

By contrast, those Shareen identifies as 'Fresh off the boat', or FOBs, are likely to be closer in economic circumstances to her own family history, arriving as economic migrants or refugees, and struggling to succeed within the interstices of the new global economy (see also Ong, 1996). The significant difference between herself and the FOBs, which is illuminated in her account, is that they, unlike her, are still without a full and comprehensive grasp of English. This apparent class deficit thus becomes one criterion for the classification and separation between 'friend' and 'foe', demarcating a legitimate 'us' versus a mockable and illegitimate 'them' ('I don't associate with them'). Once again, elements of race and class converge, where the practice of classification functions to separate both working-class subcultures from each other, as well as from more affluent groups. Shareen's classification tells us less about the specific migration histories of these particular students than about their perceived position within deeply classed hierarchies, masked as they are by racial categories.

'Signals of Risk': Living Racialized Identities in a Post-9/11 World

Shareen's efforts to distinguish a 'FOB' and a 'Honger' can be understood in part through Cohen's (1997) description of young people's separation between 'friend' and 'foe' or Bourdieu's (1984) notion of distinction. Why might it be necessary to sort friend from foe in the new global city? Our data repeatedly suggest that classifications of the illegitimate person or the deserving subject are tied in part to the subjective desires of young people to seek 'ideological solutions' (see Cohen, 1997) to their own marginalization which would allow for the possibility of new utopian futures (Althusser, 2004; see also Bettie, 2003). This need for ideological solutions emerged particularly from the tension many young people felt as they struggled to realize their own social status within their families, neighbourhoods and in the city more generally. Here, young people were attempting to resolve the contradictions they confronted and which were associated with working-class life in a radically transformed urban context with many new and 'foreign' others present.[7]

Rhetoric relating to the 'insider' versus the 'outsider' has always been central to Canadian myths concerned with nation-building. Whilst the process of producing the category of the 'foreigner' or 'stranger' has long been influential (see Honig, 2001; Walter, 2003), such symbolic referents have increased in light of both recent events (e.g. the terrorist attacks of September 11, 2001; the 7/7 London Bombing), and the growing public hysteria and moral panic over the perceived flow of non-Western migrants into Western countries. In interviews, young people who embodied the symbolic markers of such referents (such as being 'brown-skinned' or Muslim), reflected on their own struggles for legitimacy in the face of such exclusions and heightened forms of moral panic:

INTERVIEWER: I've heard people talk about 'terrorists' [...]

SHAREEN: Oh Yeah! (laughing)

INTERVIEWER: Do you get that one?

SHAREEN: 'Cause I'm Muslim! They used to bug me about 'terrorist' Osama bin Laden that I bombed them and stuff 'cause I'm Muslim and stuff.

INTERVIEWER: And how did that make you feel?

SHAREEN: I think it's funny though 'cause I'm not really Afghani.

(Shareen, aged 15)

In an interview with a young male student originally from Iraq, a similar set of conflicts emerged.

INTERVIEWER: So, you said 'terrorist. The people who are doing the suicide bombing'? And you also said [...] that some of the kids in the school say that about you, tease you guys. [...] I've heard other kids tell me that story, too. That's a pretty heavy word, right? [...]

HUSSEIN: Yeah. But I don't see it that way when people call [me], like, oh, a terrorist. [...]

INTERVIEWER: [...] How do you see it?

HUSSEIN: [...] I'm used to it, so I'll just say, ah, okay. Thank you.

INTERVIEWER: Yeah. You don't ... ?

HUSSEIN: Whatever. I don't like [fight] back.

INTERVIEWER: [...] You don't want to get back at somebody?

HUSSEIN: There's no point. [...] The guy is going to call me whatever so I'm just going to leave him alone. He thinks he's cool. [...] If people start making fun of me, I'll just go, mmm. Okay. It's good for you.

(Hussein, aged 15)

The pervasive construction of the 'foreign other', clearly intensified in times of increased emphasis upon 'national security' and surveillance, exerted material and symbolic pressures on young people within the school. In navigating the deeply troubling territory of historical and political constructions, many young participants sought out strategies to rescue their own sense of 'self-worth' in the face of the constant denigration of those 'others' with whom they were compared. Hussein takes us through what he himself defines as the terrorist:

HUSSEIN: The people who explode themselves [...]. They use babies too.

INTERVIEWER: Do they?

HUSSEIN: Yeah. They're like crawling, like in Baghdad, one baby was crawling and one guy's like, what the? Dee, dee, boom! [...] It was in like a party, too. [...] 'Cause it's for their religion because [...] heaven will take you right away. The odds of saying that's true so they can. It's all for their religion [...]. I think that's dumb.

As is evident in Hussein's account, deeply symbolic forms of racialization often resulted in classification strategies and forms of interpellation which involved both identifying themselves as important individuals, whilst simultaneously drawing upon deeply sedimented forms of symbolic racism or a kind of micro-spatial orientalism to characterize the apparent outsider. This tension resulted in the production of visual images such Figure 6.2, created by Suc, a 16-year-old first-generation Asian-Canadian.

At the centre of this image is a female figure who is both overweight

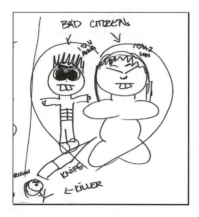

Figure 6.2 Student Image of the 'Citizen': Beacon Park. Vancouver, BC.

and 'orientalized', as in stereotypical public imaginaries of the Asian Girl. As revealed through interviews, Suc expressed deeply ambivalent positions about her weight in relation to her ethnic background, noting that

> this is an Asian school and they're all so skinny and stuff and yeah it makes me feel [bad] … I had this talk with my friend too that there's this pressure on me because I'm kind of big and I'm still Asian around them.

Here we are witness to an example of the complex ways in which young people navigate the contradictory messages of ethnicity, normalcy and belonging. In contexts where 'whiteness' remains the ideological norm of Canadian citizenship,[8] the possibility of being a 'good person' is circumscribed not only by personal behaviour, but also by a conventional embodiment of the gendered expectations of this or that ethnicity. Thus, an apparently overweight Asian girl can be depicted as a 'bad citizen' who has been unable to redeem herself or her imperfect body within the racialized hierarchy of the legitimate 'citizen' versus the 'foreigner'. Similar expectations emerged in relation to the raced and classed nature of school violence. As Andy reported in relation to the Hardcore Asians and some First Nations young males in the school (as efforts in gaining recognition):

ANDY: I don't know. Around the school it is all messed up. Like there was that machete incident at a [school nearby].
INTERVIEWER: No tell me about it. What happened?
ANDY: Some guys like bumped in the hall or something like that then they all got pissed off with each other and after school one of the guys took a machete and tried to swing it at a guy's head and then the guy does this with his hand [lifting up his hand] and he loses like three fingers

[…]. Every school is getting violent. We are like having boxing matches in the school. Before it was right at the school where we'd box each other for money. It was fun.

INTERVIEWER: When you say we, who is we?

ANDY: The [Asian] guys. […] And then people bet on who can win. […] Well, first it was like grade ten and then others jumped in. And then it's interesting to see how some people fight. Some people are so quiet and you like never expect anything from them and you think they're going to get their ass kicked and then they just burst.

[…]. Like sometimes there are people who are racist here and [the boxer] takes offence.

As the narrative accounts of our young participants suggest, official discourses and categories of race and nation, fused through the horizons of diasporic fringe experiences, continue to play a major part in legitimizing racism in schools. This is largely so because national narratives of legitimacy have deemed the white autonomous subject as superordinate and have persistently reproduced a notion of racially marginalized youth as members of the 'dangerous classes' or, more recently, as violent 'terrorists'. Heightened anxiety about the 'foreigner' – emerging as a reconfigured twenty-first-century form of moral panic – therefore penetrates the cultural landscape which young people navigate in their attempts to make sense of their legitimacy in the nation-state. The contradictory ways in which such classifications emerge strongly reflect Cohen's earlier insights about the degrees of cultural ambivalence generated through increasing class conflicts. Young people are therefore afforded only partial glimpses into the real, rather than imaginary, relations of inequality that they must endure and respond to within the symbolic constraints imposed by the new spatial relations of the global city (see Nayak, 2003a). And, as young people living at the edge of urban legitimacy, it is precisely because of these spatial relations, micro-nationalisms and geographies of difference that they are also subject to the alienations and exclusions which operate in and through the border imaginaries of the city – to new race relations, to forms of historical domination, and to conflicts which are inherited and re-contextualized in new places and times.

Many images produced by the young people in both Tower Hill and Beacon Park expose these conflicts and highlight how social class mediates the production of race through space. This kind of mediation often activated what Appadurai (1996) has named a 'community of sentiment, an articulation of individual sentiment onto a broader social plane of belonging' (cited in Stahl, 1999: 27). This affective plane of belonging set the stage for a theatre of identity performances and classifications which often brought about wider degrees of social conflict over legitimacy in highly local and trans-local ways. Importantly, though, these were not flattened planes of belonging grounded in undifferentiated signifiers of youth modalities (e.g. FOBs, Hardcore Asians). Rather, contextual and spatial variability in material and cultural realities which are both local and trans-local provide the backdrop for understanding the cultural processes underlying new class patterns of racialization among young people. In this way, we can move beyond an over-simplification of the local, and towards a more heterogeneous cartography of the urban fringe and its forms of youth cultural practice and moralizing distinctions.

Conclusions

In this chapter, we have traced the impact of symbolic racialization and forms of micro-nationalisms on the classification struggles undertaken by the young people within our study sites, with a particular emphasis resting upon the ethnographic landscape of Beacon Park. We have also attempted to show how national imaginaries and micro-nationalisms interact with social class to transform race relations beyond any elusive binary polarizations. These imaginaries necessarily operate in the gap between young people's memories of home and place and the projection of one's idea of legitimacy in relation to wider social events in the present. We therefore wish to suggest that contemporary notions of the hybridized racial subject, whilst a clearly powerful conceptual ideal, demand further theorization to address the symbolic effects of class struggle, spatiality, traces of historical time, mobile national imaginaries and the pervasive influence of widely circulating moral panics about young people in the contemporary global city.

We have also sought to reveal the manner in which young people draw upon the language of race metaphorically within a wider symbolic repertoire designed to distinguish 'friend' from 'foe'. Clearly, race is a powerful category within these distinctions, but it is by no means the only relevant distinction, and it is not without its own colonial and post-colonial slippages. As exemplified by the phenomenon of racial 'wannabes', and the incorporation of racialized 'others' into a specific subculture (e.g. the 'super white' youth who became 'officially Asian', or the Portuguese Gangsta Boy striving to be Eminem), race as a category of subcultural affiliation involves a high degree of slippage. However, this slippage does not make racial categories superfluous, nor does it point to the death of class. Rather, it is through the very powers of the slippage between past and present and space and place that racial categorizations remain significant resources for young people's classification of themselves and others, alongside the range of ways such classifications are modified to accommodate the realities of class, local histories and circulating moral discourses.

One particularly powerful moral discourse (or 'panic') currently circulating is that of 'terrorist threats'. Rather than understanding this as an isolated phenomenon unique to a post-9/11 world, we see this as a discursive strategy that links powerfully with instances of exclusion from a colonial past and present, or what Gregory (2006) has referred to as the history of the 'dark continent'. The making of the 'foreign other' represents a powerful symbolic force within Canadian histories of racism and colonialism, and this is precisely the context in which the current panic about youth and terrorist threats is permitted to emerge. This emergence of panic becomes, paradoxically, yet another cultural resource of some value (i.e. crisis content) for young people as they engage in self-making or in interpolating apparent space invaders. Thus young people report being labelled as 'terrorist' due to migration histories, accents or skin colour. We understand this naming practice as part of both larger transnational and trans-local struggles to define urban legitimacy – often perceived in relation to notions of the 'good citizen' in the shadows of the nation-state – and to differentiate this subject from the dark phantoms perceived to be threatening the well-being of 'world-class' cities. The language of the 'good citizen' within the specific national context of Canada, and its implications for young people living on the economic fringes of the global city, is the subject of the next chapter.

7

Legitimacy, Risk and Belonging in the Global City
Individualization and the Language of Citizenship

In the previous two chapters, we focused on the spatial arrangements and configurations of symbolic domination at the local level of the school and neighbourhood. In this chapter, we move towards a consideration of the symbolic role of the highly individualized liberal citizen, and his/her perceived place within the nation. In particular, we are interested in exploring how individualization, social class relations and national scripts come together in the late-modern global city and are drawn upon as symbolic references by low-income youth in their own understandings of state legitimacy. We examine these questions through two lenses: the first draws upon Goffman's traditional youth subcultural concept, 'the front', and seeks to re-contextualize its meaning for the twenty-first-century city. The second borrows from critiques of the liberal state in political theory as a means for revealing some of the symbolic meanings associated with the commonly used, but highly misapprehended term, 'citizenship'. Although apparently disparate in theoretical orientation and meaning, we suggest here that both 'the front', a cultural and class performance, and 'citizenship', as a symbolic and classifying reference of the nation, are used as cultural strategies by young people to apprehend their own and others' place in local subcultures and the national imaginary.

We begin by asking how young people have been transformed, both in their daily lives and in the broader perception of national imaginaries, by social changes associated with individualization practices operating at the edge of the neo-liberal city. This is not necessarily the form of individualization described by Beck (1992) and Giddens (1991), which is sometimes seen as an agentic means of mobility, reflexivity and freedom from traditions by which liberal citizens engage with 'do it yourself' or 'can do' biographies, or are under pressure to live out new ways of life that deviate substantially from previous traditions. Rather, the pressure to become 'the best one can be' is necessarily contorted and reconfigured when applied to the lives of low-income youth who do not see within their horizons the potential for agency, mobility and middle-class possibilities seen to be available to some of their peers. It is here that we draw upon Goffman's (1959) seminal notion of 'the front', traditionally conceptualized as young people's projection of collective experience and marginalization.

Here, while retaining some of its original conceptual force, we re-position 'the front' as a social and cultural practice which has embedded elements of individualization and risk into its own cultural narrative and set of positional rules as it is performed in the present. In the contemporary global city, we argue that the 'front' is used by low-income youth as a recuperative strategy which provides a platform for expressing and bolstering sometimes quite fierce identity claims about young people's value and legitimacy in urban contexts where they often feel devalued. Rather than reinforcing their position within subcultural groups, then, we see 'the front' as a medium and form of governance for expressing working-class distinctions intended to assert young people's individual value in a political moment and risk society where the 'do it yourself', 'can do' culture or the culture of self-perfection carry powerful symbolic and cultural weight (Rose, 1999).

At the same time, contemporary social changes simultaneously appear to be transforming the very meaning(s) of what it is to be young in relation to the state and to new patterns of social class retrenchment in urban centres. For example, young people are often characterized, on the one hand, as 'international', 'global', hybrid and mobile (see Rizvi, 2005), and, on the other, as fundamentally disenfranchised from democratic politics (Mitchell, 2003; Institute for Public Policy Research, 2006). What lies behind these recent shifts in our conceptualizations of young people? In what ways are intensified patterns of social stratification under the dynamics of global neo-liberalism re-contextualizing young people's engagement with concepts of 'citizenship', nation and state membership at local scales of the school and neighbourhood life? Finally, how do young people themselves narrate their own and others' 'citizenship'? Here we attempt to answer these questions by exploring what these converging temporal and conceptual shifts in the category youth, urbanization and the citizen might mean for young people's classification struggles within the radically transformed fringe of the late-modern Canadian city.

Our comparative analysis of youth cultures shows that the prevailing and accelerating emphasis on individualism and meritocracy has served to intensify the production of what Goffman identified in the 1950s as 'the front', particularly as a generalized response to social conflicts at the level of race, class, gender and nation as encountered within local neighbourhoods. Our approach concentrates upon how elements of youth subcultural and post-subcultural activity interact with the social structures of late-modern Canadian cities to generate new conceptions of belonging and citizenship amongst young people. This intersection between structure and youth cultural activity belies the simple injunction that young people should become more 'civically engaged', a claim which locates the problems of democratic disengagement as principally within young people themselves. By contrast, we suggest that strategic efforts to create more inclusive political environments must begin with a socio-cultural analysis of young people's national imaginaries of belonging and the state, alongside their classification struggles. Drawing upon the work of Wendy Brown (2005, 2006) and others (see Arendt, 1968), our primary argument rests upon the idea that an enduring problem with a normative, liberal conception of citizenship is its assertion of an abstract notion of individualized belonging that does little to understand or engage the highly variegated ways that such concepts are conceptualized by low-income young people living in globalizing urban centres. We therefore concentrate on how young people conceptualize not only class and race (see Chapters 4, 5 and 6), but also national scripts and citizenship as symbolic referents in their 'classification struggles' (Bourdieu, 1984).

As demonstrated in previous chapters, attempts to classify can be understood as deeply ambivalent cultural processes of struggle through which young people mark their own and other bodies as, for example, 'strange', 'foreign' or 'acceptable'. This leads us towards some understanding of young people's conceptions of the state and citizen as a ritualized component of cultural strategies which are responding to wider memories of home and nation and micro-nationalisms.[1] Against this background, we now move forward to explore: (1) the manifestations of the new individualized 'front', as expressed in relation to symbolic culture, nation and micro-nationalisms at the level of youth cultural activity; and (2) conceptions of citizenship as they are expressed, through language and through visual symbol, in the lives of our young participants in Tower Hill and Beacon Park.

Narrating Urban Conflicts and the Magical Resolutions of Youth Selfhood in the Global City: The Individualized Front

> For most kids where it's at is the street: not the romantic action packed streets of the Ghetto but the wet pavements of Wigan, Shepherds Bush and Sunderland. The major activity in this venue, the main action of British Subculture is, in fact, doing nothing.
>
> (Corrigan, 1979)

As we seek to narrate elements of youth culture in the new global city, it is hard to avoid the old adage that 'the more things change the more they stay the same'. This does not sit well with all aspects of youth culture, of course. However, one rather steadfast element of youth culture which persists strongly across time is the recognition that social conflicts of the nation and associated narrative identities remain matters for young people to resolve indirectly. For Corrigan (1979) as well as for Goffman (1959), and more recently, for McDonald (1999), Shildrick (2006) and Nayak (2003a), young people's social conflicts of the state ultimately become internalized as conflicts of the self and are performed at that level as essentially local dramas, but may also come to assume a more resonant symbolic status. This position seems particularly to hold when larger or more traditional communities of support begin to fragment or no longer exist as safe sites for the expression of social conflict. In such circumstances it becomes the burden of the individual – in this case, low-income young people – to carry the local social conflict as an embodied cultural entity, simultaneously as a form of individualized selfhood and as a form of protection. As we have noted, one way to engage in such protection whilst performing a youth subcultural identity is the phenomenological performance of a 'front'. According to Goffman's (1959) original case, the 'front' begins with the feeling of marginality, alienation or stigma (see Reay & Ball, 1997) in any one given space, and then emerges as a dramatic performance of self protection or as a position which strives to fight the effects of boredom but may ultimately lead to the reproduction of inequality.

Many of the young people in our study cited boredom, feelings of individualized failure and utopian desires for escape as the basis for an expression of a particular kind of stylish but deeply coded 'front'. The combined aim of the 'front' is both to combat boredom and to gain recognition, and further to develop cultural strategies to address this aim. The 'front' also seeks to respond – as a historical narrative – to aspects of social alienation and isolation emerging from class conflict. As Barnhart (1994: 27) writes:

> The front acts as a vehicle of standardization, allowing for others to understand the individual on the basis of projected character traits that have normative meanings. As a 'collective representation', the front establishes proper 'setting', 'appearance', and 'manner' for the social role assumed by the actor, uniting interactive behaviour with the personal front.

Barnhart (1994: 208) goes on to note that this process, called 'dramatic realization' by Goffman, is a form of 'impression management', which can be understood as 'the control and communication of information through image and performance' (1994: 208). The 'front' can therefore be understood as a cultural practice which leads to social status for a subcultural group member, as well as a strategy for acquiring enhanced value to be used for the exchange of something else (see also Skeggs, 2004). Paradoxically, as demonstrated below through interview excerpts (181–184), young people utilized the 'front' as both a means to assert their belonging within local subcultures and as a mode of asserting their unique sense of identity and potential in a society that glorifies individual effort and self-reliance above all else. This complex social mechanism originated amongst young people who were otherwise marginalized within the contemporary global city, and served to shore up individualized success (where possible, and within the boundaries of their own definitions). This seemed essential for young people as they strived to access a range of possible resources to reinforce their own sense of legitimacy in urban imaginaries grounded in high levels of economic disadvantage, diasporic transformations and vast levels of urbanization, particularly from a range of economically disadvantaged refugees and asylum seekers from Asia and, in particular, rural China.

In the following extract we see the expression of the 'front' emerging around the experience of boredom for young people who are alienated by middle-class regimes of schooling and new national narratives operating at the local level. Cognizant of the value placed on schooling as a means to establish individualized success within the global economy, low-income young people are forced to reconcile their personal experiences of schooling as alienating with the reality that they must continue to attend. As Josh notes, the only worthwhile element of schooling for him revolves around the presence of his friends, with whom he can retain some sense of his own intrinsic worth, in large part through the performance of a shared subcultural identity. Such feelings of worthiness certainly do not derive from schooling itself, against which he must position himself as a choosing subject who opts out of the system (because school is boring, and he doesn't want to work that hard), rather than as someone who has failed.

INTERVIEWER: What's the best thing about school? [...] If you want to be an electrician, it's important to finish school right? [...]
JOSH: Yeah.
INTERVIEWER: So what's the best thing about school?
JOSH: Friends.
INTERVIEWER: Friends, that's it?
JOSH: Pretty much. I don't like school that much [but I have to go]. [...] I live with just my mom, and my sister's always after me [to go to school]. If I don't go, she gets me into trouble.
INTERVIEWER: What's the worst thing about being in school?
JOSH: The work.

INTERVIEWER: The work, you don't like the work?
JOSH: No.
INTERVIEWER: You genuinely don't want to – how come?
JOSH: It's hard and it's *boring*...
INTERVIEWER: Are you passing?
JOSH: I don't know about that.
INTERVIEWER: You don't know about that?
JOSH: Probably not.

...

INTERVIEWER: So what's that gonna mean for your future?
JOSH: Pretty bad so far ...
INTERVIEWER: So what did you say you wanted to be?
JOSH: An electrician.

By the end of this excerpt, Josh has acknowledged the significance of education; he seems aware that, unlike previous generations of working-class youth (e.g. Willis' lads), taking up manual working-class employment now requires some acceptance of the correspondence principle (education = job), where his own forms of knowledge and cultural capital are constantly denigrated. Rather than submit to the assessment of his worth as defined by the level of his success in school, he draws upon the 'front' to assert his view that the only value in education comes from friendship groups, and his judgement that school is boring, and thus not worthy of his time. Nonetheless, the strength of the 'front' for self-protection remains relatively fragile, particularly in the face of broader cultural emphases on the individual success that is apparently available to anyone who strives for high levels of achievement. As Josh notes, he 'doesn't want to work that hard', yet below he goes on to describe the ambivalence he feels in trying to work out his own desire to become a successful and legitimate citizen.

INTERVIEWER: Are you planning on finishing school?
JOSH: I dunno.
INTERVIEWER: Yeah, how come [you dunno]?
JOSH: I don't know, I just don't.
INTERVIEWER: You don't like school?
JOSH: Yeah, [it's boring].
INTERVIEWER: [...] What would you rather be doing?
JOSH: I'd like to graduate, you know and get a nice job but I don't think that's gonna happen.
INTERVIEWER: How come?
JOSH: Just 'cause I'm down a lot – and – like in credits [...] and I don't think there is any way I can improve on that in any way.
INTERVIEWER: You don't think so?
JOSH: There's probably a way but I don't think I want to work that hard

[…]. [I'm sure that means I won't be anyone important in Canada but …]

Rather than work hard at school, Josh draws upon the available front in the local hyper-masculinized subculture: the Thugs. As he notes in pointing out his mates in the school corridor one day, 'Thugs are beyond school.' Thus the primary dynamics for the protection of a 'working-class failure' is a naming practice that represents in part the gender, class and race interests of the group itself. As Clarke (1976) argues, the 'front' – as one element of youth subcultural activity – becomes the representation of wider social conflict through a market of symbolic exchanges that allows young people to feel visible, connected and powerful.

At the same time, this process of performing the 'front' presents contradictions for young people faced with heightened forms of individualization, with an exaggerated sense that they should be 'somebody', even as they navigate the space of the new individualized city which is no longer an industrial landscape that honours the working-class hero. In an interview with Randy, another young man from Tower Hill:

INTERVIEWER: Are they thugs?
RANDY: Yeah, they're like gangsters […] Portuguese Gangsters […]
INTERVIEWER: Just because they're Portuguese doesn't make them gangsters or from the Ghetto?
RANDY: No it's just something they do, [out of sheer boredom] you know they act 'tough' […].

Later Randy highlights why toughness and 'just hanging about' replaces the need for school success or mediates one's relationship to boredom and schooling in a consumer-oriented society. He later tells of another Thug or Gangsta Boy who dropped out because he said the

Thug thing got to his head […]. It just got to his head and he dropped out […] too much peer pressure […]. I think the boys like to show that they're mainly one of them, like become part of the group.

Here, we see the performance of 'the front', recognized by Randy as 'just something they do', as fundamentally a dramatic performance ('they act tough'), which serves to combat abjection and middle-class accounts of academic success and to establish their own distinctness within individualized school cultures as a dramatic break from boredom in a low-income neighbourhood.

Similarly, another young Portuguese male comments about 'gangs' and hanging around outside school out of boredom as a pastime and leisure activity: 'I guess they are trying to be cool […]. They think if you carry weapons and do smoking or you do drugs [...] you'll be classified as higher than the others.' These intimations of performance, classification, theatre and drama are reinforced by comments from young people about the Gangstas and their relationship to spatial authority ('like who owns the school'). As both Arendt and Ricoeur tell us, the narrative self is pervaded by dramatic and presentational qualities which can often serve as a basis from which to challenge society's attempt to define or prescribe. This is particularly so in contexts where feelings of failure (which are structurally located and over which young people in this new age are driven to feel extreme shame) provide the basis for residually bounded community structures (as well as for the performance of some of its sedimented narratives as a means to retrieve community).

But the performance or drama of youth cultural identity does not, as Clarke (1976) suggests, necessarily achieve the retrieval of community. Rather, the Gangstas and Thugs find recourse in an image of that community effected through the re-articulation of power, style and authority. Authority over the meaning of what it is to be young thus emerges as a form of power or contestation over the style and cultural choices of those other groups operating in the same class category but who must ultimately represent a difference, a foe; as Frankie responds to a question we pose about the Ginos:

INTERVIEWER: What's a Gino?
FRANKIE: That's the total opposite [of the Thug]. They wear pegged, tight, clothing, expensive clothes and there are a lot around [...]. You know the European name, I dunno, it's like most people where I'm from, Portugal, are all big Ginos [not me]. I'm a [Thug].

Here we witness that which Clarke (1990) wrote of the subjects of his study: 'they were the dispossessed inheritors; they had received a tradition which had been deprived of its real social basis. The themes and imagery still persisted but the reality was in a state of decline and disappearance.'

The declining nature of community as well as the painful recognition of its loss was also apparent in our study. Thus it was that many of the teachers reflected on the fact that strong working-class communities were being pushed out of the neighbourhood as a result of rising market prices in the inner-city. What had once been a strong residential housing community was being appropriated by an 'arty middle class' voluble in protesting about the 'state of the neighbourhood'. Here there are echoes of that which Derek Gregory (2006) suggests is a real space for the forced construction of visibility (i.e. the front), but which is also always a space of constructed invisibility, which is to say, suffering, neglect and abandonment. The space thus serves to expose new social class relations and the redrawing of cultural borders that makes possible the simultaneous struggle to be seen – as Gino, Thug or as Hardcore Asian boxer boy – alongside a pervasive individualization which expresses itself as a form of personal consumption in the form of heightened class relations of value and exchange. As the pressures of liberal individualism mount, young people must draw upon whatever cultural resources are available to set themselves apart; otherwise, they would be forced to accept the assessment, passed on by school authorities and reinforced in broadly circulating media images, of their own individualized failure.

The Making of the Deserving and Undeserving Citizen

While the 'front' might shore up young people's sense of legitimacy within urban imaginaries which are persistently undermined, however imperfectly, it becomes increasingly difficult for them to sustain their sense of self-worth in the face of the highly individualized concept of the neo-liberal citizen. The 'front', in its strongest subcultural expressions, retains some semblance of connection between the individual and the subcultural group or even community, even if the desire is to distinguish oneself as powerful and unique within it. However, the impact of liberal individualism and the role it plays in eroding low-income young people's own and others' sense of legitimacy emerges much more significantly when young people are asked to conceptualize the abstract and often empty concept of 'citizenship'.

Here, we bring together Bourdieu's seminal concept of the 'classification struggle' (1984), as central to our conceptual focus throughout, with a political critique of liberal and neo-liberal forms of individualism and citizenship. The classification struggle represents the manner in which individuals may engage in unconscious, culturally based struggles for social positions, both with and against people of their own class, but always in explicit relation to those with whom they imagine they are in competition. In light of these persistent competitions in urban space, what we argue here is that young people's expressions of the 'good citizen' or illegitimate member of the nation-state can in no way be seen or conceptualized outside the wider frame of social and cultural relations. Hence we view young people's expressions as part of a wider symbolic order about legitimacy and as a set of hidden social relations that can be seen as less than global and more than local, particularly in relation to wider imaginaries about nation and state. Understood in this way, citizenship, as a historically inscribed colonial ideal, may be problematized within the larger context of social relations as one aspect of young people's classification struggles at the edge of the inner core of global cities.

In theorizing young people's conceptions of state belonging and citizenship, we must therefore confront two essential features of youth subjectivity: the forces of symbolic ownership which can be found in one's history and position in the state, and the ways in which young people's struggle for social status must necessarily involve an investment in a sense of self-importance, exchange value and capability over and against that of others (friend or foe) (Skeggs, 2004; Cohen, 1997). The latter, as we have shown, is often mobilized through the enactment of a 'front', and serves as a dramatic break within boredom in a highly individualized milieu. However, we must also ask ourselves how young people draw upon political categories to determine whether or not they have achieved the status of the worthy, as conceived in these terms. In so doing, we may hope to learn how some part of the naming or defining of the potentially 'deviant' or manifestly worthy citizen revolves around the control of one's own territory and the assertion of an essential self as strategies for the winning of social recognition.

In seeking to work out the manner in which such classifications may occur, we are forced to repudiate the growing literature on the relationship between young people and the state which takes it as axiomatic that citizenship should be considered in terms of young people's *responsibilities to* the nation-state. This position typically asserts that any lack of citizenship 'skills' can be traced to a dearth of 'civic knowledge' or civic disengagement (Chamberlin, 2003; Ichilov, 2005; Weller, 2003). But few existing studies are of much help in showing how the lived social and political status of young people may actively mediate larger cultural narratives of democracy and citizenship. In the absence of phenomenologically oriented interpretations of young people's narratives of citizenship, it is difficult to ascertain just how young people may make sense of such foundational political concepts.

At this level of analysis, we therefore seek to connect the cultural sociology of youth stratification, which we have explored extensively throughout the preceding three chapters, with Hannah Arendt's and Wendy Brown's (1995, 2006) work on the constraints of ethical engagement in a democratic sphere. As Arendt (1971) notes, at the root of the problem of the state lie the myths associated with liberal democracy, particularly its emphasis on 'individual freedom', and the accompanying norms which define citizenship and find their shape in the history of Western states (see also Brown, 2001, 2005). In extending our concerns about youth practices of symbolic classification to political thought, Arendt's key contribution is her belief that dominant forms of state membership have emerged as a highly individualized and banal presence within liberal democracies, politically attuned to the objectives of both nationalism and nation-building. In this context, citizenship may stand as a form of displacement rather than as a meaningful political concept (Benhabib, 2004; Honig, 2001). Indeed, as Brown (2005: 41) suggests, the inherent problems associated with liberalism have been exacerbated in recent years through neo-liberal state practices, which 'facilitate[s] competition ... and rational economic action on the part of every member and institution of society'. In such an individualizing 'risk society' (Beck, 1999), dismissing and denigrating those 'bad citizens', whose status and circumstances demonstrate that they have been the agents of their own 'bad choices', stand precisely for the symbolic classification struggle of the individual in the state. The focus on individual choice within political liberalism thus renders each person an isolated, ahistorical unit, reducing citizenship to 'the isolated action of an individual that chooses [a consumer]' (Hernández, 1997: 35). The key argument here is that wider political discourses – such as the notion of the 'good citizen' as asserted through liberal political structures – govern a young person's subjective classification struggle within the symbolic realm of culture. These political discourses do not reside outside the realm of the sociological world or specific embodiment by youth themselves. Rather, such political discourses serve a fundamentally classificatory function in regulating young people's cultural narratives of citizenship, as we endeavour to show.

Responding to researcher questions about how they understood the concept of 'citizenship', young people linked a recurring series of attributes to their descriptions of legitimacy and belonging. Some examples of this may be seen in letters written by students to an imaginary young person about to immigrate to Canada:

> First of all, obeying the law and not committing crimes. What a person does reflects the kind of person you are and how people see you. ... By getting a job you will be more respected and be making a living at the same time. Job = respect others, others respect you!
>
> (Shareen, aged 15)

> There are five qualities required. Never cheat people for money, obey the laws, which are very important. Don't commit crimes, or it'll be in your record. Don't be racist or judgemental, not many people will be attracted to you. Most importantly for socializing, respect and treat people equally, with these qualities you will have a chance to come to Canada.
>
> (Angela, aged 16)

> You may consider bringing as much money as you can possibly get your hands on. That way it's easier to start over here in Canada with money. You should also have a positive attitude. This is certainly a must because in order to succeed you have to have this quality to begin with. Another thing is you made it this far, you have to keep working hard at this to reach Canada!
>
> (Amanda, aged 15)

Significant in each of these accounts is the centrality of economic self-sufficiency and non-reliance on the state for successful integration into Canada, the importance of compliance with the law, and self-regulation and responsibility for personal well-being and one's behaviour within the state. It would seem that the aspiring citizen needs to bring 'as much money to Canada as you can possibly get your hands on' or failing that, to get a job so that he or she will 'make … a living' to 'be respected'. He or she must always 'obey the law' and 'never commit crimes'. Within the polarized frame of the 'deserving' or 'undeserving' citizen, young people repeatedly emphasized characteristics of legitimacy and belonging, rarely referencing the opportunity to participate in public life as a way to engage with or challenge the state (through, for example, community participation, activism or voting).[2] Neither did they characteristically remark upon the rights and protections to which one is entitled as a citizen of Canada, or that which Hannah Arendt referred to as the 'right to have rights' (also see Benhabib, 2004). Instead, young people more commonly narrated dominant accounts of citizenship which conformed to a highly individualized moral and political order. Here, the 'good citizen' was a person who successfully utilizes strategies of self-regulation and self-surveillance to contribute to the economy or to benefit from it, to become affluent and not become a 'burden' to the state.

The process of classifying others as legitimate (or not) seems here to be tied primarily to traditional notions of liberal individualism heavily bound to exchange values, class aspirations and class status. In this understanding, citizenship is not something that is automatically conferred by the state but is instead represented as something we ought either to benefit from or feel anxious about. As one young Anglo-Canadian male remarked:

> Being a good citizen is good […] but how like is it going to pay off really? And it's like if you're a good citizen, yeah, […] you get the satisfaction of helping people, but it's like, it's just a deal.
>
> (Mark, aged 15)

In other words, being a good citizen at the fringe of the late-modern city is perceived as a means by which to negotiate an exchange – 'it's just a deal' – rather than an inherent status that offers unconditional protections and entitlements. Subsequently, it may carry a high price tag – or be perceived as 'risk-taking' – in urban concentrations of poverty amidst the struggle to apprehend the cultural frames of legitimate citizenship and their associated classifications. And, as ever, such classifications remain bound by urban spatial arrangements and reflect young people's fears of living in urban contexts where danger may seem more omnipresent than it might have in the past: 'it's like [now] people would try [to help as citizens] and a lot of them do and end up getting like killed or something' (Mark, aged

Figure 7.1 Student Image of the 'Citizen': Beacon Park. Vancouver, BC.

15). Here citizenship is reconfigured as a 'crime [that's] going to happen. You can't stop it really [...] and it's like if you try and stop someone [or help them] and then you end up hurting them, you can end up being the one who gets punished' (Andrew, aged 15) (see also Figure 7.1).

As the image in Figure 7.1 suggests, being a 'good citizen' – particularly if one is already marginalized by the state – may not be worth the risk. One consequence of these perceived risks is that young people understand state care to be extended only to those recognizable as suitably low-risk; they see their own role within the state as likewise limited. As this interview excerpt from Debbie (aged 15) attests, public participation is seen as safe only when it happens through acts of regulated charity that are aimed at those considered to be 'deserving':

INTERVIEWER: Anything else you want to talk about for a good citizen?
DEBBIE: They just help people.
INTERVIEWER: They just help anyone?
DEBBIE: No, [they help] other good citizens, they help people that are poor, donate food to them.

Figure 7.2 documents a similar response to the question of what role the 'good citizen' might play in relation to others.

On the left side of the image, the 'good citizen' is seen engaging in a legitimate charitable act: 'helping the elderly'; on the right side of the image, we see the bad citizen (even an orientalized subject), not taking seriously his or her civic responsibility to place trash in the trash bin.

Clearly, we are not suggesting that the provision of care to, for example, 'the elderly', is undesirable. Rather, our purpose in illustrating these polarizations is to demonstrate that they often emerge as the only way that public participation and legitimacy may be imagined by young people. Moreover, these acts of charity, often seen by young people as replacing welfare entitlements in the increasingly individualized state, are only

Figure 7.2 Student Image of the 'Citizen': Beacon Park. Vancouver, BC.

extended to those considered deserving of such treatment. If those who are being considered in the struggle to classify in any way represent potential risks, the attribution of 'deserving' easily slips out of view.

It is noteworthy that such classificatory forms are often expressed by young people who themselves are living outside the comfortable affluence of many middle-class young people. Indeed, our data suggest that it is the very reality of hardship and more visible forms of retrenchment in the new global city that may heighten and intensify these polarizations. In this context, young people might seek to be recognizable to others against and above those they witness living on their neighbourhood streets or engaging in prostitution or the drug trade to survive. This is particularly the case where young people become increasingly aware of their growing invisibility under the dynamics of neo-liberalism. As the modalities of social differentiation and populist political discourses about poverty suggest, this group of young people do not direct their concerns towards the state as the locus for responsibility. They are more likely to turn them towards the new twenty-first-century individual as either free of wrongdoing and risk (and thus deserving) or as undeserving: 'they just can't stop doing the same wrong things' (Leanne, aged 16). These trends were most palpable when young people themselves felt under siege by the state, often conflating citizenship with risky business or as unfolding at the expense of those deemed as 'others', 'foes' or otherwise objects of 'disgust'.

Young people also adopted the language of the individualizing state to make sense of the degree of destitution that they were witnessing on a daily basis. They did so by drawing repeatedly upon the idea that a person's fate is exclusively the result of their own individual choices; that is, the consequence of the autonomous, self-perfecting subject who controls his or her own actions (Rose, 1999). In responding to a photograph of people sleeping outside a major sports stadium in Toronto, one student wrote:

It's these people's fault that they're sleeping on the cold ground. They can easily go find a job or can go to welfare. The reason they're there is because they're lazy. They don't care about life. They look like they're just letting it pass them by.

(Allison, aged 15)

Another young person wrote:

When you see homeless people on the street [...] you would ask yourself 'Why are they even there?' It's because they don't know what to do with their lives anymore or they are short on cash or they're just plain lazy.

(Rebecca, aged 15)

Such discourses of individual choice are, of course, highly consistent with the rational, liberal subject identified by Arendt and others as problematically located in the centre of the political history of Western states. They also hold a contradictory place in young people's classification struggles, for by suggesting that individuals are inherently responsible for their

Figure 7.3 Student Image of the 'Citizen': Beacon Park. Vancouver, BC.

Figure 7.4 Student Image of the 'Citizen': Beacon Park. Vancouver, BC.

own bad choices, they risk shifting the blame for their own potential failures within regimes of schooling and wider society onto themselves. It is for this reason that those 'foreign others', the strangers and unwelcome neighbours ('terrorists', prostitutes, 'bums'), those signals of risk described in previous chapters, must be continually reconstituted as an undeserving 'other' whose very presence can shore up young people's own sense of legitimacy within the urban hierarchies of the global city.

Conclusions

We began this chapter by asking how young people living in the new twenty-first-century global city respond to national scripts about individualization, meritocracy and prevailing conceptions of the citizen. We have answered this question by highlighting the interdisciplinary theoretical power of conceptualizations such as the 'front', as well as political critiques of citizenship and state life as a set of symbolic referents. These carry enduring ideological and cultural legacies upon which young people draw as they struggle themselves, and alongside others, in the face of novel forms of social conflict. Such struggles are necessary as young people attempt to respond to what Bourdieu (1997) has called 'positional suffering' as potentially 'undeserving' subjects within the state. We have argued that, rather than simply representing instrumental civic virtues that apparently permit or will young people into state participation, citizenship has instead come to signify and re-signify the concept of the legitimate person within the nation-state. Such legitimacy has been re-formulated by young people themselves and intensified in part through the co-opted language of individualization. The 'good citizen' thus comes to be seen as the compliant, self-regulating individual who participates in the public sphere only through acts of charity, and only if the risks to a recognizable and acceptable form of selfhood are not too great. By contrast, the 'bad citizen' may be portrayed as the victim of his or her own 'bad choices,' and/ or a foreign and intimidating object potentially unworthy of recognition.

From this perspective, citizenship must be understood as much more than an instrumental political term. Rather, it should be seen as both a cultural and symbolic marker of social division and a symbolic narrative which serves in part to regulate both the class and classifying practices of young people. We base our conclusions on the assumption that there are heightened forms of symbolic meaning operating among youth, contingent in part upon quite new forms of urban retrenchment and regeneration. Forms of residual 'surplus meaning' – temporalized notions of the nation and its legitimate citizens as enduring ideas – are therefore implicated in the processes of youth classification, presenting a new cultural and spatial 'youthscape' (Nayak, 2003a) for channelling frustrations and resentments which are deeply tied to social division on a much wider scale. These surplus meanings emerge through metaphors and signs, which arise from the raw materials of young people's life experiences, but which are also borrowed from a residual past which actively persists in the present.

Tracing these signifiers also provides a window on the cultural, embodied and deeply coded forms of 'symbolic violence' (Bourdieu, 1997) which still operate through national narratives of citizenship and their classifying functions. In referring to Bourdieu's use of the term 'symbolic violence', we are suggesting that the contemporary language of citizenship has paradoxically come to represent an 'authorized' focus for particular classifications. While some youth participants' responses (e.g. class insults, racial interpellations) are indeed cause for concern, they should not surprise us, given the degree of classification operating through the embodiment of rising retrenchment on a much larger scale. Of greater concern for the larger project of urban justice is the degree to which low-income young people may have become increasingly individualized in the new urban city, thus narrowing their potential for political action. As both Arendt and Curtis have noted, conditions of modernity have led to the attenuation of our ability to sense the nature of 'the real' (Curtis, 1997: 46; 2003), displacing the 'ethical' and the 'political' from the centre of young people's lives. Young people's capacity, therefore, to be open to difference on a much wider social scale may be curtailed by high levels of individualization and heightened forms of positional competition. Results from our ethnography suggest that such liberal conceptions, which the young people have incorporated into protective classification strategies, such as 'the front', serve to perpetuate their isolation from each other (what Arendt calls 'world alienation'), and from the public world where they might have a chance to advocate for themselves and those others with whom they are required to live. As Arendt writes: 'what has become so inhospitable about the world that humankind should desire to escape its home?' (cited in Ring, 1989: 34).

Conclusion

One becomes moral as soon as one is unhappy.

(Proust, 2003: 282)

In this book we have presented an ethnographic account of contemporary youth cultures and their accounts of living at the edge of the urban core in late-modern urban Canada. In offering these accounts, we have striven not only to shed some light on the 'structures of feeling' that underwrite young people's contemporary urban imaginaries, but also to engage dialectically with the temporal, spatial and symbolic elements of what Ricoeur refers to as the 'testimonial role of [youth] narrativization' (see also Alexander, 1995). In so doing, our goal has been to bring the otherwise isolated narratives of young lives within a systematic socio-cultural investigation of young people's social positioning in the late-modern city. At the heart of this analysis has been our attempt to make sense of the range of young people's negotiations with the city's boundaries and edges, and with their associated fantasies, imaginaries and struggles to be recognizable to themselves and to others. We have undertaken this analysis in order to explore the class effects of the dynamic relationship of past and present in urban space – as 'historical time' and 'embodied time' – upon the ambitions, potential futures and late-modern cultures of low-income and working-class youth. As Ricoeur tells us: 'Experience can be said, it demands to be said. To bring it to language is not to change it into something else, but, in articulating and developing it, to make it become itself' (1998: 115).

Throughout the work we have resisted the temptation to imagine the narratives to which we have listened as singular voices, as individualized confessions, or as empty discourses. We have, in short, turned away from – again, to use the words of Ricoeur with which we started – the 'amnesia of the now'. Our approach has rather been to engage young people's narratives as 'eclipsed moments, refiguring them as similar to our present experience (failing which we would not be able to recognize them), while simultaneously acknowledging their dissimilarity as distinct and distant' (Kearney, 2004: 100). In this way we have attempted to show how youth cultural narratives and their narrative re-appropriation in the form of ethnographic representation exercise a dual function. They operate as a form of historical narration which lives in the present, and also as a form of recognition that perceives that, while the past is always absent, its symbolic features endure through the refiguring of surplus meaning within the novel youth narratives of the urban spaces of the present. Such an approach has, we hope, helped us to avoid some of the governing effects of the theory wars which have concentrated on theoretical problems of the very existence of youth subcultures over and against post-subcultures. These conflicts, while interesting and vital within the world of theory and its interlocutors, with all its strategic assaults and territorial defences, has often served to elide or mask the cult of the 'new' as it struggles to displace the old.

Paradigm wars about youth cultures have also sometimes masked the importance of narrative in the organization of space as the arena for the intermingling of past, present and future. Guided by this understanding, we have sought to discover how youth narrations converge and are realized in the material spaces between fiction and history, experience and discourse, truth and myth and past and present (see Arendt, 1998). Once we recognize such convergences and their operative functions, we are better placed to engage the storied self, or Walter Benjamin's Storyteller, where identity operates not as a sovereign subject who is responsible for his or her own failings but instead as an expression of complex combinations of the fictive and the factual. In our understanding, 'fictional effects' (Kearney, 2004: 102) are paradoxically just those moments in which change seems attainable because in the still unknown landscape of young people's possible worlds, we can also recognize the class effects of a storied marginalization which renders both social conditions and anomie visible. In this way, a re-contextualization of youth cultures as both past and present turns us away from 'neutralizing injustice' (see Kearney, 2004: 102), from re-representing fixed and immobile accounts of young people as the new folk devils, and from simply explaining away the power of surplus meaning, the subject, the cultural ordinary and social class relations.

And, as we have learned in our comparative ethnography, multiple selfhoods, mobile forms of individualization or the 'freedom to be me' are not of course equally available to all, and nor do they always emerge in and through experience, even if the language of liberalism is spoken. Instead, in recognizing differentiation among youth cultures across place we have tried to make visible historical reference points and plots from the past which young people inherit as they interface with new worlds, much of which are not of their own choosing. It cannot then any longer be a question of merely pitting subcultures against post-subcultures, of facing-off social class against fluidity or against discourse, or inclusion against exclusion. And nor is it a question of 'intellectual strait-jacketing' which insists upon a form of social class theorizing which refuses engagement with the subjective and imaginative worlds of youth cultures (see Brown, 2005).

For us, it is rather a question of recognizing that any explanation of youth cultures and young people and their differential experiences of exclusion in the global city demands a narrative form which provides some account of the symbolic and material orders in which young people must necessarily exist. It is a matter of seeing that imagination without hope, or without fantasy and its fictional effects, risks losing the meaningfulness for which youth cultures must necessarily strive in the present moment.

Our particular task has been to take the stories of the young people we encountered in Tower Hill and Beacon Park and, through comparative cultural and spatial ethnographic lenses, to assess them against the background noise of local histories in urban spaces, and in relation to contemporary moral claims and urban class conflicts. In so doing, we have tried to create space for their 'experience ... [to] become itself'. But we have not treated these experiences as innocent, or isolated. Rather, we have seen them as tied to the 'battlefield of competing meanings' (see Kearney, 2004: 105) which underpin widespread forms of youth exclusion in the global city of the present and their links to wider circulating forms of moral anxiety operating at global scales (Ahmed, 2003).

In so doing, we have argued that subcultural theory and post-subcultural accounts comprise less a binary than a dialectic, capturing both the enduring elements of wider social class relations, together with a recognition of the symbolic cultural force of social change. In doing so, we have been constantly aware of the theoretical dangers of either overestimating change in the form of post-subcultures in the present, or 'installing traditionalism' into the centre of our theorizing 'in the place where commitment to risk and upheaval belongs' (see Brown, 1999). Rather than discarding subcultures in favour of post-subcultures, or vice versa, then, we have argued that each provides conceptual utility that contributes to a better understanding of the dilemmas of young people's lives across place. And, indeed, space and place – as class geographies of power and emotion – become crucial in apprehending the symbolic expression of youth cultures in their various formations; this necessitated the use of visual methods such as photo-narratives, timelines and archival photos. Whilst visual methodology is now employed by many researchers to great effect, our key contribution in this respect has been to synthesize the pragmatic utility of these methods at the level of ethnographic practice that recognizes their power to access youth experience at the multi-nodal levels of the temporal, the spatial and the symbolic.

In conducting this work, we have come to conceptualize loss and young people's accounts of loss as a social class relation which not only forms part of wider urban imaginaries but which speaks on a broader scale to the geographies of nation and colonialism and their surplus effects. In so doing we have found that subcultural practices can sometimes persist when cultural practices and forms of collective memory are transported across the world and are layered upon an already uneven urban space.

They may also persist in particularly traditional forms as part of strategic settlement practices associated with the disciplining categories of the state in host cities. These settlement sites often emerge as key spaces for the maintenance of collective memory, culture and the need for class protection in times of intense retrenchment as youth cultures must necessarily interface with new worlds. Subcultural expressions may also be associated with widening and concentrating class conflicts and re-circulating moral anxieties about the 'working classes', spaces of abjection and their links to particular categories of youth. And, as always, they remain powerful devices for navigating high degrees of alienation, urban risks and social fear. Here, class geographies of power and micro-nationalisms (such as the Gino and Gangsta rivalries, or degrees of orientalism operating at the urban fringe) emerged as powerful predictors of youth cultural affiliation and one's ability to free oneself from elements of tradition (such as the Ginos and Gangstas of Tower Hill).

In Tower Hill, for example, we witnessed young people navigating the sedimented effects of traditional gender and class roles alongside the apparent re-organization and re-contextualization of youth cultural practices in the forms of style (e.g. desires to be Eminem, Ginos who listen to techno and beat music) and gendered peer rivalry. Examining how conceptual ideals of femininity and masculinity were constructed, re-negotiated and monitored as part of authorized social relations in particular spaces such as the school corridor also provided a powerful spatial landscape for understanding the cultural processes underlying young people's struggles for legitimacy in subcultural groupings. Clearly, despite 'new times' and the mediating role of liberal discourses in subcultural practices, gender and class relations frequently assumed the form of ideological burdens of history and reiterations of tradition. At the same time, they also incorporated urban modalities and imaginaries drawn from the trajectories of late-modernity, horizons of contemporary popular culture and neo-liberal discourses.

We also witnessed post-subcultural effects in which diasporic and highly mobile communities of young people, such as recent migrants, indigenous peoples and long-time settler societies, vied for space and legitimacy. Here, we witnessed first-hand and close up the traces of these local, national and global histories, as well as memories of home, belonging and micro-nationalisms operating at the urban fringe. We saw how they were felt and creatively acted upon – re-enacted through youth cultures – as young people struggled to classify themselves in relation to race, citizenship and legitimacy. As told through young people's stories and visual accounts of race and place, the 'Wannabes', the 'Real and Hardcore Asians', the 'Hongers' and the 'FOBs' were often represented in the first instance as simple and essentializing racial categories. However, in the unfolding of spatial and social class relations, we witnessed complex stories about the role of class in the making of race through space. However, in these seemingly new productions of youth communities such as wannabe Asians, we also saw the continuing and re-traditionalized effects of colonial practices of classification such as the foreign other, enfolded within new stories of crisis, such as the 'war on terror'. Each of these productions existed within a specific spatial locale, the history of which was shown to be inseparable from the manifestation of locally emergent youth subcultures.

As expressed in late-modern trajectories of the young person, there is also of course a good deal of circulating rhetoric that revolves around the high modern ideal of individualization and the 'good citizen'. Here we sought to describe how young people understand this rhetoric, how they view belonging and security in the state, how they classify legitimacy and what this might mean for any kind of political engagement with the city or the state. Rather than conceding to widely circulating beliefs about the root of youth civic disengagement being caused by political apathy, we have demonstrated that young people use the idea of the 'good citizen' as a cultural and moral resource for distinguishing between 'friend' and 'foe', and in determining levels of personal risk in the late-modern city. Drawing in particular upon political critiques of liberalism and neo-liberalism, we showed how young people have incorporated micro-national anxieties and global risks into their understandings of themselves and each other at the urban fringe, including self-help above state support, and the requirement to be self-regulating and self-perfecting. The consequence of youth practices of interpellation is deep ambivalence about their own place in the world, as well as about the qualities required of the good citizen, particularly when living at the fringe of the global city. Clearly, to be engaged politically or to be a 'good citizen' is for many young people a form of risk-taking as they seek to work out their own sense of self-worth over and above those they have classified as fundamentally undeserving, or as they assess the consequences of any potential political action in an urban fringe site which carries with it the historical burden of abjection. Indeed, what we have learned is that in the late-modern city helping others or engaging with the state may be seen as dangerous, meaningless or simply a game. We also saw that the very concepts of citizen and nation assumed the symbolic meanings of micro-national struggles, migration biographies and memories of home, though not necessarily in ways which undermined racism or which could subvert the effects of the long history of colonial relations in new times.

Philosophical Reflections: Youth Cultures as Symbolic Narrations

Narratives do not impart sovereign truths. Rather, they solicit the (re)discovery of meaning. Narratives do so by depicting spectacular events unfolding in time and space. Such spectacles stand ripe for hermeneutic engagement. They solicit the exercise of interpretive skills to discern their themes, lessons, and moral bearings.

(Thiele, 2006: 1)

Perhaps Arendt, more than any other political theorist, observed that narratives are incapable of imparting sovereign truths even as they speak to the power of wider moral economies of the nation. Perhaps youth studies and even present-day youth cultural studies, with their focus on transitions, new times, new subjects and presentism, are not much interested in narrative even when it is defined as something fundamentally sociological. However, in reviewing our findings and in recognizing the necessary dialectic between subcultural and post-subcultural theorizing, we believe there is now a case for moving beyond the idea of youth culture as only spectacular as a classed 'revolt into style' or as somehow fundamentally disembedded from tradition. Instead we wish to argue that youth cultures can be seen as forms of symbolic narration which are unfolding, polyvalent, deeply connected to urban imaginaries and paradoxical; this is principally because these unfolding narratives always hold within them the spatial and sometimes mobile mark of others we may not have known in past time, and the anticipation of a future that can never be known. The narrative of youth cultures – as in life itself – must therefore necessarily exceed the frontiers of identity and of theory. It is, in other words, through a phenomenological understanding of such identity claims around youth cultures themselves that we are forced to move beyond their essential *authority* (that is the 'authority of the sovereign', or what 'commends a text (a life) to memory'; see Felman, 2002: 228). In so doing, we open ourselves to the dramatic tensions of that agonistic space which bridges the duality of youth cultural expression and life itself, and which characterizes a storied life in all its manifestations. These dilemmas are both relational and spatial in that we both benefit and suffer from the *conflict of interpretations* once the spatial expression of a text – for example, to be a Gina, a Hardcore Asian or a Gangsta – begins its journey through successive audiences, present and future, known and unknown in particular contexts: 'where dialogue ends, hermeneutics begins' (Ricoeur, 1981).

In this way, being young or performing youth culture is, therefore, something quite different from the historical meaning(s) or even current uses of the phrase 'youth identity' or even youth subcultures. It is in this recognition of a storied 'who' and its governing processes (who we could not narrate without others both dead and alive, past and present) that allows us to acknowledge difference (in the life of the text), and therefore of the impossibility of youth 'cultures' as a truly essential form. Youth cultures, as a form of identification, necessarily exceeds the essential boundaries of youth identity or any sovereign self (see Hall, 1996a, 1996b, 1997). Here we see youth cultures performing 'human time', constituting 'the time of our existence and our experience', but also a time that encompasses and overflows them.[1] In this respect, a 'critical consciousness' of our language-use and its representational effects in terms of young people's experience of past and present lives proved to be a necessary precursor for seeking a fuller understanding of youth cultures in the present. And this necessity must co-exist with a fuller understanding of urban space as something which is necessarily tied to class conflicts on a wider scale.

Following Miller and Rose (2008), then, we do not wish to ask the question of what youth cultures are as an object of analysis. Rather, we wish instead to ask what forms of governance does the power of *identity*, as a highly symbolic entity, possess within the imaginary nucleus of youth cultures? What multiple readings do we need to engage with to render identity as a technique of cultural power within the very nucleus of youth cultures and in representations of young people across time? How does the very technique and power of identification shape and change the ways in which young people struggle to classify themselves and others at the fringe of the global city? Which moral claims about identity emerge in these new spaces as the most legitimate form of power?

In engaging with social and cultural theory, both with and beyond established theories of youth cultures and youth exclusion, the scholarship of theorists such as Hannah Arendt, Paul Ricoeur, Adriana Caverero and Wendy Brown has been particularly helpful in relating questions about the representation of youth in research, particularly concerning the ways in which the multiple stories of young people might be narrated in and through the medium of time, and through the widening of analytical justice by way of narrative and historiography. For Arendt and Ricoeur, a paramount element of a selfhood that is inescapably situated (in other words relational) as well as reflexive, lies in its ethical striving towards that responsibility which is expressed by the verb 'I can'. The 'I can' (not I am) of a deeply situated self, narrated within the contexts of time and place 'can be read in terms of four verbs, which the "I can" modifies: *I can speak, I can do things, I can tell a story,* and *I can be imputed,* and action can be imputed to me [in part] as its author' (Ricoeur, 1992: 16; 2002: 280). This is not a singular 'I' in a free world without constraints and it is not an 'I' on its own, for to 'say I is to never say me' as a liberal mediation (see Ricoeur, 1992). These statements instead represent the active and discursive space within which the capacities of an active and unfolding form of youth culture can be recognized. Arguably, then, our task as researchers has been to represent this process of becoming as a temporal unfolding which is only a partial draft of cultural identity – an *interesse* – not only in relation to those whom we seek to represent but also as a debt to a history which may have eluded us and which always forms part of the future or the 'not yet' (see Simon, 2005).

Research engaging with youth cultures should, in our view, seek to capture this 'space of experience' as the past made present. In this way, associated analyses might strive towards representing

> the weight of our past on our future ... obligat[ing] us, in historical responsibility, not only to take our past into account in what we do today but also to respect it for tomorrow in ways which a critique of its language forms [solely as identity] may in some manner undermine.
>
> (Dauenhauer, 2000: 242; brackets our addition)

It is for this reason that singular theoretical interpretations of youth culture remain inadequate for the task of interpretation. In this recognition, we might consider moving towards a better understanding of the ontology of youth narratives over time (and their powerful modes of operation through the practice of youth cultures). Such narratives can of course surpass conventions but still function in 'communities of practice' (Paechter, 2003) as both micro and macro forms of symbolic dominance (*pace* Bourdieu) and as techniques of governance (*pace* Foucault), even if we are not always conscious of them.

We need to find ways – youth culture research certainly constitutes a good case for this – of embedding diverse and polyvalent meanings from the past more explicitly within youth research in the present, as well as developing a 'historiographical radicalism' of the field (see Felman, 2002). Such temporal reflexivity calls upon us to 'know something about the past made present' or that 'absent cause' which has remained hidden from us through the very practices of doing research. This knowledge continues to encourage us that there will likely be elements of many theoretical worlds – both past and present – that can assist us with this task. Such work can only be done, we believe, through an interdisciplinary bridging which takes as axiomatic that narrowly defined subjects inherited from particular traditions of thought and practice – for example, sociology, cultural geography, gender studies, cultural studies – are unlikely to expand the ethical dimensions of research without research detours into an ethical temporality or a relational dialogue with its others, without which we would not be who we are (Skocpol, 2005). To the extent that we remain bound by terms which enable the 'endless repetition of a catastrophic past that is locked up in trauma and repetition [...] which could prevent a grasp' (Felman, 2002: 228) of something new or unprecedented, or indeed to break fresh ground in relation to young people themselves, then we must risk those elements of our past – in this case – our research *identities* and the sedimentations of power that accrue through our affective investments in them. In the words of Richard Kearney (2004: 32): 'it is only by distancing the self from the original ego that the interpreter can hope to recover a new sense of subjectivity: enlarged, decentred and open to novel possibilities of self interpretation.' And, in so doing, we can witness a relational account of youth culture which 'borrows from the imaginative power of re-description' as it appears to us in space and time. In this way, youth cultures can be seen as the 'infinite imaginative variations of a story' ... but this story (if it can be freed from a moralizing politics and forms of heightened moral anxiety) is always both new and re-appropriated from past time and within particular geographical arrangements of power (Kearney, 2004: 54).

Socio-cultural Reflections

Temporality and Representation: Youth Cultures Possessing and Repossessing the Past

In respect of both temporality and representation, then, connections may be sought between the young people's symbolic order of any given time and place, the social imaginaries circulating about young people, and the reconstructed experience of being young. One way to imagine youth culture as a temporal entity inherited from the past and grounded in authorized spaces, therefore, is through the concepts of 're-staging' and surplus meaning – that is, as a theatrical and dramatic re-staging (indeed a re-contextualized front) of an existing social narrative that has been reconstructed for a particular public audience in order to retrieve that which might be lost through the processes of social change. As Kearney writes (2004: 54): 'For a human being-in-the-world in its most everyday sense [...] involves a process of temporalization which makes our present actions meaningful by interpreting them in terms of a recollected past and a projected future.'

We might join Ricoeur and others in arguing that the performance of youth cultures is 'bound up in narrative imagination', and in this narration it becomes evident that the 'self flows toward another', the 'moi into a soi', providing an encounter with 'foreign worlds, enabling us to tell and listen to other stories' (see Kearney, 2004: 33). If young people who live on the margins of legitimacy are to avoid becoming merely a spectacle of constant resimulation, a reproduction of a colonial folk devil, or the 'dark phantom of race relations' in new times, then we are now, more than ever, in need of the powers of a narrative imagination.

More importantly, what we learn from narrative imagination as part of the practice of representation and temporality is that we can only speak of youth representation – such as the Hardcore Asians – as an outcome of a narrative act (not only or ever just a subjective 'I'), which releases a certain force of representing which is modern (i.e. something modern in the making), changing, enduring and historical. The narratives young people offer always therefore have more to give us than a mere account of their lives. They are engagements in what Paul Ricoeur identifies as the wider notion of *représentance*, 'representation by replacement', re-contextualization, or by encountering something anew. Here, narrative construction with representative force in urban space takes the place of a simple notion of representation or fixed accounts of an unchanging person or a developmentally sequenced sovereign subject: 'History operates through an irreducible course of reconstruction, which is its only instrument for seeking truth' (cited in Kearney, 2004: 369). Hence, youth cultures provide us with an indirect way of witnessing the power of time in relation to young people's changing self-understandings and not a simple narrative of sociological change or presentism. It is precisely in this way that it becomes even more urgent that we recognize that the sociologist, the geographer, the cultural studies scholar and the historian cannot continue to hold a distanced approach from each other, and that we learn more about the dangers of merely reconstructing a narrative of young cultures as a single and de-contextualized snapshot in time. Indeed, in holding on to such intellectual distancing we may fail to grasp key sociological questions such as those pertaining to generational conflict, migration narratives, the power of the diaspora to transform national imaginaries of space, and the enduring symbolic force of youth cultures. This approach to youth culture – time, space, change and ultimately the subjective – also allows us to see that young people do not own, as it were, their symbolic expressions as a statement of selfhood; rather, they also carry the durable and sedimented effects of quite mobile and trans-local social orders with them as they attempt to live their lives in a radically changing world. And, as McLeod and Yates (2006) argue, against the paradigmatic dominance operating in the late-twentieth century about constant change, the concept of new times and radical change may indeed be overstated.

In summary, then, we have learnt that young people may be seen as neither author nor subject of their own narratives, but always subjected to, and subjectified within, a particular time and place. A temporal and spatial understanding of how diverse young people struggle to hold together the imagined identities they construct for themselves and others as they navigate complex and exclusionary social terrain is central to the project of understanding how youth cultures are made and remade. It also succeeds in showing how a reconfiguration of past time or even lost time in youth narratives leads to the interruption of traditional systems of meaning which change the course of existing youth cultures. Social change, temporality, urban space and youth subjectivity therefore emerge as mediators of social meaning.

Youth can no longer be seen as a 'truth', a simple construction through discourse, a future or a simple narrative of marginality which we must observe as some objective category in constant need of scrutiny or repair. Instead, it must be seen as a cultural medium and expression of temporal existence. Change needs to be understood within the context of time and the discursive tropes that figure the youth narrative itself (Ricoeur, 1976, 1992; see also Simon, 2000). We cannot find this narrative simply as a sociology of youth in the present. Inevitably, some elements of the narrative serve the purpose of desirable myths and longstanding colonial projects, as well as lost histories and 'great nations', and some elements serve the purpose of 'truth' in the loose sense of meaning expounded in young people's stories of exclusion in the global city. However, if we are to get past the long listing of often paralysing youth narratives which hang endlessly off the pages of the plethora of research studies charting the voices of young lives, we must attempt to locate such lives within spatial sites of meaning which help us better to understand the world that young people face as part of history as well as of the present. This is not a tale of narrative comfort; we do not always feel at home as we read narratives of exclusion and struggle at the edge of the global city. But the power of young people's narratives must reach beyond itself, enabling us to learn something new. As Clifford Geertz has so aptly suggested, progress in any field often lies in conjunctions (history, geography *and* sociology *and* youth studies): 'take care of the conjunctions and the nouns will take care of themselves' (Geertz, 2000: 334).

Epilogue on Space, Moralizing Subjects and the Global City

The stories that the young people told us about themselves, their lives, and their experiences of local neighbourhoods, homes and the cities in which they live constitute the narrative identity that Ricoeur describes, and with which we began the book. Our goal in appropriating Ricoeur's idea of the symbolic narrative in youth cultural research was to erase the spectre of 'lost youth' from its maligned media and popular culture frame, and offer an account that served as a reconstitution of the 'who-ness' (Arendt, 1998) of these young people, and the making and remaking of both space and self. Faithful to Arendt's notion of the 'space of appearances', we recognize that widely circulating one-dimensional representations of young people – which often sway public opinion in unfortunate directions – have the potential to undermine young people's potential for action within the public realm, or their ability to be seen as the subjects of thoughtful action by others. In other words, contemporary representations of 'lost youth' function as a form of *symbolic violence* (Bourdieu, 1997), resulting in practical harms directed towards young people in the forms of regressive policies, increasing criminalization and in their associated feelings of abjection about themselves and others. It is our hope that this book has offered a partial response to these forms of injustice.

The other spectral player is, of course, the 'global city' itself, that apparently unwieldy and fluctuating concept that encapsulates both the promise of a utopian future and the dystopic realities of stratification, urban decay and rising inequality. Through the phenomenological accounts of our youth participants, we have, we believe, shed some light on this new urban constellation in relation to wider-circulating moral claims about young people in late-modernity. As seen through the eyes of young people – through their stories of local neighbourhoods, their photo-narratives, their captioning of local archival footage and, above all, through their highly territorial place-based classification struggles – the edge of the global city has been illuminated as a site of profound ambivalence and for the creation of class fantasies and new antagonisms impacting on youth cultures. The global city for these young people is one populated by an increasing and vaguely threatening homeless population; it is a place that is marked by the stigma of visible drug-use and prostitution near their schools and homes. It represents the threat of both criminalization and of abandonment. It creates, in other words, a feeling of loss but one which cannot be named and for which there may be no language, and where young people feel that they may not be redeemed from anonymity and namelessness.

For these young people, there are personal prices to be paid for these spatial arrangements. For many youth participants, the global city was not seen as the desirable destination of 'world-class' status, as represented by global rankings directed at middle-class professionals or multinational corporations looking for new cities in which to make profit. Rather, it represented a space of increasing marginalization, representing a continuity of uneven processes that have been pushing low-income young people and their families to the urban fringes for over three decades. These fringes are neither innocuous nor irrelevant. They carry with them affective investments, diasporic formations and class struggles which shape the way young people imagine themselves and others in the present and future.

In assessing fringe imaginaries, we learn that the search for magical resolutions to class conflict is not dead and nor is social class. Instead, it may very well be that theory to greater or lesser degrees is responsible for the death of social class or has functioned, in Nayak's (2009) words, to 'erase old registers' of substantial significance in the present. It may also be that the very idea of cosmopolitan life in the world-class city is not only elusive but particularly dangerous as it clearly does not apply to many of the young people in our study. This is so because cosmopolitan subjects often rest alongside the kinds of moralizing politics that have shaped the very organization of the city in relation to working-class communities, particularly when tied to moralizing strains of potentially new folk devils. As Skeggs (2004) suggests, we see that space and its inhabitants are tied to wider forms of symbolic and moral evaluations which lead to the attribution of value. Clearly, as our work has shown, young people are using different forms of cultural exchange and classification which are embedded in high degrees of moral regulation and cultural norms which are spatially contingent. Here class 'insinuates itself' into the very spatial practices of youth cultures as they seek to understand who has more or less moral value in a rapidly changing place (Skeggs, 2004). In such cases, we learn that urban change is all-too-often premised on the needs of outsiders rather than the needs of those young people who must navigate this space and attempt to apprehend it. We also learn of the sheer power of symbolic and moral distinctions to shape young people's place and self-making projects (e.g. Boxer boys) and to wider questions about who can be a good citizen in the new global city.

Young cultural expression is therefore a form of social translation which makes visible the past and the present in dialectical tension. It is in this very tension that we are able to read and respond to the inequalities which young people face in the apparently new 'global city'. Unfortunately, at this stage, we do not have a series of solutions to offer in the form of prescriptions. Instead, we must close by insisting that there is political value in gaining some grasp in youth cultural studies on what really is 'the time of the now', and a historicity of space as it relates to young people in the present. We have been concerned therefore with the problem of how we might address youth exclusion in a manner that abandons the fictions associated with the death of class, the death of history and by engaging with the horizons of the possible and the new. For us, and with a deep commitment to the work of Paul Ricoeur what we have learned is that the time of youth culture is also our time and the problems young people encounter are not theirs in any singular sense. They belong to us as we read them against the global city and in our struggle to redeem lost time in the symbolic horizons of the present.

Notes

Introduction

1. Intimations of the scale, character and potential of such threats have in recent years been relayed with substantial force through an increasingly sophisticated and globalized visual, electronic and print media.
2. Ricouer (1991) defines narrative identity as:

   the kind of identity that human beings acquire through the mediation of the narrative function. I encountered this problem at the end of *Time and Narrative* volume III, when, after a long journey through historical narrative and fictional narrative, I asked the question of whether there was any fundamental experience that could integrate these two major types of narrative. I then formed the hypothesis that the constitution of narrative identity, whether it be that of an individual person or of a historical community, was the sought-after site of this fusion between narrative and fiction. We have an intuitive pre-comprehension of this state of affairs: do not human lives become more readily intelligible when they are interpreted in the light of the stories that people tell about them? And do not these 'life stories' themselves become more intelligible when what one applies to them are the narrative models – plots – borrowed from history or fiction (a play or a novel)? The epistemological status of autobiography seems to confirm this intuition. It is thus plausible to endorse the following chain of assertions: self-knowledge is an interpretation; self interpretation, in its turn, finds in narrative, among other signs and symbols, a privileged mediation; this mediation draws on history as much as it does on fiction, turning the story of a life into a fictional story or a historical fiction, comparable to those biographies of great men in which history and fiction are intertwined.

   (As cited in Wood, 2004: 188)

3. These storied youth narratives – encoded and recoded in human time – point us towards a sociology of young people which does not use the category of 'change' as a fetish which endeavours to position young people solely as the vehicles of transition, future citizenship and progress, or, by contrast, as leisure loving, club-going, knife-bearing footballers and sink estate kids (Muggleton, 2000; Shildrick, 2006).
4. And if we are to equip ourselves with a figure of that 'something' that makes up the 'lost youth' which figures so strongly in public consciousness, then we will also be obliged, following Ricoeur, to turn back in time towards those longstanding middle-class representations of youth in the past which continue to underpin the classificatory tenor of contemporary media accounts and the public record.
5. These ideas are also expressed in the work of Deleuze and Guattari (1987) as 'structured planes of affect'.
6. As Grossberg (1997: 16) has suggested, 'bespeaking the body, embodying release from boredom, from ennui, from anomie – from, that is to say, the sometimes repressive, imprisoning routines of everyday life.'
7. Mattering maps are, according to Deleuze and Guattari (1987), 'maps people fabricate in order to articulate what matters most to them in their everyday lives'.
8. The Canadian case of Amir Khadr who is imprisoned at Guantanamo Bay is informative

here (http://varifrank.com/archives/2006/06/canada_17_more_1.php, accessed 17 October 2008), as is the recent case of the young Muslim convert suffering from Asperger's Syndrome who was made to appear in the media as a primitive warrior working on behalf of Jihad (i.e. conflated with a primitive culture, www.dailymail. co.uk/news/article-1077808/How-Muslim-convert-set-bombs-error-open-toilet-door.html, accessed 17 October 2008).

9. For notable exceptions to this, see Gallagher, 2007.

10. We also endeavour to map some of the contemporary dimensions of social class relations and forms of classifications and negotiations operating between young men and women against the backdrop of globalizing forces and their manifestation at the local level.

11. For example, in keeping with the findings of earlier subcultural research work, our study shows that, in particular spatial urban contexts, highly traditional (rather than re-traditionalized) notions of youth subcultural configuration remain very powerful in shaping the positional rules and practices of subcultural activity. By contrast, in areas where wider global changes have radically reconfigured the spatial structures of localities in ways which interface with powerful forms of middle-class consumption and new forms of governance, currents of fragmentation, increased forms of self-governance and fluidity attesting to post-subcultural effects may present themselves (see also Buckingham et al., 2009; Kehily & Nayak, 2009).

1. Theoretical 'Breaks' and Youth Cultural Studies: Post-Industrial Moments, Conceptual Dilemmas and Urban Scales of Spatial Change

1. DAY OF TERROR BY SCOOTER GROUPS: YOUNGSTERS BEAT UP TOWN – 97 LEATHER JACKET ARRESTS

The Rockers wore black leather and studs, had anti-authority beliefs, and projected an easy rider nomadic romanticism. [...] It was under this glare of publicity that the idea of scooter gangs – Mods – versus motorbike gangs – Rockers – really flourished. Until then they had not been rigidly separate groups: the conflict was more a case of rivalry between Londoners and local groups which came in for the weekend from villages in the surrounding counties of East Anglia. Then, as later, there were no massed opposing groups of scooter riders and motorbike riders. The truth was, especially in cities, the groups were inter-related, often from the same housing estates; only separated by fashion or generations. [...] Whilst the division of these particular minorities of British youth into factions emerged at Clacton, it's true to say that stylistic differences had already emerged in the early 60s. An 'Italianate' or 'Modern' style of designer dressing and an attraction to R&B [...] had given birth to the Mod, though they were lumped in under the general heading of Teddy Boys at the time. [...] Which is all rather too neat, as the Mods, at least, fractured into a variety of sub-groups almost from the beginning. There were the scooter boys, all flapping jeans and anoraks, centring on art-school types. Then there were the short-haired hard Mods, who wore jeans suspended from braces, and weighty boots. They are the ones who seem to have been at the centre of the violence, and they are thought to have been the precursors of the crop-headed, violent Skinheads [...]. Again, there were smooth Mods, usually slightly older and better-off, who paid close attention to their dress, cruising the boutiques by day and the clubs by night. [...] Ironically, the Mods were largely absorbed, while the Rockers went on virtually unaltered, apart from the odd name change. The annual battles on the beaches had ceased long before, and the war between Mods and Rockers that had raged on our TV screens was already fading from popular memory. Did it actually ever happen or was it just a media creation?

(http://en.wordpress.com/tag/mods-and-rockers/, accessed 18 March 2009; see also http://news.bbc.co.uk/onthisday/hi/dates/stories/may/18/newsid_2511000/2511245. stm, accessed March 18, 2009)

2. Up to the late 1980s, in part what we might have witnessed in the field of youth cultural studies may best be seen as the impact of residual surplus meanings flowing over from the combined effects of both the dominating effects of class theory and post-war moralizing fears about young people. We can also now see the ways in which the effects of post-war identity politics impacted not only on the ways in which theorists thought about youth groupings or the category 'youth', but also upon explanatory theories themselves, with intellectuals coming to perceive youth subcultures as primarily organized in relation to social class (and in many ways divided from each other).

3. This notwithstanding, a consequence of this turn has been that much of the more recent work on how to 'read' research in youth subcultural and post-subcultural studies has circled around a deeply polarized debate about the *death of class* as a substantial explanatory factor in the framing of contemporary youth cultures on the one hand, and residual structural manifestations of class on the other.

4. It should be clarified that phenomenology is, to some degree, making a 'comeback' in both social and educational theory.

5. For a magnificent challenge to some of the recent theoretical work on post-subcultures, see Louis Theroux's 2008 documentary work on the male inmates at San Quentin, see http://news.bbc.co.uk/1/hi/magazine/7181055.stm, accessed 20 March 2009.

6. Even within the field of youth studies, one can find accounts of youth culture which have evacuated social class from their frameworks and become tied to culture and hybridity as locally derived sets of discourses or as inherited social practices which regulate young people's commitments to this or that post-subcultural identity. Here, youth subjectivity is typically seen as ever-changing, fluid and unstable, operating not as a form of local historical sedimentation, but as a feature within that which Nayak (2003a) has referred to as a hybridized 'youthscape'. On the other hand, we have more recent and broadly structuralist positions such as high modernist or late-modern approaches which suggest that youth identity is shaped largely by elements of late-modern social change, heightened retrenchment and global structures which are outcomes of what Beck (1999) has termed reflexive modernization. On this view, youth identities are seen as moving in response to advanced forms of modernization which are quite oblivious to entrenched class histories or unique local cultural communities. From this perspective, wider global forms of class stratification and de-ritualized forms of change become the focal point of interest, and it is the identification of future transitions and pathways which becomes the key concern.

7. For example, the working-class subcultures of Ginas, Thugs and Gangstas from our Toronto study site fit this description. This will be explored in greater detail in the second part of the book.

8. Strictly speaking, *Making Modern Lives* by McLeod and Yates is not about youth culture but it does speak indirectly to it through longitudinal and comparative research.

9. This also applies to Arendt's critique of metaphysics and the false idea of a true independent self free from the social conditions or the forms of intersubjectivity shaping the self in any 'social life world' (see Arendt, 1971).

10. To put this another way, post-subcultural formations can be seen to exist in particular spatial contexts in the new global city which are bound by profound, but sometimes invisible, historical effects which are not necessarily always, or directly, attached to liberal individualism or radical change as it impacts upon youth cultures.

11. In so doing, our position is that elements of youth individualization and the

emergence of quite new youth identities, together with sedimented class positions and spatial forms of meaning-making, may be seen to be simultaneously at work.

12. An additional difficulty in developing ethnographies which reflect phenomenological principles is that the representation of young people as marginalized is often now perceived as a problematic and unethical way of representing youth inequality. Much of the concern over objectifying social inequality through ethnographic representation stems from postmodern or cultural concerns with representation as itself a problem in reproducing the very conditions of inequality which ethnographers had hoped to eradicate. We argue that the key difficulty with the abandonment of ethnography as a phenomenological enterprise has been the resultant inability within the sociology of education to examine the 'reach and structure of [youth] experience' (to quote Geertz, 2000: 9) and to follow Geertz further, to anticipate that answers to 'the most general questions of why [young people do what they do] – to the degree that they have answers – are to be found in the fine detail of lived life'.

13. Historical time refers to expressions of narrative identity which carry with them 'a trace of the past' (Walter Benjamin, Paul Ricoeur) or a crystallization of the past in the temporal present.

14. Simms, 2003: 102–103.

2. Spatial Landscapes of Ethnographic Inquiry: Phenomenology, Moral Entrepreneurship and the Investigation of Cultural Meaning

1. Thompson (1981) argues that Ricoeur's philosophy presupposes that the social sciences (including intellectual history) themselves are a form of hermeneutics, in spite of repeated attempts to reconcile their methods and findings with positivist criteria of scientificity and objectivity (e.g. that of generality and falsifiability) (Thompson, 1981).

2. Thompson, 1981: 2.

3. Rose (2007) tells us that making images as a way of answering a research question is relatively rare but is crucial in understanding social differences and in visualizing these differences as a form of cultural expression.

4. Such visual accounts possess the power to open a window upon the field of moral identification to which young people have access as they navigate the urban city.

5. Our argument is that, if methods of studying youth cultures are to continue to mature analytically, then we should not view circulating approaches as oppositional. That is, that we should not view, for example, language versus temporality or deconstruction versus phenomenological interpretation as in either decline or ascendance, as they are conceptual terms within a methodology that are much more like twins or deeply connected relatives to each other in intellectual history than we may have previously thought or understood.

3. Lost Youth and Urban Landscapes: Researching the Interface of Youth Imaginaries and Urbanization

1. In this study, the urban fringe represents a mixed neighbourhood of largely working-class and migrant communities which is located on the edge of the inner-city but does not represent the inner-city. The reason for this is that inner-cities within a global context tend to be 'regenerating' – in order to appear 'world-class' and competitive, in a similar vein as the nation has been competitive in the past – so that low-cost housing has been converted into high-cost rentals, with the result that low-income communities have been forced to move to the fringe. Often the fringe in a late-modern Canadian city houses well-established working-class communities who represent a mix of post-war immigrant communities who migrated in the early post-

war period or even at the turn of the twentieth century, as well as those who see themselves as 'arty' or fringe in style and professional status, and those individuals who are being displaced from council housing or single-night dwelling establishments originally located at the urban core.

2. See, for example, http://en.wikipedia.org/wiki/Shangri-La_Hotels_and_Resorts, accessed 18 March 2008.

3. Similar changes have taken place near Bloor, King and Queen Street and near City Hall in Toronto, Ontario. As the *Toronto Star* reports in an article entitled 'Toronto Ranks 15th in Global City Survey':

> VANCOUVER – Toronto is the second-best city in Canada to live in, according to a global survey released today. [...]. Vancouver rates 3rd internationally and tops in Canada in annual review of 215 urban areas: For the second year in a row, Toronto ranks fifteenth among cities around the world in overall quality of life, according to the annual review by Mercer Human Resource Consulting, which operates in 40 nations.

4. Vancouver is the best place to reside in Canada, the survey says, ranking third in the world – just behind the Swiss cities of Zurich and Geneva. Other Canadian cities in the survey were Ottawa at 18th internationally, Montreal at 22nd and Calgary at 24th. [...] 'Generally speaking, Canadian cities did really well,' Danielle Bushen, a principal at Mercer in Toronto, told the Star's Joanna Smith. 'Toronto's traffic and muggy summers with poor air quality played a role in its ranking. The city placed 21st internationally in the category of health and sanitation.' There are a significant number of days in Toronto, particularly in the summer time, when there are air quality advisories. So while overall quality of life is great, in that one area Toronto rates a little bit lower,' Bushen said.

(www.thestar.com/News/article/198438, accessed 8 December 2008)

5. As is well documented in the business awards literature around the world, Shangri-La Resort is owned by Robert Kuok and first began as part of a company based in Malaysia entitled Shangri-La Asia Limited. It is also incorporated in Bermuda and in Thailand under a slightly different title. The key point here is that this company has designed itself as a growing international resort which is not housed in one nation but is a global company operating in world-class cities. It is also designed to house those entrepreneurial individuals who also move globally (Yoon, 2008). See www.ir.shangri-la.com.

6. This latter set of moral discourses was proliferating in the early part of the twentieth century as the rise of a notion of legal regulation of citizens was put in place and the First World War was on the horizon. These discourses must not always be seen as straightforwardly progressive (e.g. the official formation of 'slums' or youth poverty). However, earlier periods of social welfare must be read against the contemporary tide of neo-liberal policies which have eliminated the visibility of economically disadvantaged youth in Canadian society. In 1999, for example, Bill 8 (in Ontario) (i.e. anti-panhandling legislation) enforced, through law, a 'clean-up' of the streets, or what might be more appropriately described as a removal of economically disadvantaged youth from the only space where they remain visible to the larger public. A report by CERA (Canadian Housing Equality Resources Association) exposes this concern in the following quotation:

> Bill 8 [...] conforms with the emerging patterns of Canadian legislators to show less and less concern about alleviating poverty and more interest in legislating poverty into invisibility. This hostility towards economically disadvantaged young people

has manifested itself in unprecedented cuts to social assistance [...]. In promoting a society which is marred by depths of poverty that have not been seen in a generation in Ontario at the same time as criminalizing the poor in an unprecedented manner, this government is taking us back to the outlook of previous centuries.
(See website: www.equalityrights.org/cera/docs/Bill8Submission.html, November 1999)

7. The first anti-panhandling law (1999/2000) passed in Canada took place in Ontario under the premiership of Mike Harris. But the local/national and arguably global impact of this law has meant that some youth subcultures were being criminalized for innocuous activity. The following excerpt from a blog following the details of these laws highlights the impact these acts and laws had on young people themselves: since then, similar laws have been passed in many provinces in Canada.

But what of the Charter? From the article in the *Toronto Star*, the ruling construed that the Charter 'extended to those groups on the basis of personal characteristics, such as race, sex, ethnic origin, or age'. Squeegee kids are not identified by their personal characteristics, but the activity they are engaged in. Is this a proper interpretation of our rights and freedoms, or a cop out by a panel of judges unwilling to change a law that may anger business owners and city officials? The Charter itself is meant to defend citizens from a tyranny of the majority. The spirit of the Charter is to act as the codified defence of the individual, regardless of 'personal characteristics'. I, for one, think the Charter helps to force people to look beyond personal characteristics, and treat everyone fairly. The ruling continues to raise questions. Is a law that targets the poor discrimination? Is 'squeegeeing' a form of expression? Are our streets any safer without squeegee kids?
(www.blogt.com/city/2007/01/squeegeekids_get_no_quarter, accessed November 2009)

8. Another implication of the increasing labour mobility experienced by young people and their parents was that some young people felt a particular kind of urban alienation, often being obliged to cross neighbourhoods and suburban boundaries in order to get to schools or to see friends. As a result, many of the young people were spending increasing amounts of time alone, travelling long distances to and from school either by foot or by transport, or isolated from their peers.

9. The neo-liberal policies associated with very substantial retrenchment in cities are most commonly linked to Mike Harris, Ontario's premier during the mid-1990s until 2002. Wikipedia has this lay comment to make about Harris:

Michael Deane Harris (born January 23, 1945, in Toronto, Ontario) was the twenty-second Premier of Ontario from June 26, 1995 to April 15, 2002. He is most noted for the 'Common Sense Revolution', his government's program of deficit reduction in combination with lower taxes and significant cuts to some government programs.

10. These issues will be discussed in much more detail in Chapters 4–7.

11. This neighbourhood is making transitions, with a larger number of Portuguese immigrants arriving into the neighbourhood from those parts of Africa colonized by the Portuguese (known as the Portuguese diaspora). As housing prices have continued to increase at the urban core and fringe, the neighbourhood was becoming increasingly mixed, with some middle-class professionals moving to the edges of this neighbourhood (Teixeira, 2007). Noteworthy too was that many Portuguese families were moving out of the neighbourhood because of increases in rental costs for businesses and homes. This particular Portuguese community is commonly referred to as the 'mother of all communities' and has been seen, up until recent years, as an ethnic enclave for almost five decades. We define *neo-liberalism* broadly as a set of free-market policies which are premised upon the economic concepts of choice, competi-

tion, and risk. Within the context of education, the aims of neo-liberalism are largely achieved through increases in standardized testing, school choice policy and reduced public spending.

12. We use the term 'working class' in the way that British youth cultural theorists have to politicize the significance of young people's class history in shaping their lives in a stratified economic order. In so doing, we do not wish to undermine other forms of identification but rather to make the case that identification as a young person is deeply linked to class formations.

13. League tables refer to the ranking of schools by municipality on achievement scores emerging from both provincial testing and graduating averages.

14. According to one study, only 62% of Vancouverites reside in acceptable housing, defined here as housing in adequate condition, of suitable size and affordable (Engeland et al., 2005). This figure is the lowest of all the major cities in Canada.

15. While there has been little research on the social effects of this service-based economy in Vancouver, some have argued that 'one of the key characteristics of service-based globalizing cities is a tendency towards labour market polarization between high wage professional, technical and managerial sectors and lower wage workers' (Sassen, 1996, 1998, 2000a, 2000b).

16. www.english-vancouver.com/canada-human-development/ (downloaded 5 April 2006). Ranking as follows: First by Condé Nast Traveler Magazine; second in 1996 by UN Human Development Index; and third by Mercer Human Resources Consulting in 2005.

4. Warehousing 'Ginos', 'Thugs' and 'Gangstas' in Urban Canadian Schools: Gender Rivalries and Subcultural Defences in Late-Modernity

1. Earlier versions of this concept were linked to Cohen's (1986, as cited in Cohen, 1997) notion of 'symbolic control'.

2. The style originated in the culture of prison, where inmates were given ill-fitting uniforms and, for safety reasons, not permitted to wear belts.

3. As Kearney (2004: 45) writes about Ricoeur's notion of the symbolic imagination: '[it is] by beginning with the idea that symbols are already out there [...] that we have something to think about.'

4. It is now well established that in global cities around the world – or apparently 'world-class' cities – the gap between social classes has widened considerably since the 1960s (see the *Observer*, 9 May 2009). These gaps are largely paralleled in most affluent, large cities across the world.

5. Examples of these are the urban border zones between Little Italy or Little Portugal in many East Coast cities of North America or between the Vietnamese Nammers who relate more to Japan than to the West when compared with Cambodian girls.

6. Like other contemporary youth theorists, we too seek to suggest that theories of de-traditionalization have exaggerated the degree to which gender norms have been reconfigured along with the so-called 'freedoms' which such marginalized groups are thought to have.

7. As previously noted, the majority of data for this chapter is drawn from the Toronto site. Although related dynamics were witnessed within the Vancouver site via different subcultural groupings, it was observed to a much greater extent – and better documented through transcripts and fieldnotes – in Toronto.

8. Slim Shady ('Sun' is the term used by Tony) is one of Eminem's aliases. It also refers to the release of his second LP, widely seen as a hip-hop classic. It has several references to drugs and violence, and was an extremely popular album among the Gangsta boys.

9. It is noteworthy that each of these classifications, albeit mediated by contemporary

change and popular culture, has a history in other forms of material culture in the UK, Australia and Canada.

10. Based on a recent survey of young girls' and women's attitudes about working life and their futures, a *Guardian* journalist reported that little transformation across three decades has taken place in working-class communities in relation to notions of gendered work (e.g. such as hair-dressing). The argument here was that, unlike the gains made by middle-class girls through the feminist movement and equal opportunity policies directed towards them, working-class girls have fallen outside the remit and patterns of academic and professional mobility because of urban retrenchment policies, educational choice practices and cuts to social support in urban centres.

5. Urban Imaginaries and Youth Geographies of Emotion: Ambivalence, Anxiety and Class Fantasies of Home

1. The Prisoner's Cinema is a term used to refer to the visual experiences reported by prisoners when they have been exposed to little light or have survived darkness for long periods. The outcome of such confinement is that they see spots or lights that seem to appear out of nowhere. These images have a form but they are difficult to identify.
2. In Vancouver, for example, Youth Cops had replaced youth workers once they were cut by municipal policy-makers and the government, as described in Chapter 3.

6. Impossible Citizens in the Global Metropolis: Race, Landscapes of Power and the New 'Emotional Geographies' of the City

1. See Louis Theroux on the 'Gangs' of San Quentin Prison: http://news.bbc.co.uk/1/hi/magazine/7181055.stm, accessed 20 March 2009.
2. Instead we draw upon the class imaginary as a way of reading the cultural production of race as a 'structure of feeling'.
3. In so doing, we wish to move away, not unlike our repositioning of youth cultural theory, from a focus on racial identity or post-race accounts of youth culture.
4. Paul Ricoeur's metaphor of 'oneself as another' seems apropos here. This metaphor is designed to point to the cultural detours one takes as they encounter new and powerful worlds which they wish to belong to such that they too can become powerful.
5. It is for this reason that it is important to take a middle line here as it is not clear that we are talking either about a subcultural or a post-subcultural moment but perhaps a reconfiguration of groupings which allow both the history of membership and the present to co-exist in particular kinds of tension.
6. Such changes are very recent, however. For example, it was only 40 years ago, in 1967, that Canadian immigration policies eliminated explicit references to race in their designations (Abu-Laban, 1998).
7. In recent years, a safe injection site has been operating in the neighbouring DTES under the auspices of a 'Harm Reduction' programme. Since its opening a more aggressive policing system has been implemented such that drug-users are charged with a crime if they are found in possession of drugs. Before the injection site opened, individuals were rarely charged with possession or the use of drugs on the street (Graham, 2007). Consequently, many users living in the DTES were migrating towards the neighbourhood where many of our participants were students and living with their families.
8. All teachers in this study were white, which stood in stark contrast to the very diverse youth participants who participated in this study.

7. Legitimacy, Risk and Belonging in the Global City: Individualization and the Language of Citizenship

1. These are nationalisms which are operating in particular neighbourhoods but which are not necessarily tied to the nation in which the neighbourhood resides.

2. One exception to this was a young Aboriginal student who included the importance of 'voting' within her list of strategies for being a good citizen, making note of this after the injunctions to obey the law and 'do good deeds'. Noteworthy is that this participant had engaged in activities at the Aboriginal Friendship Centre, where she may have been given some alternative education in the importance of asserting her social and political rights within Canada.

Conclusion

1. Hall, S. (1997). *Representation: Cultural representations and signifying practices.* London: Sage.

References

Abu-Laben, Y. (1998). Keeping 'em out: gender, race, and class biases in Canadian immigration policy. In V. Strong-Boag, J. Anderson, S. Grace & A. Eisenberg (Eds.), *Painting the maple: Essays on race, gender, and the construction of Canada*. Vancouver, BC: UBC Press.

Adkins, L. (2002). *Revisions: Gender and sexuality in late modernity*. Buckingham: Open University Press.

Ahmed, S. (1999). Passing through hybridity. *Theory, Culture and Society, 16*(2), 87–106.

Ahmed, S. (2000). *Strange encounters: Embodied others in post coloniality*. London: Routledge.

Ahmed, S. (2003). The politics of fear in the making of worlds. *International Journal of Qualitative Studies in Education, 16*(3), 377–398.

Ahmed, S. (2004a). Affective economies. *Social Text, 22*(2), 121–139.

Ahmed, S. (2004b). *The cultural politics of emotion*. Edinburgh: Edinburgh University Press/ London: Routledge.

Alexander, J.C. (2004a). Cultural sociology. *European Journal of Social Theory, 7*(1): 45–65.

Alexander, J.C. (2004b). Toward a theory of cultural trauma. In Jeffrey C. Alexander, Ron Eyerman, Bernhard Giesen, Neil J. Smelser & Piotr Sztompka (Eds.), *Cultural Trauma and Collective Identity* (pp. 1–30). Los Angeles: University of California Press.

Alexander, R.M. (1995). *The 'girl problem': Female sexual delinquency in New York, 1900– 1930*. Ithaca and London: Cornell University Press.

Althusser, L. (2004 [1970]). Ideology and ideological state apparatus. In A. Easthope & K. McGowan (Eds.), *A critical and cultural theory reader*. Toronto: University of Toronto Press.

Anti-Poverty Coalition Report. (2007). *Roundtable on Solving Poverty*. National Council of Welfare, Ottawa: The Conference Publishers Inc.

Apparadurai, A. (1990). Disjuncture and difference in the global culture economy. *Theory, Culture, Society, 7*, 295–310.

Appadurai, A. (1996). *Modernity at large*. Minnesota: University of Minnesota Press.

Appadurai, A. (2000). Grassroots globalization and the research imagination. *Public Culture, 12*(1), 1–19.

Arendt, H. (1968). *Between past and future: Eight exercises in political thought*. New York: Viking Press.

Arendt, H. (1971). *The life of the mind*. New York: Harcourt Brace & Jovanich.

Arendt, H. (1998 [1958]). *The human condition* (2nd ed.). Chicago: University of Chicago Press.

Austin, J.L. (1975). *How to do things with words*. J.O. Urmson and Marina Sbisà (Eds.). Cambridge: Harvard University Press.

Back, L. (1996). *New ethnicities and urban cultures: Racism and multiculture in young lives*. London: UCL Press.

Baert, P. (1992). *Time, self and social being*. Aldershot: Avebury.

Baert, P. (1998). *Social theory in the twentieth century*. Cambridge: Polity Press.

Baird, B. (2008). The child. *Australian Feminist Studies, 23*(57).

Barnhart, A. (1994). On Goffman: *The self in everyday life*. Retrieved 17 June 2009, from http://employees.cfmc.com/adamb/writings/goffman.htm.

Baumann, Z. (2007). *Liquid times: Living in an age of uncertainty*. Cambridge: Polity Press.

BBC News. (2005). Retrieved 22 June 2009, from http://news.bbc.co.uk/onthisday/hi/witness/may/18/newsid_3014000/3014033.st.

Beck, U. (1992). *The risk society: Towards a new modernity.* London, Newbury Park, New Delhi: Sage.

Beck, U. (1999). *World risk society.* Malden: Blackwell.

Beers, D. (2007) *Homes Now.* thetyee.ca/blogs/.../2009/06/../povertcoalitionreducton plan.

Benhabib, S. (2004). *The rights of others: Aliens, residents and citizens.* Cambridge: Cambridge University Press.

Benjamin, W. (1968). *The work of art in the age of mechanical reproduction.* New York: Schocken Books.

Bennett, A. & Kahn-Harris, K. (2004). *After subculture: Critical studies in contemporary youth cultures.* New York: Palgrave and Macmillan.

Berelowitz, L. (2005). *Dream city: Vancouver and the global imagination.* Vancouver: Douglas & McIntyre.

Bettie, J. (2000). Women without class: Chicas, cholas, trash and the presence/absence of class identity, *Signs: Journal of Women in Culture and Society, 26*(1) 1–35.

Bettie, J. (2003). *Women without class: Girls, race and identity.* Berkeley: University of California Press.

Binnie, J. & Skeggs, B. (2004). Cosmopolitan sexualities: disrupting the logic of late capitalism, *Sociological Review, 52*(1), 39–62.

Bloom, A. (1998). *Under the sign of hope: Feminist methodology and narrative interpretation.* Albany: Suny Press.

Bogatsu, M. (2002). 'Loxion Kulcha': Fashion and black youth culture in post-apartheid South Africa. *English studies in Africa, 45*(2), 1–12.

Bourdieu, P. (1984). *Distinctions: A social critique of the judgement of taste.* (R. Nice, Trans.). Harvard: Harvard University Press.

Bourdieu, P. (1997). *Pascalian Meditations.* (R. Nice, Trans.). Stanford: Stanford University Press.

Bourdieu, P. (1999). Site effects. In P. Bourdieu et al. (Eds.), *The weight of the world: Social suffering in contemporary society.* (P.P. Ferguson, Trans.). Stanford: Stanford University Press.

Bourdieu, P. (2001). *Masculine Domination.* (R. Nice, Trans.). Stanford: Stanford University Press.

Bourdieu, P. (2006). *The weight of the world: Social suffering in contemporary society* (3rd ed.). Oxford: Blackwell.

Bourdieu, P. & Wacquant, L.J.D. (1992). *An invitation to reflexive sociology.* Chicago and London: University of Chicago Press.

Bouthius, U. (1995). Youth, the media and moral panics. In J. Fonas & G. Bolin (Eds.), *Youth culture in late modernity.* London: Sage.

Bowden, M. (2007). Policing and youth question: Civil society and the state in the urban periphery in Ireland (PhD thesis submitted to the Department of Sociology, Trinity College Dublin).

Brake, M. (1985). *Comparative youth culture: The sociology of youth cultures and youth subcultures in America, Britain and Canada.* New York: Routledge.

Britzman, D.P. (1995a). Beyond innocent readings: Educational ethnography as a crisis of representation. In W.T. Pink & G.W. Noblit (Eds.), *Continuity and contradiction: The futures of the sociology of education.* Cresskill, NJ: Hampton Press.

Britzman, D.P. (1995b). *Practice makes practice: A critical study of learning to teach.* New York: State University of New York Press.

Britzman, D. (1998). *Lost subjects, contested objects: Toward a psychoanalytic inquiry of learning.* New York: Suny.

Brown, W. (1995). *States of injury: Power and freedom in late modernity.* Princeton: Princeton University Press.

Brown, W. (2001). *Politics out of history.* Princeton: Princeton University Press.

Brown, W. (2005). *Edgework: Critical essays on knowledge and politics.* Princeton: Princeton University Press.

Buchan, R.B. (1985). Gentrification's impact on neighbourhood public service usage (MA thesis). Vancouver, BC, Canada: University of British Columbia.

Buckingham, D., Bragg, S. & Kehily, M.J. (2009). *Rethinking youth cultures in the age of global media* (Seminar Series, funded by the Economic and Social Research). London: Institute of Education.

Burawoy, M., O'Riain, S., Blum, J. George, S. & Gille, Z. (2000). *Global ethnography: Forces, connections and imaginations in a postmodern world.* Berkeley: University of California Press.

Campaign. (2000). *Child Poverty in Canada. Report Card 2000.* Toronto: Ontario. United Way of Canada. Retrieved 18 October 2009, from www.campaign2000.ca/rc/00/index.html.

Canada's Mortgage and Housing Group. (2008). www.cmhc-schl.gc.ca/en/.

Canadian Council on Learning. (2008). The costs of dropping out of high school. www.cclcca.ca/CCL/Reports/Other+Reports/20090203CostofDroppingOut.htm

Canadian Council on Social Development (CCSD, 2000). *Thinking Ahead: Trends Affecting Public Education in the Future.* (www.ccsd.ca/pubs/gordon/part2.htm).

Canadian Housing Observer (2008). *The state of Canada's housing: An overview,* Canada Mortgage and Housing Corporation, Ottawa, Ontario.

Canadian Press. (2008, 31 May). Teens face violence and death as they look to gangs for acceptance: Retrieved 18 January 2009, from www.canadiansafeschools.com/content/documents/Link/Safe%20Schools%20in%20the%20News/teensface violenceanddeath-may3108.pdf.

Canadian Social Trends (2006). Winter, 82 (524, Canada). Catalogue 11-008. Statistics Canada, Government of Canada, Ottawa, Ontario.

Canadian Social Trends (2009). Summer, 7 (524, Canada). Catalogue 11-008. Statistics Canada, Government of Canada, Ottawa, Ontario.

Canguilhem, G. (1989). *The normal and the pathological* (translated from French). Cambridge: Zone Books.

Carrim, N. (1998). Anti-racism and the 'New' South African educational order. *Cambridge Journal of Education, 28*(3), 301–320.

Carrim, N. & Soudien, C. (1999). Critical antiracism in South Africa. In S. May (Ed.), *Critical multiculturalism: Rethinking multicultural and antiracist education* (pp. 153–171). London and Philadelphia: Falmer Press.

Carter, P.L. (2006). Straddling boundaries: Identity, culture and school. *Sociology of Education, 79*(4), 304–328.

Castells, M. (1978). *City, class and power.* London, New York: Macmillan.

Cavarero, A. (2000). *Relating narratives: Story-telling and selfhood.* New York: Routledge.

Chamberlin, R. (2003). Citizenship? Only if you haven't got a life: Secondary school pupils' views of Citizenship Education. *Westminster Studies in Education, 26*(2), 87–97.

Chari, S. (2005). Grounds for a spatial ethnography of labour, *Ethnography,* 6(3), 267–281.

Chatterton, P. & Hollands, R. (2003). *Urban nightscapes: Youth cultures, pleasure spaces, and corporate power.* London: Routledge.

City of Vancouver. (2006). *2005/06 Downtown Eastside Community Monitoring Report* (10th ed.). Vancouver: City of Vancouver.

Clarke, J. (1976). The skinheads and the magical recovery of community. In S. Hall & T. Jefferson (Eds.), *Resistance through rituals: Youth subcultures in post-war Britain.* London: Hutchinson.

Clarke, J., Hall, S., Jefferson, T. & Roberts, B. (1976). Subcultures, cultures and class. In S. Hall & T. Jefferson (Eds.), *Resistance through rituals: Youth subcultures in post-war Britain.* New York: Routledge.

Cohen, P. (1972). *Sub-Cultural Conflict and Working Class Community.* Working Papers in Cultural Studies. No.2. Birmingham: University of Birmingham.

Cohen, P. (1997). *Rethinking the youth question: Education, labour and cultural studies* (2nd ed.). Houndmills: Macmillan.

Cohen, S. (2002 [1972, 1987]). *Folk devils and moral panics: The creation of the Mods and Rockers.* New York: Routledge.

Community Action Publishers. (2004). *Welfare Families No Better Off With National Child Benefit.* National Council of Welfare's report. Ottawa, Canada, August 16.

Community Statistics Census Data. (2008). *Community Webpages, Grandview-Woodland.* Retrieved 27 August 2008, from http://vancouver.ca/commsvcs/planning/census/ 2006/ localareas/grandview.pdf.

Connell, R.W. (2005). *Masculinities.* Berkeley: University of Berkeley Press.

Connell, R. (2007). *Southern theory: The global dynamics of knowledge in social science.* Crows Next, NSW: Allen and Unwin.

Corrigan, P. (1979). *Schooling the Smash Street kids.* London: Macmillan.

Curtis, K. (1997). Aesthetic foundations of democratic politics in the work of Hannah Arendt. In C.J. Calhoun & J. McGowan (Eds.), *Hannah Arendt and the meaning of politics* (pp. 27–52). Minneapolis: University of Minnesota Press.

Curtis, K. (2003). *Our sense of the real: Aesthetic experience and Arendtian politics.* Ithaca: Cornell University Press.

Dauenhauer, B.P. (2000). Ricoeur and the tasks of citizenship. In John Wall, William Schweiker & W. David Hall (Eds.), *Paul Ricoeur and Contemporary Moral Thought.* New York: Routledge.

Davies, B. (1990). *Frogs and snails and feminist tales.* New York: Unwin Hyman.

Davies, B. & Harré, R. (1991/1992). Contradiction in lived and told narratives. *Research on Language and Social Interaction, 25,* 1–35.

Dei, G. & Karumanchery, L. (1999). Social reforms in Ontario: The marketization of education and the resulting silence on equity. *Alberta Journal of Educational Research, 45*(2), 111–131.

Deleuze, G. & Guattari, F. (1987). *A thousand plateaus: Capitalism and schizophrenia, and more.* Minneapolis: University of Minnesota Press.

Dillabough, J. (2008). History and temporality as ethical reflexivity in social science research. In K. Gallagher (Ed.), *The methodological dilemma: Critical and creative approaches to qualitative research.* New York: Routledge.

Dillabough, J. & van der Meulen, A. (2007). Female youth homelessness in urban Canada: Space, representation and gender identity. Rethinking the representation of youth homelessness in the public record. In J. McCleod and A. Allard (Eds.), *Learning at the Margins.* New York: RoutledgeFalmer.

Dillabough, J., Wang, E. & Kennelly, J. (2005). 'Ginas', 'Thugs', and 'Gangstas': Young people's struggles to 'become somebody' in working-class urban Canada. *Journal of Curriculum Theorizing, 21*(2), 83–108.

Douzinas, C. (2007). *Human rights and empire: The political philosophy of cosmopolitanism.* London: Routledge.

Downtown Eastside Community Monitoring Report. (2000). *A review of demographic data for Chinatown, the Downtown Eastside, Gastown, Strathcona, Victory Square* (Vancouver Municipal Working Paper series). Vancouver, BC, Canada.

Durham, M & Kellner, D. (2001). *Media and Cultural Studies: Keyworks.* New York: Routledge.

Eby, D. and Misura, C. (2006). *Cracks in the foundation: Solving the housing crisis in Canada's poorest neighbourhood.* Vancouver: Pivot Legal Society.

Edginton, D.W., Goldberg, M.A. & Hutton, T. (2003). *The Hong Kong Chinese in Vancouver.* Vancouver: Vancouver Centre of Excellence for Research on Immigration and Integration in the Metropolis.

Engeland, J., Lewis, R., Ehrlich, S. & Che, J. (2005). *Evolving housing conditions in Canada's Census Metropolitan Areas, 1991–2001.* Ottawa: Statistics Canada.

Evans, S. & Hall, S. (2007). *Visual culture reader* (2nd ed.). London: Routledge.

Felman, S. (1992). *The juridical unconscious: Trials and traumas in the twentieth century.* Cambridge: Harvard University Press.

Felman, S. (2000). Theaters of justice: Arendt in Jerusalem, the Eichmann trial, and the redefinition of legal meaning in the wake of the Holocaust. *Theoretical Inquiries in Law, 1*(2). Retrieved from www.bepress.com/til/default/vol1/iss2/art8.

First Call: BC Child and Youth Advocacy Coalition. (2008). *BC campaign 2000: 2008 child poverty report card.* Vancouver.

Foucault, M. (1977 [English translation, 2007]). *Security, territory and population* (Lectures from the College de France). London: Palgrave, Macmillan.

Foucault, M. (1978 [French publication, 1976]), *The history of sexuality*, Vol. I. (Robert Hurley, Trans). New York: Pantheon.

Foucault, M. (1980). *Power/knowledge: Selected interviews and other writings, 1972–1977* (Colin Gordon, Ed.). London: Harvester.

Foucault, M. (1984). *The care of the self: The history of sexuality*, Vol. III. (Robert Hurley, Trans.). New York: Pantheon.

Foucault, M. (1985 [1984]). *The use of pleasure: The history of sexuality*, Vol. II. (Robert Hurley, Trans.). New York: Pantheon.

Fowler, D. (2008). *Youth culture in modern Britain, c.1920-c.1970.* New York: Palgrave Macmillan.

Frankish, C.J., Hwang, S. & Quantz, D. (2005). Homelessness and health in Canada: Research lessons and priorities. *Canadian Journal of Public Health, 96*, March/April, 523–529. Report for the Secratariat on Youth Homelessness.

Fyfe, G. & Law, J. (1988). *Picturing power: Visual depiction and social relations.* New York: Routledge.

Gallagher, K. (2007). *The theatre of urban: Youth and schooling in dangerous times.* Toronto: University of Toronto Press.

Geertz, C. (2000). *Available light: Anthropological reflections.* Princeton: Princeton University Press.

Giddens, A. (1991). *Modernity and self identity: Self and society in the late modern age.* Cambridge: Polity.

Gille, Z. & O'Riain, S. (2002). Global ethnography. *Annual Review of Sociology, 28*, 271–295.

Gilroy, P. (2000). *Between camps: Nations, cultures and the allure of race.* London and New York: Routledge.

Gilroy, P. (2004). *After empire.* London: Taylor & Francis.

Goffman, E. (1959). *The presentation of self in everyday life.* Woodstock: Overlook Press.

Graham, E. (2007). Rounding 'em up on the East Side of the Wild West: Four pillars? Or one big corral? (Unpublished Masters thesis). University of British Columbia: Vancouver, BC, Canada.

Gregory, D. (2006). *The colonial present.* Oxford: Blackwell.

Griffin, C. (2008). Imagining new narratives of youth: Youth research, the 'new Europe' and global youth. *Childhood, 8*, 147–166.

Griffin, C. (2009). What time is now? Research about youth and culture beyond the Birmingham school. Paper presented at the *Rethinking youth culture in the age of global media ESRC seminar series.* London: The Knowledge Lab.

Grossberg, L. (1997). *Dancing despite myself: Essays in popular culture.* Durham: Durham University Press.

Grossberg, L. (2005). *Caught in the crossfire: Kids, politics, and America's future.* Boulder: Paradigm Publishers.

Halberstam, J. (1998). *Female masculinity.* Durham: Duke University Press.

Hall, S. (1980). Cultural Studies: Two Paradigms. *Media, Culture and Society, 2*, 57–72.

Hall, S. (1992a). The question of cultural identity. In S. Hall, D. Held & T. McGrew (Eds.), *Modernity and its futures* (pp. 274–325). Cambridge: Polity Press in association with Blackwell Publishers and the Open University.

Hall, S. (1992b). New ethnicities. In J. Donald & A. Rattansi (Eds.), *'Race', Culture and difference*. London: Sage.

Hall, S. (1996a). *Critical dialogues in cultural studies* (David Morley & Kuan-Hsing Chen, Eds.). London: Routledge.

Hall, S. (1996b). Introduction: Who needs identity? In S. Hall & P. du Gay (Eds.), *Questions of cultural identity* (pp. 1–17). London: Sage.

Hall, S. (1997). *Representation: Cultural representations and signifying practices* (Culture, Media and Identities series). Milton Keynes: Open University.

Hall, S. & Jefferson, T. (1976). *Resistance through rituals: Youth subcultures in post-war Britain*. New York: Routledge.

Harris, A. (2004). *Future girl: Young women in the twenty-first century*. New York and London: Routledge.

Harris, A. (2009). *New wave cultures*. New York: Routledge.

Harrison, B. (2002). Photographic visions and narrative inquiry. *Narrative Inquiry, 12*(1), 87–111.

Harvey, D. (1990). *The condition of postmodernity: An enquiry in the origins of cultural change*. Cambridge: Blackwell.

Hebdige, D. (1979). *Subculture: The meaning of style*. New York: Methuen & Co., Ltd.

Hier, S. (2002). Conceptualizing moral panic through a moral economy of harm. *Critical Sociology, 28*(3), 311–334.

Heir, S. (2003). Risk and panic in late modernity: implications of the converging sites of social anxiety. *British Journal of Sociology, 54*(1), 3–20.

Heisz, A. (2006). *Canada's global cities: Socio-economic conditions in Montreal, Toronto and Vancouver*. Ottawa: Statistics Canada.

Hernández, A. (1997). *Pedagogy, democracy and feminism: Rethinking the public sphere*. Albany: State University of New York Press.

Hey, V. (1997). *The company she keeps: An ethnography of girls' friendships*. Buckingham: Open University Press.

Hoerder, D., Hébert, Y. & Schmitt, I. (Eds.) (2005). *Negotiating transcultural lives: Belongings and social capital among youth in transnational perspective*. Göttingen: V+R Unipress.

Hollands, R. (1997). From shipyards to nightclubs: Restructuring young adults' employment, household, and consumption identities in the North-East of England. *Berkeley Journal of Sociology, 41*, 41–66.

Holloway, S. & Valentine, G. (2000). *Children's geographies: Playing, living, learning*. London: Routledge.

Honig, B. (1995). *The agonistic feminist politics of Hannah Arendt*. Ithaca: Cornell University Press.

Honig, B. (2001). *Democracy and the foreigner*. Princeton: Princeton University Press.

Hou, F. & Picot, G. (2004). Visible minority neighbourhoods in Toronto, Montreal & Vancouver. *Canadian Social Trends*, Spring, 8–13.

Housing Again: Resources. (2001). *Ontario's 'safe streets act' constitutional challenge, factum (2/2001)*. Retrieved 8 December 2008, from http://action.web.ca/home/housing/resources.shtml?x=67173&A.

Human Resources and Development Canada. (1997). *Concentrations of poverty and distressed neighbourhoods in Canada*. Ottawa, Canada: Government of Canada Publication.

Human Resources and Development Canada. (2001). *A study of family, child care and well-being in young Canadian families*. Ottawa, Canada: Government of Canada Publication.

Human Resources and Development Canada. (2007). *A study of poverty and working poverty among recent immigrants to Canada*. Ottawa, Canada: Government of Canada Publication.

Human Rights Watch. (2009). *World Report 2009*. Retrieved 16 June 2009, from www.hrw.org/world-report-2009.

Ichilov, O. (2005). Pride in one's country and citizenship orientations in a divided society: The case of Israeli–Palestinian Arab and Orthodox and Non-Orthodox Jewish Israeli youth. *Comparative Education Review, 49*(1), 44–61.

Institute for Public Policy Research. (2006). *Childhood is changing, but 'paedophobia' makes things worse.* Retrieved 16 October 2006, from www.ippr.org.uk/pressreleases/?id=2388.

Jameson, F. (1991). *Postmodernism, or, the cultural logic of late capitalism.* Durham: Duke University Press.

Jameson, F. (1998a). *Brecht and method.* London and New York: Verso.

Jameson, F. (1998b). *The cultural turn: Selected writings on the postmodern 1983–1998.* London and New York: Verso.

Jameson, F. (2000). Globalization and political strategy. *New Left Review, 4.*

Jameson, F. (2002). *A singular modernity: Essay on the ontology of the present.* London and New York: Verso.

Kaplan, D.H. & Li, W. (2006). *Landscapes of the ethnic economy.* New York: Rowman & Littlefield.

Katz, C. (1994). Playing the field: Questions of fieldwork in geography. *The Professional Geographer, 46,* 67–72.

Kearney, R. (2004). *On Paul Ricoeur: The owl of Minerva.* Aldershot: Ashgate.

Kehily, M. & Nayak, A. (2009). Global femininities: Consumption, culture and the significance of place. In J. Dillabough, J. McLeod & M. Mill (Eds.), *Troubling gender in education.* London: Routledge.

Kelly, D.M. (2000). *Pregnant with meaning: Teen mothers and the politics of inclusive schooling.* New York: Peter Lang.

Kelly, D.M., Pomerantz, S. & Currie, D. (2005). Skater girlhood and emphasized femininity: 'You can't land an ollie properly in heels'. *Gender and Education.* Retrieved 14 January 2009, from www.informaworld.com/smpp/title~content=t713422725.

Kennelly, J. (2008). *Citizen youth: Culture, agency, and activism in an era of globalization* (unpublished PhD Dissertation). University of British Columbia.

Kennelly, J. & Dillabough, J. (2008). Young people mobilizing the language of citizenship: Struggles for classification and new meaning in an uncertain world. *British Journal of Sociology of Education, 29*(5), 493–508.

Kenway, J., Kraak, A. & Hickey-Moody, A. (2006). *Masculinity beyond the metropolis.* New York: Palgrave-Macmillan.

Lather, P. (2007). (Post) critical feminist methodology: Getting lost. Paper presented to the American Educational Research Association. Chicago.

Lawler, S. (2005). Disgusted subjects: The making of middle-class identities. *The Sociological Review, 53*(3), 429–446.

Lawler, S. (2008a). *Identity: Sociological perspectives.* Cambridge: Polity.

Lawler, S. (2008b). Stories in the social world. In M. Pickering (Ed.), *Research in cultural studies.* Edinburgh: Edinburgh University Press.

Lawler, S. (2009). The middle classes and their aristocratic others: Nature as culture in classification struggles. *Journal of Cultural Economy, 1*(3), 245–261.

Lee, M., Villagomez, E., Gurstein, P., Eby, D. & Wyly, E. (2008). *Affordable EcoDensity: Making affordable housing a core principle of Vancouver's EcoDensity Charter.* Vancouver: Canadian Centre for Policy Alternatives.

Lefebvre, H. (1991). *The production of space.* (D. Nicholson-Smith, Trans.). Cambridge: Blackwell.

Lesko, N. (2000). *Act your age: A cultural construction of adolescence.* New York: Routledge.

Levi, M. & Wall, D.S. (2004). Technologies, security and privacy in the post-9/11 European information society. *Journal of Law and Society, 31*(2), 194–220.

Lyon, D. (2004). Globalizing surveillance: Comparative and sociological perspectives. *International Sociology, 19*(2), 135–149.

McCrae, L. (2006). The Redhead Review: Popular cultural studies and accelerated modernity. *History of Intellectual Culture, 6*(1). http://www.ucalgary.ca/hic/website/2006vol6no1/forum/forum_mcrae.html.

McDonald, K. (1999). *Struggles for subjectivity: Identity, action and youth experience.* Cambridge: Cambridge University Press.

MacDonald, R. (1999). The road to nowhere: Youth, insecurity and marginal transactions. In J. Vale, J. Wheelock & M. Hill (Eds.), *Insecure times: Living with insecurity in contemporary times.* London: Routledge.

MacDonald, R., Mason, P., Shildrick, T., Webster, C., Johnston, L. & Ridley, L. (2000). Snakes & ladders: In defence of studies of youth transition. *Sociological Research Online, 5*(4). Retrieved from www.socresonline.org.uk/5/4/macdonald.html.

McDowell, L. (2000). The trouble with men? Young people, gender transformations and the crisis of masculinity. *International Journal of Urban and Regional Research, 24*(1), 201–209.

McLeod, J. & Yates, L. (2006). *Making modern lives: Subjectivity, schooling, and social change.* New York: State University of New York Press.

McNay, L. (2000). *Gender and agency: Reconfiguring the subject in feminist and social theory.* Cambridge: Polity Press.

McNay, L. (2008). *Against recognition.* Cambridge: Polity Press.

McRobbie, A. (1982). The politics of feminist research: Between talk, text and action. *Feminist Review, 12,* 46–62.

McRobbie, A. (1991). *Feminism and youth culture: From* Jackie *to Just Seventeen.* Boston: Unwin Hyman.

McRobbie, A. (2004). Notes on 'What Not to Wear' and post-feminism symbolic violence. In L. Adkins and B. Skeggs (Eds.), *Feminism after Bourdieu.* London: Blackwell.

McRobbie, A. (2005). *The uses of cultural studies.* London: Sage.

McRobbie, A. (2008). *Displacement feminisms.* London: Sage

McRobbie, A. (2009). *The aftermath of feminism: Gender, culture and social change.* Los Angeles: Sage.

Marques, D. & Medeiros, J. (1984). Portuguese immigrants in Toronto. *Polyphony,* summer, 154–158.

Mason, V. (2004). Strangers within in the 'lucky country': Arab-Australians after September 11. *Comparative Studies of South Asia, Africa and the Middle East, 24*(1), 233–243.

Massey, D. (1994). *Space, place and gender.* Cambridge: Polity Press.

Massey, D. (1995). The conceptualization of place. In D. Massey & P. Jess. (Eds.), *A place in the world?* Milton Keynes: Open University Press.

Massey, D. (1999). Imagining globalization: Power-geometries of time–space. In Brah, A., Hickman, D. & Mac an Ghaill, M. (Eds.), *Global futures: Migration, environment and globalization.* London: Macmillan.

Mauss, M. (2006). *Techniques, technology and civilization.* Berghahn and Durkheim Press.

Medonos, J.C. (2007). *Conceptions of space – The smoking place, a view from a skidoo & playgrounds in Sisimiut.* Retrieved from http://blogforyouthstudies.blogspot.com/2007/11/conceptions-of-space-new-article-for.html.

Miller, P. & Rose, N. (2008). *Governing the present.* Cambridge: Polity Press.

Mills, S. (1996). Gender and colonial space. *Gender, Place and Culture, 3*(2), 125–147.

Mitchell, K. (2003). Educating the national citizen in neoliberal times: From the multicultural self to the strategic cosmopolitan. *Transactions of the Institute of British Geographers, 28,* 387–403.

Muggleton, D. (2000). *Inside subculture: The postmodern meaning of style.* London: Berg Publishers.

Muggleton, L. (2003). *The post-subculture reader.* London: Berg.

Muggleton, D. & Weinzierl, R. (2003). *The post-subcultures reader.* New York: Berg.

Nayak, A. (2003a). 'Boyz to men': Masculinities, schooling and labour transitions in de-industrial times. *Educational Review, 55*(2), 147–159.

Nayak, A. (2003b). Last of the 'Real Geordies'? White masculinities and the subcultural response to deindustrialization. *Environment and Planning D: Society and Space, 21,* 7–25.

Nayak, A. (2003c). *Race, place and globalization: Youth cultures in a changing world.* New York: Berg.

Nayak, A. (2009). Rewinding the past, fastforwarding the future: Youth cultural studies in a global age. Paper presented to the *Rethinking Youth in the Age of Global Media* ESRC series. London: The Knowledge Lab.

Neumann, Michael. (2004). A happy compromise: Hate crime reporting in the *Globe* and *Mail. Counterpunch.* Retrieved 22 February 2008, from www.counterpunch.org/neumann04152004.html.

Novi, E. (1997). *Inside ethnic families: Three generations of Portugese-Canadians.* Montreal, Quebec: McGill Queens University Press.

Ong, A. (1996). Cultural citizenship as subject-making: Immigrants negotiate racial and cultural boundaries in the United States. *Current Anthropology, 37*(5), 737–762.

Paechter, C. (2003). Masculinities and femininities as communities of practice. *Women's Studies International Forum, 1,* 69–77.

Parnaby, P.F. (2003). Disaster through dirty windshields: Law, order and Toronto's squeegee kids. *Canadian Journal of Sociology, 28*(3), 281–307.

Parnaby, P.F. (2006). Crime prevention through environmental design: Discourses of risk, social control, and a neo-liberal context. *Canadian Journal of Criminology and Criminal Justice, 48*(1), 1–29.

Parnaby, P.F. (2007). Crime prevention through environmental design: Financial hardship, the dynamics of power, and the prospects of governance. *Crime, Law, and Social Change, 48*(3–5), 73–85.

Pearson, C. (1983). *Hooligan: A history of respectable fears.* London: Macmillan.

Pellauer, D. (2007). *Ricoeur.* London: Continuum.

Pendakur, K. & Pendakur, R. (2004). *Colour my world: Has the majority–minority earnings gap changed over time?* Vancouver Centre of Excellence Research on Immigration and Integration in the Metropolis, Working Paper series, No. 04–11.

Pilkington, H. (2002). *Looking West? Cultural globalization and Russian youth cultures.* University Park: Pennsylvania State University Press.

Pilkington, H. (2004). Youth strategies for glocal living: Space, power and communication in everyday cultural practice. In A. Bennett & K. Kahn-Harris (Eds.), *After subculture: Critical studies in contemporary youth culture* (pp. 118–134). London: Palgrave Macmillan.

Pilkington, H. (2006). Beyond 'peer pressure': Rethinking drug use and 'youth culture'. *International Journal of Drug Policy, 18*(3), 213–224.

Pilkington, H. & Johnson, R. (2003). Peripheral youth: Relations of identity and power in global/local context. *European Journal of Cultural Studies, 6,* 259–283.

Pillow, W.S. (2004). *Unfit subjects: Educational policy and the teen mother.* New York and London: RoutledgeFalmer.

Pinney, C. (2001). Public, popular, and other cultures. In Dwyer, R. & Pinney, C. (Ed.), *Pleasure and the nation: The history, politics and consumption of public culture in India* (pp. 1–34). New Delhi, Oxford: Oxford University Press.

Poynting, S. (2006). What caused the Cronulla riot? *Race & Class, 48*(1), 85–92.

Poynting, S. & Morgan, G. (2007). *Moral panics in Australia: Social problems in mass media.* Hobart: ACYS Publishing.

Proust, M. (2003 [1927]). *In search of lost time* (box set). New York: Random House.

Read, W.J. (2002). In the land of paradigms, method rules. *Qualitative Social Work, 1*(3), 291–295.

Reay, D. (2008). Psychological aspects of white middle-class identities: Desiring and defending against the class and ethnic 'other' in urban multi-ethnic schooling. *Sociology, 42*(6), 1072–1088.

Reay, D. and S.J. Ball (1997). Spoilt for 'choice': The working classes and education markets. *Oxford Review of Education 23*(1), 89–101.

Reay, D. & Lucey, H. (2000). 'I don't really like it here but I don't want to be anywhere else': Children and inner city council estates. *Antipode, 32*(4), 410–428.

Reay, D. & Lucey, H. (2003). The limits of 'choice': Children and inner city schooling. *Sociology, 37*(1), 121–142.

Redhead, S. (1993). *Rave off: Politics and deviance in contemporary youth culture* (2nd ed.). Aldershot: Ashgate.

Redhead, S. (1995). *Unpopular cultures: The birth of law and popular culture.* Manchester: Manchester University Press.

Redhead, S. (1997). *Subculture to clubcultures.* Oxford: Blackwell.

Redhead, S. (2004). *Repetitive beat generation.* Edinburgh: Rebel Inc/Canongate.

Ricoeur, P. (1967). *The symbolism of evil.* Boston: Beacon.

Ricoeur, P. (1976). *Interpretation theory: Discourse and the surplus of meaning.* Fort Worth: The Texas Christian University Press.

Ricoeur, P. (1981). *Hermeneutics and the human sciences.* (J. B. Thompson, Trans.). Cambridge: Cambridge University Press.

Ricoeur, P. (1989). *Time and narrative,* 3 vols. (Kathleen McLaughlin and David Pellauer, Trans.). Chicago and London: University of Chicago Press.

Ricouer, P. (1991). From text to action: Essays in hermeneutics II. (K. Blamey and J. Thompson, Trans.). London: Athlone Press.

Ricoeur, P. (1992). *Oneself as another.* Chicago: University of Chicago Press.

Ricoeur, P. (1998a). *Critique and conviction* (Kathleen Blamey, Trans.). New York: Columbia University Press.

Ricoeur, P. (1998b). *Hermeneutics and the human sciences* (J.B. Thompson, Trans.). Cambridge: Cambridge University Press.

Ricoeur, P. (2000). *The just.* Chicago: Chicago University Press.

Ricoeur, P. (2002). Ethics and human capability: A response. In John Wall, William Schweiker & W. David Hall (Eds.), *Paul Ricoeur and contemporary moral thought* (pp. 279–290). New York: Routledge.

Ricoeur, P. (2004). *Memory, history, forgetting.* Chicago: University of Chicago Press.

Ring, J. (1989). On Marx and Arendt. *Political Theory, 17*(3), 432–448.

Rizvi, F. (2005). International education and the production of the cosmopolitan identity. *RIHE International Publication Series, 9,* 77–92.

Roberts, K. (2009). *Youth in transition: Eastern Europe and the West.* Basingstoke: Palgrave Macmillan.

Rose, G. (2007). *Visual methodologies: An introduction to the interpretation of visual materials* (2nd ed.). London: Sage Publications.

Rose, N. (1999). *Powers of freedom: Reframing political thought.* Cambridge: Cambridge University Press.

Rose, N. (2000). Government and control. *British Journal of Criminology, 40*(2), 321–339.

Ross, A. (1988). *Universal abandon? The politics of postmodernism.* Minneapolis: University of Minnesota Press.

Roy, A. & Al-Sayad, N. (2004). (Eds.) *Urban informality in an era of liberalization: Transnational perspectives from the Middle East and Latin America.* Lanham: Lexington Books.

Ryan L. (2007). Squeegee kids get no quarter. *BlogTO.* Retrieved 15 March 2009, from www.blogto.com/city/2007/01/squeegee_kids_get_no_quarter/.

Said, E.W. (1993). *Culture and imperialism: The T.S. Eliot Lectures at the University of Kent.* New York: Knopf/Random House.

Said, E.W. (1995 [1978]). *Orientalism: Western conceptions of the Orient.* Harmondsworth: Penguin.

Sassen, S. (1994). *Cities in a world economy.* Thousand Oaks: Pine Forge Press.

Sassen, Saskia. (1996). *Losing control? Sovereignty in an age of globalization*. New York: Columbia University Press.

Sassen, S. (1998). *Globalization and its discontents*. New York: New Press.

Sassen, S. (2000a). *Cities in a world economy* (new updated edition). Pine Forge: Sage Press.

Sassen, S. (2000b). *The global city: New York, London, Tokyo* (new updated edition). Princeton: Princeton University Press.

Sassen, S. (2007). *A sociology of globalization*. New York: W.W. Norton.

Scheibelhofer, E. (2009). Understanding European emigration in the context of modernization processes: Contemporary migration biographies and reflexive modernity. *Current Sociology, 57*(1), 5–25.

Sekula, A. (1984). *Photography against the grain: Essays and photo works, 1973–1983*. The Nova Scotia series: Source materials of the contemporary arts. Press of the Nova Scotia College of Art and Design.

Sekula, A. (1986). *The body and the archive*, October, 39, 2–65.

Shildrick, T. (2006). Youth culture, subculture and the importance of neighbourhood. *Young, 14*(1), 61–74.

Shildrick, T. & MacDonald, R. (2006). In defence of subculture: Young people, leisure and social divisions. *Journal of Youth Studies, 9*(2), 125–140.

Simms, K. (2003). *Paul Ricoeur*. London: Routledge.

Simon, R. (2000). The touch of the past: The pedagogical significance of a transactional sphere of public memory. In P. Trifonas (Ed.), *Revolutionary pedagogies*. New York: Routledge.

Simon, R. (2005). *The touch of the past: Remembrance, learning and ethics*. London: Palgrave Macmillan.

Simpson, G. (2004). *Great powers and outlaw states*. Cambridge: Cambridge University Press.

Skeggs, B. (1997). *Formation of class and gender: Becoming respectable*. London: Sage.

Skeggs, B. (2004). *Class, self, culture*. London and New York: Routledge.

Skeggs, B. (2005). The making of class through visualising moral subject formation, special edition 'Class, culture and identity'. *Sociology, 39*(5), 965–982.

Skeggs, B. & Binnie, J. (2004). Cosmopolitan sexualities: Disrupting the logic of late capitalism. *Sociological Review, 52*(1), 39–62.

Skeggs, B., Moran, L., Tyler, P. & Binnie, J. (2004). Queer as folk: Producing the real of urban space. *Urban Studies, 41*(9), 1839–1856.

Skelton, T. & Valentine, G. (1998). *Cool places: Geographies of youth cultures*. London & New York: Routledge.

Skocpol, T. (2005). *Vision and method in historical sociology*. London: Sage.

Smith, H. (2004). *The evolving relationship between immigrant settlement and neighbourhood disadvantage in Canadian cities*. Vancouver Centre of Excellence Research on Immigration and Integration in the Metropolis, Working Paper series, No. 04–20.

Sommers, J.D. (2001). *The place of the poor: Poverty, place and the politics of representation in downtown Vancouver, 1950–1997* (unpublished PhD dissertation). Burnaby, BC: Simon Fraser University.

Spooner, C. (2006). *Contemporary gothic*. London: Reaction Books.

Stahl, G. (1999). Still 'Winning space?' Updating subcultural theory. *Invisible Culture*. Retrieved from www.rochester.edu/in_visible_culture/issue2/stahl.htm.

Stanley, T. (2003). White supremacy and the rhetoric of educational indoctrination: A Canadian case study. In J. Barmen & M. Gleason (Eds.), *Children, teachers, and schools in the history of British Columbia*. Calgary: Detselig Enterprises Ltd.

Strange, C. (1998). *Toronto's girl problem: The perils and pleasures of the city, 1880–1930*. Toronto: University of Toronto Press.

Steedman, C. (1986). *Landscape for a good woman*. London: Virago.

Steedman, C. (1995). *Strange dislocation: Childhood and the idea of human interiority 1780–1930*. Cambridge: Harvard University Press.

Steedman, C. (2000). *Enforced narratives: Stories of another self*. London: Routledge.

Sturken, M. and Cartwright, L. (2001). *Practices of looking: An introduction to visual culture.* Oxford: Oxford University Press.

Szklarski, C. (2003). Neighbours warned against vigilantism: Child's murder, abduction attempts have west-end residents frightened. *Toronto Star.* Retrieved 16 June 2003, from http:torontostar.ca/NASApp/cs/ContentServer?pagename=thestar%2Futilities%2 FJavaSearch&searchstring=holy+jones.

Tagg, J. (1993). *The burden of photographic representation: Essays on photographies and histories.* Minneapolis: University of Minnesota Press.

Teixeira, C. (2007). Toronto's Little Portugal: A neighbourhood in transition. Published Report for the Centre for Urban and Community Studies, University of Toronto: Toronto, Canada, March.

Thiele, L. (2008). *Arendt, action and narrative.* Allacademic Research. Online publication. Retrieved 16 June 2009, from www.allacademic.com//meta/p_mla_apa_research_citation/1/5/0/6/5/pages150655/p150655-1.php.

Thompson, E.P. (1981). *The making of the English working class.* London: Penguin Books.

Thompson, K. (1998). *Moral panics.* London: Routledge.

Thompson, R. & Holland, J. (2003). Hindsight, foresight, and insight: The challenges of longitudinal qualitative research. *International Journal of Social Research Methodology, 6*(3), 233–244.

Thomson, R. & Tayor, R. (2005). Between cosmopolitanism and the locals. *Young, 13*(4), 327–342.

Thornton, S. (1996). *Club cultures: Music, media and subcultural capital.* Middletown: Wesleyan University Press.

Thornton, S. (1997). Introduction to Part 1. In K. Gelder & S. Thornton (Eds.) *The subcultures reader.* London & New York: Routledge.

Threadgold, S. & Nilan, P. (2009). Reflexivity of contemporary youth, risk and cultural capital. *Current Sociology, 57*(1), 47–68.

Tupechka, T., Martin, K. & Douglas, M. (1997). *Our own backyard: Walking tours of Grandview Woodland.* Vancouver.

Tyler, I. (2006). Chav scum: The filthy politics of social class in contemporary Britain. *M/C Journal, 9*(5). Retrieved 21 October 2009, from http://journal.media-culture.org.au/0610/09-tyler.php.

Ungar, S. (2001). Moral panic versus the risk society: The implications of the changing sites of social anxiety. *British Journal of Sociology, 52*(2), 271–291.

Villa, D.R. (1997). Hannah Arendt: Modernity, alienation, and critique. In C. Calhoun & J. McGowan (Eds.), *Hannah Arendt and the meaning of politics* (pp. 179–205). Minneapolis: University of Minnesota Press.

Walkerdine, V. & Lucey, H. (1989). *Democracy in the kitchen: Regulating mothers and socializing daughters.* New York: Random House.

Walkowitz, J. (2007). The cultural turn and a new social history: Folk dance and the renovation of class in social history. *Journal of Social History, 39*(3): 51 pars. Retrieved from www.historycooperative.org/cgibin/justtop.cgi?act=justtop&url=http://www.historycooperative.org/journals/jsh/39.3/walkowitz.html.

Walter, P. (2003). Literacy, imagined nations, and imperialism: Frontier College and the construction of British Canada. *Adult Education Quarterly, 54*(1), 42–58.

Weis, L. (2008). *The way class works: Readings on school, family, and the economy.* New York: Routledge.

Weller, S. (2003). 'Teach us something useful': Contested spaces of teenagers' citizenship. *Space and Polity, 7*(2), 153–171.

Williams, R. (1973). *The long revolution.* Harmondsworth: Penguin Books.

Williams, R. (1977). *Marxism and literature.* Oxford: Oxford University Press.

Williams, R. (1989). *Resources of hope: Culture, democracy, socialism.* New York: Verso.

Willis, P. (1977). *Learning to labour: How working class kids get working class jobs.* London: Saxon House.

Willis, P. (2000). *The ethnographic imagination.* Cambridge: Polity Press.

Willis, P. (2003). Foot soldiers of modernity: The dialectics of cultural consumption and the 21st-century school. *Harvard Educational Review, 73*(3), 390–415.

Wilson, E. (1995). The rhetoric of urban space. *New Left Review,* Volume A, 209, 146–160.

Wood, D. (2004). *On Paul Ricoeur: Narrative and interpretation.* New York: Routledge.

Wright, T. (1997). *Out of place: Homeless mobilizations, subcities, and contested landscapes.* Albany: State University of New York Press.

Wyn, J. (2000). The post-modern girl: Education, 'success', and the construction of girls' identities. In J. McLeod & K. Malone (Eds.), *Researching youth.* Hobart: Australian Clearinghouse for Youth Studies.

Yoon, E. (2008). *Urban conditions and changes in DTES, Vancouver, and Metro Vancouver, and Junction, Toronto and Metro Toronto.* Unpublished working paper, 22 August 2008.

Zlomislic, D. (2003). Grief, memories help bond Holly's family. *Toronto Star.* Retrieved 16 June 2003, from http:torontostar.ca/NASApp/cs/ContentServer?pagename=thestar/layout/article_printedfriendy&c=article&cid=1052251583342&call_pageid=968332188492.

Index

Numbers in **bold** indicate figures in the text.

eBooks – at www.eBookstore.tandf.co.uk

A library at your fingertips!

eBooks are electronic versions of printed books. You can
store them on your PC/laptop or browse them online.

They have advantages for anyone needing rapid access
to a wide variety of published, copyright information.

eBooks can help your research by enabling you to
bookmark chapters, annotate text and use instant searches
to find specific words or phrases. Several eBook files would
fit on even a small laptop or PDA.

NEW: Save money by eSubscribing: cheap, online access
to any eBook for as long as you need it.

Annual subscription packages

We now offer special low-cost bulk subscriptions to
packages of eBooks in certain subject areas. These are
available to libraries or to individuals.

For more information please contact
webmaster.ebooks@tandf.co.uk

We're continually developing the eBook concept, so
keep up to date by visiting the website.

www.eBookstore.tandf.co.uk